GOLD

NEW EDITION

C1 Advanced

CONTENTS

INTRODUCTION

Rationale

Welcome to *Gold C1 Advanced New Edition*, the innovative and engaging course for students preparing to sit Cambridge English Qualifications C1 Advanced, or general English students studying at C1 level on the common European framework. *Gold C1 Advanced New Edition* follows the same approach as previous editions but has been revised and updated following extensive research with users throughout the world. The new material includes additional progress tests, a unit-by-unit Grammar reference with check exercises and a complete Cambridge English Qualifications C1 First Practice Test.

Students will finish the *Gold C1 Advanced New Edition* course confident of both their English level and knowledge of the best strategies for each exam task. The language and skills taught in the units are supported by comprehensive reference sections for Grammar, Writing and the exam. *Gold C1 Advanced New Edition* provides a complete package of printed and digital components that can be used individually or in different combinations to suit the students' needs and the teaching environment. The overview on pages 4–5 explains how the *Gold C1 Advanced New Edition* components fit together. The teaching notes include many ideas for how and when to use the different components to provide an integrated and easy-to-use course package that teachers will find invaluable.

Main features of the course

Dynamic learning

Gold C1 Advanced New Edition helps teachers to deliver stimulating, discussion-rich lessons with lots of personalisation. There is a strong emphasis on communicative practice and the development of natural speaking skills to build student confidence.

Better class flow

Each unit in *Gold C1 Advanced New Edition* contains practice for all papers of the Cambridge English Qualifications C1 Advanced exam, and every lesson includes an integrated range of skills with plenty of discussion. The material is divided into lessons on spreads or pages, each with a carefully structured progression through a variety of activities including individual, pair- and whole-class work.

Vocabulary presented in chunks

In *Gold C1 Advanced,* phrasal verbs, collocations, idioms and other vocabulary are presented and practised in context to help students understand and remember them better.

Comprehensive exam practice and support

Gold C1 Advanced New Edition ensures that both teachers and students know what to expect in the exam and how to deal with each part effectively, thanks to the carefully staged exam tasks and comprehensive Exam Focus section detailing strategies for every part of the exam, as well as extra tips with exam tasks. Support levels are graduated through the book to help prepare students for tackling the tasks independently in the exam. The *Gold C1 Advanced New Edition Coursebook* also contains a complete Cambridge English Qualifications C1 Advanced Practice Test, putting another exam preparation tool at the teacher's disposal. The *Exam Maximiser* also provides comprehensive revision, practice and extension, as well as a complete Practice Test, additional Use of English sections and advice on how to avoid making common exam errors. The *Gold C1 Advanced New Edition MyEnglishLab* component provides further online practice of the skills students will need to excel in the exam, as well as two further Cambridge English Qualifications C1 Advanced Practice Tests.

Extensive digital package

The *Gold C1 Advanced New Edition* digital components include *eText* for students, App for students including audio and video, *ActiveTeach* IWB software, *MyEnglishLab*, and downloadable teacher's resources including the *Testmaster*, photocopiable worksheets and all *Coursebook* and *Exam Maximiser* audio and video. You will find many ideas of how and when to use these included in the *Teacher's Book* along with other suggestions for incorporating technology.

OVERVIEW OF COURSE COMPONENTS

Coursebook

- Twelve engaging units with authentic texts
- Exam-style practice and exam tips
- Extensive reference section including Grammar reference, Exam focus and Writing reference
- Download the class audio from **www.pearsonELT.com/gold**

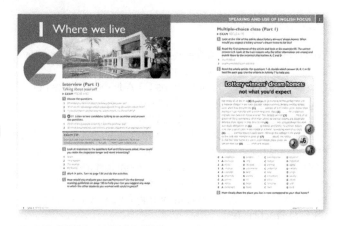

Exam Maximiser

- Complements and consolidates the *Coursebook* material
- Additional practice of skills, exam tasks and language points
- Activities follow on from but are not dependent on the *Coursebook*
- Six additional Use of English spreads and a complete Practice Test
- With- and without key versions
- Students download the *Exam Maximiser* audio material for self-study from **www.pearsonELT.com/gold**

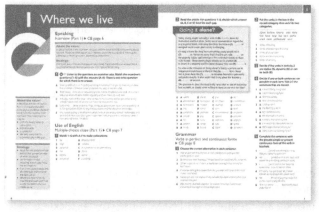

MyEnglishLab

- Online Learning Management System which complements and consolidates the *Coursebook* material
- Interactive versions of all *Exam Maximiser* activities
- Large bank of extra practice activities provides comprehensive training in the subskills and areas of language that underpin the exam
- Video presentations explain each part of the exam
- Three full practice tests
- Automatic activity grading and instant rich feedback
- Gradebook to track students' progress
- Common Error Report identifies areas for improvement

eText for students

- Digital version of the *Coursebook*
- For use at home or in class, on desktop, laptop or mobile devices
- Students can listen to the audio as many times as they need to and read along with the audio script

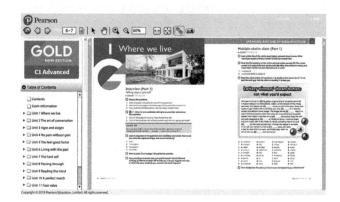

Teacher's Book

- Your complete guide to using all of the *Gold C1 Advanced New Edition* components in a blended classroom
- Lesson plans with answers, audio scripts and writing task sample answers
- Cross-references to all of the *Gold* components
- Supplementary ideas for warmers and extension activities
- Advice on using the digital components and other ideas for a blended classroom
- Three engaging photocopiable activities per unit with detailed teaching notes to revise and extend the *Coursebook* material
- Comes with *Teacher's Resource Disc*

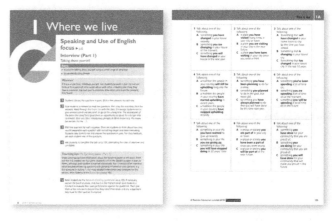

Teacher's Resources

- Available offline (*Teacher's Resource Disc*) or online
- See instructions inside the front cover for how to download.
- *Coursebook* and *Exam Maximiser* audio
- *Testmaster* with customisable versions of all the course tests in Word format, with audio:
  - 2 Placement Tests
  - 12 Unit Tests
  - 4 Progress Tests
  - 1 Exit test
  - Versions of all tests for students with dyslexia
- Speaking test videos with printable worksheets
- PDF versions of the *Teacher's Book* photocopiable activities (online only)
- Wordlists

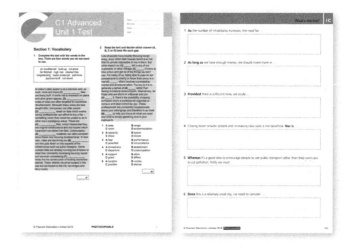

ActiveTeach

- Interactive whiteboard software to help teachers get the most out of the course
- Complete interactive versions of the *Coursebook* and *Exam Maximiser* – with integrated audio – for classroom presentation
- *Coursebook* teacher's notes and photocopiable activities
- Answer-reveal feature
- Extra interactive activities and games for every unit
- *Testmaster* with audio
- Speaking test videos with printable worksheets
- A host of useful classroom tools, including a digital whiteboard and pens; link-embedding capability; timers and scoreboards for games

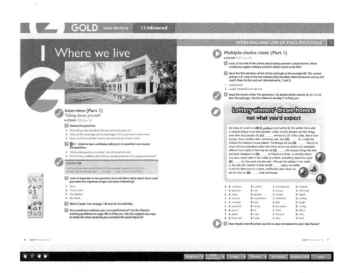

Recommended with Gold C1 Advanced New Edition

Longman Dictionary of Contemporary English

The sixth edition of the *LDOCE* is a must-have for students preparing for examinations.

- Over 65,000 collocations
- Over 18,000 synonyms, antonyms and related words
- Academic Word List highlighted
- Register notes focus on the difference between spoken and written English

The new online site offers the entire content of the dictionary plus additional innovative functionality, including *Study Centre* which has thousands of exercises, including exam practice for Cambridge English Qualifications.

Practice Tests Plus C1 Advanced New Edition

The *Practice Tests Plus Advanced New Edition* offers comprehensive practice for each exam paper and includes:

- seven complete practice tests, two with exam guidance and question-specific tips
- audio and visual materials for students to practise for the speaking and listening papers at home
- a guide to the Cambridge English Qualifications C1 Advanced exam
- answer key and audio script to support teachers doing exam practice in class.

Practice Tests Plus Advanced New Edition online materials include:

- filmed examples of the speaking exam
- writing samples
- teaching tips and activity ideas

Teaching strategies

The *Gold C1 Advanced New Edition Testmaster* includes two Placement Tests which may be used as aids to establish whether a student is at an appropriate level for the *Gold C1 Advanced New Edition* course. Even if two students were to attain an identical numerical score, no two learners are exactly the same and, consequently, it is natural that every teacher has to manage a degree of diversity in their class due to variation in prior knowledge, learning pace and style and motivation. A key aspect to successfully teaching a multi-level class is to know your learners.

Ideas to help you know your learners

Student reflection
Ask students to reflect on and describe their own goals, strengths and weaknesses in their personal English-learning journey. This works well as an initial writing assignment for the first day's homework on the course.

Test to help you teach
The *Gold C1 Advanced New Edition Testmaster* includes a range of assessment resources including Placement and Exit Tests, twelve Unit Tests and four Progress Tests, including versions for students with dyslexia. Using these tests can help you focus your classes more precisely to your students' needs.

Make time to listen
During group discussions and pairwork, take the opportunity to circulate and listen. Make notes on what you hear, especially any areas that require targeted development to deal with later in the lesson or at a future point.

Read student writing regularly
Each *Gold C1 Advanced New Edition* unit includes a writing assignment. By giving individualised feedback, you will learn a lot about each student as a writer. Make sure you keep in mind what you notice to include in future teaching.

Tutorials
Some teachers find meeting with students individually in a tutorial beneficial for monitoring and discussing progress. You could allow 15 minutes once a month for this.

Record-keeping
Records can be as simple as a page for each student in the class register binder, or could be kept electronically in a document or spreadsheet. Having a place to keep notes on each student including goals, test scores and writing feedback makes it easier to remember the details of individuals, as well as to write reports.

Managing multi-level classes

Plenty of pairwork
Working in pairs and small groups gives students the opportunity to learn reciprocally. Discussing reasons for their answers in an activity can be particularly useful by providing both the challenge of articulating a reason effectively and the support of having someone else's thought process explained. The lesson plans in the *Gold C1 Advanced New Edition Teacher's Book* include pairwork in every lesson.

Mix them up
The more diverse your class, the more important it is to change partners regularly to ensure students get a range of practice with people with different strengths. This is particularly important when preparing for the speaking paper of Cambridge English Qualifications C1 Advanced, where students will be paired with someone who may have a different level than themselves. Repeating an exercise with a new partner is a strategy that is often used in the *Gold C1 Advanced New Edition Teacher's Book*, which gives students of all abilities the opportunity to improve their first performance.

Offer choices
Many students respond well to choices that help them make a decision about their own learning. For example: 'OK, I'm going to offer you a choice here. For those who would like to look at the third conditional in more detail, I'm going to work through the Grammar reference now. If you feel you are already familiar with the third conditional, you can start the exercise on p.X.'

Have a plan for fast finishers
If your class is particularly diverse, there may be a significant variation in the time it takes for students to complete an exercise, especially during timed tests or writing activities. One option is to write the day's homework on the board before class, and let students know that if they finish class exercises early they can begin working on their homework. Another option for fast finishers is for them to design a few extra questions/exercises on the lesson topic. You could also have English newspapers/magazines/readers available.

Provide extra support
Some additional suggestions for students who are finding the course very challenging include:

- giving students the opportunity to rehearse before discussion activities, e.g. 'You're going to speak with your partner about the photos on p.X. Take a minute now to look at them and think about what you're going to say. I'll let you know when to begin.'

- for writing activities, eliciting sentence starters on the board which students may choose to use

See page 6 for some recommended additional resources.

Teaching with MyEnglishLab

MyEnglishLab: Gold C1 Advanced New Edition complements the *Coursebook* and allows you to provide students with a blended learning experience. In addition to being an interactive alternative to the *Exam Maximiser*, the *MyEnglishLab* component contains a large bank of additional Cambridge English Qualifications C1 Advanced exam practice activities. It also includes video introductions to each part of the exam and two full practice tests. You and your students can access these materials wherever there is an internet connection.

Using *MyEnglishLab* allows you to spend less time marking exercises in class, which frees up classroom time for more communicative activities, project work and so on, and students receive instant detailed feedback which is relevant to the answer they gave.

Introduce MyEnglishLab to your students
After you have registered and created your course, students can register using the unique access code from their *Coursebook* and your Teacher's course code.

Introducing the purpose of *MyEnglishLab* to your class is essential. Discuss how you intend to use it and why it is beneficial: they'll have access to additional practice of the key skills they'll need to excel in the exam; they can get instant feedback on their answers; they can track their progress very easily with the onscreen indicators.

Assign work regularly
You can make all of the material available for students to work through in their own time or assign specific activities as you go through your course. You can assign tasks to the whole class, to groups of students with different needs or to individual students. The *Gold C1 Advanced New Edition Teacher's Book* includes suggestions for specific *MyEnglishLab* activities to consolidate the *Coursebook* content in the *Additional practice* sections of the teacher's notes, where 'MyEnglishLab' is abbreviated to 'MEL'.

Make the most of the gradebook
Check the gradebook regularly to see how your students are doing. You can export the gradebook as an Excel file to make life easy when you need to write student reports. The Common Error report shows the frequency and types of errors students have made on an exercise. This makes it easy for you to identify areas for further remedial teaching.

Messages
MyEnglishLab: Gold C1 Advanced New Edition enables you to send and keep track of messages to your students. You can remind them about their homework, offer guidance, and have one-to-one exchanges. There is also a folder where you can upload documents for the class such as reading material, sample answers or notices.

Where we live

Speaking and Use of English focus ▶ p.6

Interview (Part 1)

Talking about yourself

Aims

- to practise talking about yourself using a varied range of language
- to use introductory phrases

Warmer

If this is a new class, introduce yourself. Ask students to work in pairs to find out three or four pieces of information about each other, including one thing they have in common. Ask each pair to introduce themselves and share the similarity they found.

1 Students discuss the questions in pairs. Elicit a few answers to each one.

2 Give students a moment to read the questions, then play the recording. Elicit the answers. Read through the Exam tip with the class. Encourage students not to give answers which are very brief, or go on for a long time. The second part of the exam (the Long Turn) gives them an opportunity to speak for a longer time (a minute). Elicit any other introductory phrases students know (e.g. *You know, Let me see, For me …*).

3 Elicit the question for each response. Then ask students to think about how they would respond to each question with something longer and more interesting. Students take turns to ask and answer the questions in pairs. For class feedback, ask each student one of the questions.

4 Ask students to complete the task on p.134, alternating the roles of examiner and candidate.

Teaching tip: the Speaking paper (Part 1)

Share some background information about the Speaking paper of the exam. Point out that it is divided into four parts. Students will sit the Speaking paper in pairs or threes, although each student is marked individually. Part 1 consists of an interview which involves answering questions with personal information and opinions, e.g. the questions in Activity 1. For more detailed information and strategies for this section, refer students to the Exam focus on p.182.

5 Refer students to the General marking guidelines on p.185. If necessary, explain the band structure, and that 5 is the highest band. Give students a moment to evaluate their own performance against the guidelines. Then give them a few minutes to discuss how they rated themselves and any suggestions they have for their partner to improve.

Alternative

If students don't feel confident making suggestions to each other at this early stage of the course, ask them to just reflect on their own performance, and share something they would like to improve with the other students they worked with.

Answers

2 1 Question 1: What did you like most about the area where you grew up?

2 Karl provides answers of appropriate length. He gives two utterance answers. He either first answers the question and then provides more information e.g. 'I'm German. I live just outside Berlin now but I grew up in the centre of the city.' Or he prefaces his answer with a comment that allows him to show the range of language he has at his disposal and then goes on to provide an answer e.g. 'Well, there are so many things, really, but I suppose the one that really stands out for me is living so close to a great city like Berlin.'

Teaching Tip: Recording spoken tasks

If students have mobile devices, encourage them to record themselves talking in Activity 5. Then ask them to listen to the recording and reflect on what they did well and what they could improve on. Encourage students to save the recording to play to themselves later in the course so that they can hear their own progress.

Multiple-choice cloze (Part 1)

Aim

- to complete an exam-style multiple-choice cloze task (Reading and Use of English Part 1)

Teaching tip: The Reading and Use of English paper (Part 1)

Tell students that the Reading and Use of English paper of the exam is divided into eight parts. Part 1 is a multiple-choice cloze: a gapped text with a choice of four options for each gap. For more information, refer students to the Exam focus on p.178.

6 Focus students' attention on the title of the article. Elicit the meaning of *lottery* (a game used to make money for a state or a charity in which people buy tickets with a series of numbers on them – if their number is picked by chance, they win money or a prize). Put students into pairs to discuss the question (without looking at the text).

Additional activity: Reading for gist

Ask students to read the article quickly without worrying about the gaps to see what kind of home a real lottery

winner chose. Ask them to compare it to their own ideas from Activity 6.

7 Point out that this task type focuses on whether students can understand subtleties in meaning between words of a very similar meaning. Do this activity as a class.

8 Students complete the article then compare their answers in pairs before checking as a class.

9 Students discuss the question in pairs, then elicit a few responses.

Answers

7 1 C   2 D and A

8 1 B (*only* means that there were no other winners)

2 D (*opted* is the only verb on the list which is followed by *for*)

3 A (*uncommon* and *unlikely* are not usually used as stand-alone adjectives for people. *Unfamiliar* as a stand-alone adjective for a person means not known to you, which doesn't make sense here.)

4 C (*take into account* is a collocation)

5 A (*proximity* has the best meaning and it is the only noun from the list which is followed by *to*)

6 D (*afford* = to have enough money to pay for something)

7 C (*fantasise* is the only verb listed which is followed by the preposition *about*)

8 B (*loved one* is a compound word meaning a person you love, usually a family member)

Additional activity

Put students into pairs and allocate each pair one of the sets of words from Activity 8 (or for a shorter alternative, two words from a set). With their partner, students discuss the differences in meaning and use between the alternatives then look up the definitions in the Longman Dictionary of Contemporary English at www.ldoceonline.com. Ask students to briefly present the differences to the class. Alternatively, students could post their findings to a private class online space.

Teaching tip: Setting up an online space

Set up an online space for your class, for example, in your school's learning management system, MyEnglishLab, or on a social media site. You can use the space to communicate notices to students, for students to submit work, provide links to useful resources, and for online discussion.

ADDITIONAL PRACTICE | Maximiser p.6, Speaking | **MEL** Unit 1, Speaking | **MEL** Extra practice, Speaking 1 Giving good Part 1 answers | **Active Teach** Game: Sheep out!

Grammar focus ▶ p.8

Warmer

Ask students to discuss in pairs whether they think it would be more dangerous to live in a small town or a city. Reveal that it is generally more dangerous to live in a small town than in a city and ask students to speculate why this might be (e.g. because of fewer hospitals or medical resources; rural drivers go much more quickly).

1 Put students into pairs and encourage them to think of at least three advantages and disadvantages of living in a small town. Then ask students for a show of hands to indicate whether they consider themselves a *city person* or a *small-town person.* Invite a few students to give reasons for their choices.

2 Play the recording and elicit whether the speaker mentioned any of the things that were talked about in Activity 1. Elicit any other advantages or disadvantages she talked about.

Verbs in perfect and continuous forms

Aim

- to differentiate between the use of perfect and continuous forms

Refer students to the Grammar reference section on verbs in perfect and continuous forms on p.149. Go through the notes and examples. Ask them to do the exercise on p.150.

Teaching tip: A 'flipped classroom' approach

You could ask students to read through the relevant Grammar reference sections before the lesson. This will allow more time for students to think about the grammar at home, and will also allow more time for questions and communicative activities during class.

Grammar reference answers

1 have been having
2 is working
3 has lived
4 are always complaining
5 have just had

3 Point out that all of these sentences are grammatically correct and, at this level, the focus is more about understanding and conveying subtle differences using the appropriate tense.

4 Students discuss the difference in meaning between each pair of sentences before comparing ideas as a class.

Answers

3 **1 A** They are still discussing where to move. **B** They've finished discussing where to move.

2 A The focus is on the total distance covered at the end of the journey. **B** The focus is on repeatedly covering the same distance every day.

3 A The suggestion is that the process of wondering about leaving had come to an end when she was offered the job. **B** The suggestion is that when she received the job offer she was still wondering about leaving the city.

4 **1** I had been telling **2** I had, in fact, always been **3** both **4** both **5** both, have discovered **6** will have been

Forms used by speaker:

1 I had been telling (past perfect continuous) **2** I had, in fact, always been (past perfect simple) **3** will have been living (future perfect) **4** I've been looking back (present perfect continuous) **5** I've spent, have discovered (present perfect simple) **6** will have been (future perfect)

ADDITIONAL PRACTICE | **Active Teach** Extra activity Grammar Focus 1

Stative verbs

Aims

- to understand that verbs are not used with a stative meaning in continuous forms
- to identify a range of stative verbs

Refer students to the Grammar reference section on stative and dynamic verbs on p.150. Go through the notes and examples. Ask them to do the exercise.

Grammar reference answers

1 ~~I'm loving~~ I love living in London at the moment. It's great.
2 ~~They're having~~ They have three children: Hanna, Charlie and Aurora.
3 She denies having had anything to do with the robbery. (= correct)
4 This soup tastes a bit strange. (= correct)
5 ~~He's not understanding~~ He doesn't understand anything about technology.

5 Talk through the Language tip and find out if students can think of any other examples of verbs with both stative and dynamic meanings (e.g. *have, be, think*).

Check that students understand the terms *stative verb* (a verb that describes a state of being) and *dynamic verb* (a verb that describes an action). Ask them to divide the stative verbs into groups, then check answers as a class.

6 Students complete the activity then compare their answers in pairs before you check answers as a class.

7 Give students a moment to think about the question and the verb forms. Share an example (e.g. *I've been living in my rock star mansion for a year now. I've been swimming in my huge pool every morning before class*). Students discuss their ideas in pairs or small groups, then elicit some ideas.

Answers

5 Emotions: care, like, love

Knowledge: believe, know, understand

Possession: belong, own, possess

Communication: agree, deny, promise (also possible: understand)

Senses: hear, smell, taste

6 **1** think (expressing an opinion)

2 am thinking (considering)

3 am seeing (for an arrangement in the future)

4 see (understand or appreciate an opinion in the present)

5 are tasting (for an action in progress)

6 tastes (for a permanent state or quality)

ADDITIONAL PRACTICE | Maximiser p.7, Grammar | **MEL** Unit 1, Grammar | Photocopiable 1A *This is me* | **Active Teach** Extra activity Grammar Focus 2

Listening focus ▶ p.9

Multiple matching (Part 4)

Aim

- to complete an exam-style multiple matching task (Listening Part 4)

Teaching tip: The Listening paper (Part 4)

Tell students that the Listening paper consists of four parts. Refer students to read Part 4 of the Exam focus on p.182 and then elicit a summary (Part 4 focuses on understanding informal speech and involves reading

two tasks of eight statements each, then listening to five short monologues on a related topic and matching one statement from each task to one of the speakers).

1 Read the Exam tip with the class. Students answer the questions in pairs, then elicit answers from the class. Check students understand the idea of *downsize* (to move to a smaller home).

2 Play the recording twice. Go through the answers.

3 Read the question and, if students want you to, replay the recording. Ask students to discuss the question in pairs then elicit a few opinions about each.

Answers

2 **Task 1 1** G **2** C **3** H **4** E **5** D

Task 2 6 G **7** F **8** B **9** E **10** D

Vocabulary

expressions with *space* and *room*

Aim

- to expand students' knowledge of expressions with *space* and *room*

Additional activity

Ask students to write their own sentences with *space* and *room*, and then work in pairs to share their sentences and try to give their own explanations of how the words are the same, and what differences there are. Conduct whole-class feedback. (Suggested answer: the words are different in the contexts they can be used in, which is what this activity aims to practise).

4 Students complete the activity, then compare in pairs before you check as a class.

Additional activity

Ask students to take turns to guess who each speaker in Activity 4 might be talking to and what the situation is, e.g. *I think the first speaker might be talking to her partner or flatmate. Maybe they have a really cluttered flat and are having a big clean out.* Then ask each pair to choose one of the phrases and role-play the next part of the conversation. Invite pairs to share their conversations with the class.

As an extension, get students to try and articulate how the words *space* and *room* are different. (i.e. *space* talks about an area, *room* often talks about what an area can be used for).

5 Students turn to p.144 and work in pairs to ask and answer the questions using expressions with *space* and *room*. Elicit an answer to each question, along with the meaning of the words in italics: *room service*, *room temperature*, *no room to swing a cat*, *roomy*, *room and board* and *leg room*.

> **Answers**
>
> 4 **1** both **2** both **3** room **4** room **5** both
>   **6** space **7** room **8** space

ADDITIONAL PRACTICE | Maximiser p.10, Listening | **MEL** Unit 1, Listening | **MEL** Extra practice, Listening 1 Speaker purpose | **Active Teach** Game: Noughts and crosses

Reading focus ▶ p.10

Multiple choice (Part 5)

> **Aim**
>
> • to complete an exam-style multiple-choice reading task (Reading and Use of English Part 5)

> **Teaching tip:** The Reading and Use of English paper (Part 5)
>
> Refer students to the Exam focus on p.179 and give them a few minutes to familiarise themselves with the section on Part 5.

1 Students discuss the questions in pairs. Elicit a few ideas for each question. Then ask: *How has technology changed the way people navigate?* Try to use or elicit words which are coming up in the reading text: *GPS, coordinates, Google Earth, interactive.*

2 Give students a minute to read the title and first paragraph, then elicit a few predictions of what the whole article will be about. Give students five minutes to read the article quickly to check their predictions.

3 Read the Exam tip with the class.

> **Additional activity**
>
> As an example of the Exam tip, give students the following statement: *The writer of this article thinks that we rely on technology so much that we would easily get lost without it.* Get students to try and guess what the answer would be based on their own beliefs, and then skim read to find out (answer = *no*). Then ask the class whether students' own feelings about the question affected their decision.

Ask students to read the questions and underline key words before reading the text one more time. Tell students that as they answer each question, they should find and mark the part of the text that each question relates to, then reread it in detail. After students have answered the questions, they compare their answers in pairs. As you go through the answers, elicit evidence for each one.

4 Students discuss the questions in pairs. Conduct whole-class feedback.

> **Answers**
>
> 2 C
>
> 3 **1** C **2** B **3** D **4** B **5** A **6** B

5 Tell students that working out meaning from context is an important reading skill. Brainstorm strategies for deducing the meaning of an unknown word, e.g. understand the context, read the whole sentence, work out the word class (is it a verb, noun, etc.?), look for connections to words in other languages you know. Students match the underlined words with the meanings. They compare their answers in pairs, then as a class.

6 Remind students that writing their own examples is a good way to help them remember words and phrases.

> **Answers**
>
> 5 **1** frequent **2** detachment **3** feat **4** archly
>   **5** reconaissance **6** fabric **7** parameters
>   **8** intersect

ADDITIONAL PRACTICE | Maximiser p.8, Reading | **MEL** Unit 1, Reading | **MEL** Extra practice, Reading 1 Predicting the text A | **Active Teach** Extra activity Reading Focus – meanings in context

Vocabulary focus ▶ p.12

Compound words

> **Aim**
>
> • to expand students' awareness of compound words

> **Warmer**
>
> Ask students to show each other a photo (on their phones) of their town/city or a well-known landmark, and get their partner to describe it.

1 Put students into pairs or small groups to discuss the questions. If all students are from the same city, they could each choose another city they are familiar with to discuss.

2 Give students a few minutes to read the text and clarify any unknown vocabulary. Elicit the meaning of *a mecca* (a place that attracts a lot of people), *endowed* (with a good quality), *asset* (something that is useful), *slogan* (a short phrase used in advertisements) *and bylaw* (a law which applies to a city or small area rather than the whole country).

3 Read through the Language tip with the class. Point out that compound words can combine a range of word classes, e.g. noun, adjective, adverb, verb. Ask students to look at the first underlined word in the text (*landmark*), elicit the word class of the word (a noun), and the words it combines (the nouns *land* and *mark*). Direct students to the next underlined word (*world-renowned)*. Elicit the word class (adjective) and the words it combines (the noun *world* and the adjective *renowned*). Ask students to look at the remaining underlined compound words and answer the question. Elicit the answer.

4 Tell students that this list is of some other common compound adjectives. Students match the adjectives to the nouns then check as a class.

5 Students complete the activity, then compare answers in pairs before you check as a class.

6 Focus on the first word *air-conditioned* and elicit some possible sentences using it, e.g. *My apartment isn't air-conditioned*; *When I go on holiday, I always ask for an air-conditioned room*. Encourage students to write and compare their own sentences.

Additional activity

Students could turn their sentences from Activity 6 into gapped sentences by removing one part of each compound word (or for more of a challenge, the whole compound), then swap these with a new partner. They try to guess the missing item in their partner's sentences.

Teaching tip: Recording vocabulary

Suggest students choose a place to record new vocabulary and collocations. It could be a digital record or physical notebook, but it is important that it is in one central place and doesn't get lost!

Answers

3 landmark, theatre-goers, bylaws

4 1 E long-standing friendship   2 F run-down area
  3 C cut-price airline tickets   4 D drop-down menu
  5 B middle-aged man   6 A part-time job

6 1 air   2 mass   3 far   4 highly   5 high   6 life
  7 interest   8 built

ADDITIONAL PRACTICE | Maximiser p.8, Vocabulary | **MEL** Unit 1, Vocabulary | Photocopiable 1B *Matching halves* | **Active Teach** Game: Pelmanism

Grammar focus ▶ p.13

Warmer

Write *take a trip down memory lane* on the board, and elicit what it means (when you spend some time remembering the past). Ask students to take a moment to think back to their childhood and choose a place that has happy memories for them, e.g. a holiday spot or place they used to play or somebody's home. Divide students into small groups to briefly describe that place and its significance to them. Finish by asking: *Have you been back to that place? How has it changed?*

1 Put students into pairs to discuss the statement then conduct whole-class feedback.

2 Give students a few minutes to read the text and clarify any unknown vocabulary.

1 (Suggested answer) What happened in the past would not happen now. The way things are now is very different from the way they were in the past.

2 (Suggested answer) The house itself had changed, so had the garden and so had the beach. The new owners didn't seem to care about preserving what was appealing about the house.

Conjunctions

Aim

● to use a range of conjunctions which show contrast, give conditions and add information

Ask students to read the Grammar reference section on conjunctions on p.150 and complete the exercise on p.151.

Grammar reference answers

1 yet 2 whereas 3 provided that 4 As 5 If only
6 as 7 nor

3 Students match the conjunctions to their function, then check answers as a class. Elicit other conjunctions that are used for each function (referring students back to the Grammar reference on p.150 if necessary).

4 Students complete the activity, compare answers in pairs, then check answers as a class.

5 This exercise showcases a number of useful phrases using *as* that function as conjunctions. Ask students to read the sentences and match each phrase to its meaning from the box. Check answers as a class. Tell students that they could consider using some of these *as* phrases in their essay in the next lesson (on p.14).

Additional activity

Ask students to work in teams to think of ideas to improve the city they are currently in. Each team should decide on an idea, and prepare to present their arguments to the class in a formal way, e.g. using some of the conjunctions from the lesson.

Answers

3 1 whether, whereas 2 Provided, as long as 3 nor

4 1 nor 2 as yet 3 As long as 4 whereas
   5 Provided 6 as long as

5 1 While 2 Regarding 3 until now 4 current 5 Since
   6 Starting on

ADDITIONAL PRACTICE | Maximiser p.10, Grammar | MEL
Unit 1, Grammar | Photocopiable 1C *What's the link?* | **MEL**
Extra practice, Use of English 9 Connectors | **Active Teach** Game:
Stepping stones

Writing focus ▶ p.14
Essay (Part 1)

using the task input to help you plan

Aim

- to plan and write a well-structured exam-style essay (Writing Part 1)

Warmer

Students discuss the following question in pairs: *How well do you know your neighbours? Do you think knowing neighbours is important?*

Teaching tip: The Writing Paper

Point out that the writing paper is in two parts: Part 1 is a compulsory essay; Part 2 is a choice of three tasks which could include an email/letter, a report/proposal, or a review. For more information, refer students to the Writing reference on essays on p.168.

1 Play the recording and elicit a few opinions on how people in students' neighbourhoods would react to such a scheme.

2 Students work in pairs and follow the instructions. Conduct whole-class feedback.

3 Ask students to read the plans and the checklist on p.166. Students discuss the question in pairs. Then elicit the answer.

4 Tell students to use Plan A in Activity 3 as a model as they plan the essay in Activity 2. Give them a few minutes to make their plan individually, then put them into small groups to compare ideas.

5 For this plan, give students a five-minute limit to read and plan the task. Emphasise that the plan should follow the same structure as Plan A in Activity 3 although the points can be in note form rather than full sentences. Read the Exam tip with the class. Point out that this is so that students can show their range of language. Elicit some paraphrases for each opinion in the discussion.

6 Set the essay as homework. Encourage students to show their draft to two other students for advice and make changes before you collect the essays in to provide individual feedback.

Teaching tip: Align your feedback

When giving feedback on written work, make it more meaningful by matching it to the lesson content. For example, for this essay, provide feedback on whether students have planned their essays before writing, or whether their essays show signs of good organisation.

Answers

3 Plan B is poor: It only addresses one side of the argument, i.e. the writer's opinion and it doesn't assess the potential effectiveness of the plan.

6 Model answer

   Too much traffic is a major headache for everyone in the city due to the noise, pollution and, of course, terrible delays during the rush hour. How can the government reduce traffic and dissuade people from driving their cars into the centre every day? In this essay, I will discuss two possible approaches to this pressing yet complex issue.

The first option to consider is an education campaign which could comprise visual and radio advertising, presentations to businesses and special designated days such as 'Walk to Work Day'. Compared to the high cost of significantly upgrading our public transport system, advertising is relatively low-cost and straightforward to implement. On the other hand, it is difficult to gauge the effectiveness of such a campaign in advance because it relies on individuals changing their ingrained habits.

A second alternative would be to levy a tax on parking in the city. This could be applied both to businesses and directly to consumers. While I acknowledge that it may be unpopular, it would have immediate gains in revenue and would likely make residents reconsider other transport options.

In my view, a multi-faceted education campaign would be the most effective starting point. In the future, a tax could be a possible option but it would be tolerated better once citizens are educated about the benefits of fewer cars and a more pedestrianised centre.

ADDITIONAL PRACTICE | **Maximiser** p.11, Writing | **MEL** Unit 1, Writing | **MEL** Extra practice, Writing 1 Understanding the marking criteria

Review ▶ p.15

Aim

- to revise the structures, vocabulary and exam tasks covered in Unit 1

1 – **3** Ask students to complete the activities, monitoring them to provide assistance. Alternatively, set this as a homework activity. Ask students to compare their answers in pairs before doing a class check.

Alternative: Use the Review for fast finishers

Set the review activities for fast finishers during other lessons and make the answers available in your online space for students to mark themselves.

Answers

1 **1** smell **2** is tasting **3** am seeing **4** is smelling
   5 are thinking **6** tastes

2 **1** is not enough room to

   2 provided (that) it doesn't rain

   3 has been ironing/doing his ironing

   4 will have been living

   5 as long as I have

   6 and I do

3 **1** D **2** B **3** A **4** D **5** C **6** C **7** A **8** B

2 The art of conversation

Speaking and Grammar focus ▶ p.16

Long turn (Part 2)
giving opinions

Warmer

Focus students' attention on the title of the unit and ask: *What is the art of conversation?* (the ability or skill involved in conversation). Put students into pairs to discuss the following question: *What skills make a good conversationalist? How does the art of conversation change between a face-to-face and online communication?*

1 Students work in pairs to discuss the question. Elicit a few ideas. Then ask the class: *Have you ever been stuck somewhere without a phone or internet access? Can you see any benefits from being without these things? Would you like to try it?*

2 Ask students to read the statements, then play the recording while they mark whether each speaker agrees or disagrees.

3 Play the recording again for students to complete the expressions. Students compare their answers in pairs then check as a class.

Teaching tip

Encourage your students to use a range of phrases more often by recording them somewhere, e.g. in their vocabulary notebook/file, or post these phrases to your private online space, and display them again during future Speaking Part 2 practice.

4 Direct students back to the statements in Activity 2. Encourage students to use the expressions from Activity 3. Students discuss the statements in pairs. Conduct whole-class feedback.

5 Focus students on the exam task. Elicit how many things they are asked to do and what they are.

Teaching tip

Refer students to the Exam focus for the individual long turn on p.183 and ask them to read the strategy section. Invite students to summarise this in their own words.

6 Ask students to read the questions and elicit which of the things will help the student get a good mark. (1, 2 and 3 are desirable, but 4 is not.) Remind students that for detailed marking criteria, they can look at the Marking guidelines on p.185. Play the recording for students to listen and answer the questions. Check answers as a class.

Additional activity

Ask students to work in pairs. Students take turns to be the candidate doing the task in Activity 5, and the examiner. They should try to improve on the student in the recording's answer.

The examiner could use the questions in Activity 6 to provide feedback for their partner.

7 Tell students that they are each going to practise another task. After students have completed the task, encourage them to reflect on their performance against the questions in Activity 6.

Answers

2 1 A 2 D 3 A 4 D

3 1 speaking 2 argue 3 way 4 goes 5 far 6 fair

5 Three things: Look at the pictures. They show people using their phones. I'd like you to compare two of the pictures and say why people might be communicating in this way and how effective this form of communication might be.

6 1 yes 2 no 3 no 4 yes

ADDITIONAL PRACTICE | Maximiser p.12, Speaking | **MEL** Unit 2, Speaking | **MEL** Extra practice, Speaking 4 Strategies for dealing with Part 2 questions

Review of narrative tenses

past simple, past continuous, past perfect

Aim

• to review uses of the past simple, past continuous and past perfect

Refer students to the Grammar reference section on narrative tenses on p.151. Ask students to read the notes and complete the exercise on p.152. Put students into small groups to compare their answers then check answers as a class.

Grammar reference answers

1 didn't realise, had left, got

2 got on/used to get on, would/used to, went/were going

3 Wasn't there/Didn't there use to be

4 hadn't been living, met

5 had been thinking/was thinking, gave

8 Give students a minute to read the text to find out the problem.

9 Point out that each of the narrative tenses can be used for a variety of reasons. Students match examples (1–8) to the reasons A–H, then compare answers in pairs before checking as a class. Go through the Language tip.

10 Students complete the remaining gaps. Students compare in pairs then check as a class.

11 Encourage students to use the phrases from Activity 3 in this discussion. Elicit some opinions.

12 Ask students to read the paragraph opener and elicit some possible reasons from the class (e.g. perhaps a friend needs some urgent advice or help, there's no answer at the end of the line and other mysterious things start happening). Be sensitive to the fact that some students may have received bad news on the phone late at night and offer the alternative sentences in the box below. Circulate while students write their paragraphs, assisting with tense choice as required. Ask students to work in pairs to see how many tenses have been used and check each other's tenses. Students share their paragraphs in small groups.

Alternative

Offer two alternative sentence starters for students to pick from for their paragraph.

1 I had just turned away from the table for a split second, but when I turned back, my phone was gone ...

2 I looked down at the message and could only see the first few words. 'Congratulations, you have won ...'

8 1

9 1 B 2 D 3 F 4 C 5 A 6 H 7 G 8 E

10 9 learnt 10 had booked 11 emailed 12 had flooded 13 communicated 14 had been planning 15 called 16 had managed

12 Model answer

Last night I woke up suddenly because my phone was ringing. I didn't pick it up in time, and then it stopped. I checked the voicemail messages. It was my friend Sarah who hadn't contacted me for months. Her message said 'Call me. I need to talk to you.' I was completely confused by this. We had been very close at school but since she'd moved to another city, I had hardly seen her. I knew she'd been working for her uncle and that she'd also been travelling a lot. It was 3 o'clock in the morning. I couldn't call her back in the middle of the night, could I? While I was trying to decide what to do next, the phone rang again.

ADDITIONAL PRACTICE | Maximiser p.13, Grammar | **MEL** Unit 2, Grammar | Photocopiable 2A *Tell the truth* | **MEL** Extra practice, Use of English 15: Review of tenses | **Active Teach** Extra activity Grammar Focus 1

Listening focus ▶ p.18

Multiple choice (Part 1)

ADDITIONAL PRACTICE | Maximiser p.13, Listening | MEL Unit 2, Listening | MEL Extra practice, Listening 3: Listening for detail and inferring meaning

Aim

- to complete an exam-style multiple-choice listening task (Listening Part 1)

1 Give students a few minutes to complete the questionnaire individually, then put students into pairs to compare their answers. Make sure they realise that being an introvert or extrovert are not 'good' or 'bad', just different. Ask: *Is it possible to have both introvert and extrovert characteristics?* (Most psychologists consider introversion/extroversion a spectrum rather than two separate categories. An *ambivert* is a person with a balance of extrovert and introvert features.)

2 Brainstorm what students already know about the multiple-choice listening task. Then invite students to compare their ideas with the Exam focus on p.181. Point out that students will only get 45 seconds before listening, so they will need to be ready to read as soon as they are allowed to and to read quickly. Time students for 45 seconds for them to read then play the recording.

3 Play Extract 1 again while students listen for the paraphrases of *unsure* and *relieved*, and the words which are summarised by *normal*. Elicit the answers as a class.

4 Students match the phrases A–E from the recording with the correct answers in Activity 2. Allow students time to compare their answers in pairs before you check as a class.

Answers

2 **1** C **2** A **3** B **4** A **5** B **6** C

3 unsure = sceptical

relieved = reassuring

normal = absolutely nothing wrong with that at all

4 **A** 3 **B** 2 **C** 5 **D** 6 **E** 4

Additional activity

Students discuss the following questions in small groups.

1 How helpful do you think learning about personality types is?

2 To what extent do you agree that everyone presents a certain cultivated image of themselves online?

3 How strict are you with yourself about your social media use?

Use of English focus ▶ p.19

Word formation (Part 3)

Aim

- to complete an exam-style word formation activity (Reading and Use of English, Part 3)

1 Direct students to the emojis and ask students to discuss the questions in pairs. Elicit the answers. Find out if students can come up with the adjective and the noun for each one. As an extension, ask: *What do you think is the most common emoji?* Get students to guess then check their answer online.

Background: Emoji

An emoji /ɪˈməʊdʒi/ is an icon used in electronic messages. They were invented in 1999 in Japan. The word *emoji* comes from the Japanese words *e* (picture) and *moji* (character). The similarity to the English word *emotion* is just a coincidence!

2 Ask students to complete the sentences. Write up the correct answers, then have students discuss the questions in pairs. Conduct whole-class feedback.

3 After students have quickly read the text, elicit the problems and some opinions.

4 Tell students to read the Exam tip. Remind students that they may need to add a prefix to some of the words. Students complete the gaps.

5 Students work through their answers against the checklist. Then check as a class.

Answers

2 **1** communicators (noun) **2** uncommunicative (adjective) **3** communication (noun)

3 only using emojis literally, not understanding how to use emojis ironically, trying too hard to use an appropriate emoji

4 **1** embarrassing **2** unexpected **3** misunderstandings **4** enthusiastic **5** ironically **6** impression **7** meaningful **8** effective

Additional activity

Write the following adjectives from the text on the board. Check the pronunciation of *subtle* /'sʌtl/: *subtle, evident, relevant, impossible, spontaneous.*

Ask students to discuss what each adjective means and for the noun form (subtlety, evidence, relevance, impossibility, spontaneity).

ADDITIONAL PRACTICE | **Maximiser** p.15, Use of English | **MEL** Unit 2, Use of English | **MEL** Extra practice, Use of English 4: Word building

Reading focus ▶ p.20

Gapped text (Part 7)

Aim

* to practise using reference words and context to select missing paragraphs in an exam-style gapped text task (Reading and Use of English Part 7)

1 Allow students a couple of minutes to discuss their answers. Conduct whole-class feedback.

2 Give students about two minutes to read the article on p.21 quickly to find out what the writer thought of the conversation class.

3 Remind students that Part 7 of the Reading and Use of English paper is a task which involves reading a text from which six paragraphs have been removed and jumbled, then deciding where each of the paragraphs fits. There is one extra paragraph that is not used. Brainstorm the kinds of strategies that students could use to work out which paragraph fits in each gap. Refer students to Exam focus on p.180 to compare their ideas.

Ask students to re-read the first two paragraphs then elicit the answer.

4 Read the Exam tip through with the class. Elicit what *reference words* mean, then ask students to read A–G to select the correct paragraph.

Teaching tip: Reference words

Point out that writers use reference words to refer to words or ideas at a prior or future point in the text. In the gapped text activity, it is useful for students to recognise reference words like *it, these, this* and work out what they could refer to in the missing paragraph. Point out that students can also use reference words in their own writing

to avoid repetition and improve cohesion. Substitution and ellipsis will be covered in more detail in Unit 5.

5 Students complete the task, then compare their answers and reasons in pairs before checking answers as a class.

6 Remind students that working out meaning from context is useful for the exam and in real life. Give students a few minutes to work out the meanings of the underlined words and then compare with a partner. Check answers with the class.

Additional activity

Write the following questions (that include the underlined words from the text) on the board for students to discuss in small groups. Conduct whole-class feedback.

1 *What would you do if you were out to dinner with friends and conversation began to dwindle?*

2 *Do you enjoy friendly banter? How could you tell if banter is making someone feel uneasy?*

3 *Which of these qualities do you think will get you the furthest: wit, eloquence or empathy?*

7 Students discuss the questions in pairs. Conduct whole-class feedback.

Answers

2 The writer thought the course was too theoretical rather than practical.

3 2

4 G

5 1 G (*this* (paragraph G, line 1) refers to the topic 'How to have a conversation' in the first paragraph.)

2 E (The second paragraph talks about people's views on the negative effect of technology on conversation with two quotes. Paragraph E continues this topic with an additional quote.)

3 A (The topic of the third paragraph is people's reasons for attendance. *These aims* (line 1) in paragraph A refers to the classmates' reasons in the third paragraph.)

4 D (*Then* (paragraph D, line 1) links the fourth paragraph to *After an enjoyable ten minutes spent chatting to my classmates.* The fifth paragraph refers to the discussion described in D.)

5 B (*these ideas* (in the sixth paragraph) refers to 1–6 in paragraph B. Paragraph G has similar content to B, however *this* in *the basics of this* has nothing to refer to.)

6 F (*this enjoyable burst of role play* (paragraph F) is described in the sixth paragraph: *try out ideas for unusual openings.*)

6 witty: clever and funny
empathise: understand the feelings of others
eloquence: the ability to express yourself articulately
banter: friendly, teasing conversation
unease: feeling of discomfort
dwindle: fade, grow weaker

ADDITIONAL PRACTICE | **Maximiser** p.14, Reading | **MEL** Unit 2, Reading | Photocopiable 2B *Ten perfect pairs* | **MEL** Extra practice, Reading 2 Predicting the text B | **Active Teach** Reading Focus – matching

Vocabulary focus ▶ p.22

1 Ask students to read the statements. Point out that *shout the loudest* in the second sentence needn't be taken literally and elicit the meaning (It can mean people who aren't afraid to make themselves heard, or complain, make the most fuss, etc.). Elicit the meaning of *gossip* (information that is passed from one person to another about other people's behaviour and private lives, often including unkind or untrue remarks).

Students discuss the statements in pairs. Conduct whole-class feedback.

Communication collocations

Aim

* to expand students' knowledge of collocations with *make, have, give, hold* related to communication

2 Students match the collocations, then compare answers in pairs before checking as a class. To extend in a strong class, give students a few minutes to try, in their pairs, to think of two more collocations related to communication with the verbs *make, have, give* or *hold* (e.g. *make a phone call, make excuses, make enquiries, hold/have/give an interview, give a tour, hold/have/give a demonstration, give an introduction*).

Teaching tip

Encourage students to try recording vocabulary in a visual way. Draw a mind map on the board with *communication* at the centre with the verbs *make, have, give, hold* radiating from it. Ask students to draw the same mind map and then add the nouns from Activity 2 to radiate from the relevant verb.

3 Students choose the correct alternatives, then compare answers in pairs before checking as a class. Check students know what CEO is an abbreviation for (Chief Executive Officer).

Answers

2 make: conversation (no article), a speech, a statement

have: a chat, a conversation, a debate, a discussion, a gossip, a talk

give: a presentation, a speech, a statement, a talk

hold: a debate, a discussion

3 1 speech 2 conversation 3 talk 4 discussion
5 debate 6 conversation 7 debate 8 conversation

ADDITIONAL PRACTICE | **Active Teach** Game: Noughts and crosses

Adjectives: ways of speaking

Aim

* to use a wide range of adjectives to describe voices

4 Ask students to read questions 1–5 and, if necessary, pre-teach *trustworthy* and *authoritative*. Play the recording while students answer the questions. Students compare their answers with a partner.

5 Students work in pairs to work through the exercise. If necessary, students could use a dictionary to assist with meaning.

Additional activity

Play recording 08 again and ask students to use some of the adjectives in the box to describe each speaker's voice.

6 Students discuss the questions in pairs. Conduct whole-class feedback.

7 Students complete the sentences, then compare answers in pairs before checking as a class.

8 Students answer the questions then check answers as a class.

Answers

5 1 positive: deep, husky, lively, mellow, soft, soothing, warm
2 soft, soothing, warm
3 man: lively, mellow, warm, soothing
woman: husky, lively, mellow, warm, soothing

7 1 soothing 2 nasal 3 husky 4 wobbly 5 flat 6 harsh

8 1 deep, mellow, soft, soothing, warm 2 flat, harsh, monotonous, soft 3 deep, lively, mellow, soft, warm
4 flat, lively, monotonous

Additional activity

If your students don't take themselves too seriously, try this light-hearted game to finish the class. Write on the board the following phrase: *This voice is …*

Ask students to work in pairs. Student A chooses one of the adjectives and says the phrase in that manner, e.g. in a deep voice: *This voice is …* and student B has to guess the adjective (*deep*).

Invite students to share some of their phrases for the rest of the class to guess.

ADDITIONAL PRACTICE | **Maximiser** p.16, Vocabulary | **MEL** Unit 2, Vocabulary | Photocopiable 2c *Who fits which role?* | **Active Teach** Game: Pelmanism

Grammar focus ▶ p.23

Defining and non-defining relative clauses

Aim

* to review defining and non-defining relative clauses

Refer students to the Grammar reference section on defining and non-defining relative clauses on p.152 and ask students to read the notes and complete the exercise.

Grammar reference answers

1 whose   2 whom   3 where   4 which   5 that   6 who

Warmer

Draw the following table on the board and fill in the left column. Ask students to complete the right column with relative pronouns.

defining	non-defining
who / that / omitted pronoun	who
which / that / omitted pronoun	which
when / omitted pronoun	when
whose	whose
whom / omitted pronoun	whom
where / omitted pronoun	where

Point out that *whom* is the object form of *who*. In everyday spoken or written English, people usually use *who* rather than *whom*: *Who did you send it to?* (Instead of *To whom did you send it?*). *Whom* is usually used only in the phrases *one of whom, none of whom, some of whom*, etc. (e.g. *She brought with her three friends, none of whom I had ever met before.*).

1 Students discuss the questions in pairs. Go through the answers. Point out that *who's* and *whose* are pronounced in the same way. Point out that commas can change the emphasis. For example, focus students on sentence 4. Write it on the board. Then add commas: *The girl, whose brother is a professional football player, scored the winning goal.* Now the fact that her brother is a professional football player is additional information, rather than defining information. Read through the Language tip with the class. Invite students to complete the phrase *Something that most people find annoying is …* with their own ideas. Elicit some ideas.

2 Students read the sentences and choose the correct alternatives. They then compare their answers in pairs before checking as a class. Ask: *In which sentence could the relative pronoun be omitted?* (Sentence 5).

Additional activity

If students have found Activity 2 challenging, review relative pronouns with the following exercise. Write uses 1–7 below on the board. Working in pairs, ask students to match each pronoun from Activity 2 with its use, then check as a class.

1 *to refer to things*
2 *to refer to people*
3 *to refer to people or things*
4 *used after nouns referring to a place*
5 *used after nouns referring to a time*
6 *used to show possession*
7 *refers to people who are the object of a sentence*

Answers: **1** which   **2** who   **3** that   **4** where   **5** when   **6** whose   **7** whom

3 Students match the sentences with the meanings. Ask them to compare answers in pairs before checking as a class.

4 Direct students to the title of the article and elicit the meaning of *holding you back* (preventing you from making progress). Ask the class to predict some ways that someone's voice might hold them back, then get them to quickly read the article to check.

5 Students complete the activity, then compare answers in pairs before you check as a class.

6 Students compare their ideas with a partner.

Answers

1 **1** Non-defining **2** Defining **3** Non-defining **4** Defining

2 **1** who/that (D) **2** where (D) **3** whom (D) **4** whose (D)
5 that/which (D) **6** which (ND) **7** when (D) **8** which (ND)
9 whose (D) **10** who (D)

3 **1** A **2** B

4 Problems on the telephone, at work or in job interviews.

5 **1** which **2** where **3** who **4** whose
5 which **6** when **7** which **8** why

Additional activity

Students complete the following sentences so that they are true for themselves.

The person with whom I have the most in common is ...

Someone who I'd like to have a conversation with would be ...

A job that I'd love to do would be ...

Some of the reasons why I'm taking this course are ...

Elicit whether the relative pronoun can be omitted in each. (Yes, because these relative pronouns introduce defining relative clauses.) Put students into small groups to share their sentences.

ADDITIONAL PRACTICE | **Maximiser** p.16, Grammar | **MEL** Unit 2, Grammar | **MEL** Extra practice, Use of English 12: Relative clauses with relative pronouns | **Active Teach** Extra activity Grammar Focus 2

Writing focus ▶ p.24

Proposal (Part 2)

organising your ideas

Aims

- to review the structure of a proposal
- to write an exam-style proposal (Writing Part 2)

Warmer

Write the scenarios below on the board. Working in pairs, students decide what future action or 'proposals' they would recommend to each person. Conduct whole-class feedback.

1 *My inbox is bursting at the seams and most of the emails are from people who work in the same office!*

2 *My colleague talks too quietly.*

3 *My colleague constantly interrupts and talks over me.*

4 *My boss never seems to say anything positive – it's always complaints.*

Alternatively, put students in four groups and assign each group one scenario. The group brainstorms advice, then selects their best three pieces of advice to share with the class.

Teaching tip: The Writing paper (Part 2)

Remind students that the Writing paper is divided into two parts. Part 1 is a compulsory essay and Part 2 is a choice of three tasks which could include an email/letter, a report/proposal, or a review.

1 Read through the two statements with the class and elicit which one refers to a proposal and which one refers to a report. Refer students to the Writing reference on p.174 to see a sample proposal and useful advice. Consider asking students to read it in more detail for homework.

2 Give students a few minutes to look at the exam task, the tips for writing a proposal and the candidate's answer. Then elicit which of the tips the candidate has not followed. Ask students to look at the language used in the recommendations.

3 Read the Exam tip aloud. Then ask students to look at the exam task and follow the steps to prepare to write. Remind students of the useful language for proposals on p.175. Set step 3 (writing the first draft) as a homework activity. Ask students to re-read their proposal and assess it against the checklist in Activity 2.

Additional activity

To practise the language for the *recommendations* section of a report, get students to work in small groups to write a bullet point list of recommendations. Each group chooses one of the following topics:

- *How to make friends when you're busy*
- *How to cope with gossip*
- *How to improve communication at your school*
- *How to get your ideas heard*
- *How to conquer phone addiction*

They brainstorm ideas and then choose the best three ideas to write bullet points for. They could incorporate some of the phrases for recommendations and suggestions on p.175. Ask each group to present their key recommendations to the class.

Answers

1 **1** proposal **2** report

2 The candidate has not followed tip 5.

3 Model answer

Helping with student presentations: a proposal

Introduction

In this proposal I will describe some of the difficulties students at this school have with making presentations in English and conclude by making a series of recommendations on how teachers could assist students with overcoming the obstacles to giving a successful presentation confidently.

Current situation

A student survey indicates that many students are nervous or overwhelmed when faced with presenting in English. Students are concerned about making pronunciation and grammar mistakes and they are unsure about how formal their language should be. Some students need additional assistance with structuring their presentations.

Key needs to be addressed

Students require additional help with confidence building and opportunities need to be provided for students to gain experience speaking in front of others.

Recommendations

I would suggest the following actions to teachers at the school:

- Students could be provided with a list of useful expressions for use in presentations.

- Extra drop-in sessions could be offered where students could get help on all aspects of their preparation.

- Teachers could allocate more class time to practice. For example, students could deliver their presentation in front of a small group the day before the final presentation to the whole class.

- A greater variety of lower stakes speaking opportunities should be provided in all classes to get students accustomed to speaking in front of others.

If these suggestions are implemented, it will lead to increased student confidence and performance for giving a presentation in English.

MyEnglishLab tip: Gradebook

The MyEnglishLab exercises are marked automatically so that students can have immediate feedback. Log on and check the gradebook to see their progress.

ADDITIONAL PRACTICE | **Maximiser** p.17, Writing | **MEL** Unit 2, Writing | MEL Extra practice, Writing 12: Knowing the difference between a proposal and a report

Review ▶ p.25

Aim

● to revise the structures and vocabulary covered in Unit 2

1 – **4** Ask students to complete the activities, monitoring them to provide assistance. Alternatively, set this as a homework activity. Ask students to compare their answers in pairs before doing a class check.

Answers

1 1 including 2 administrative 3 addiction 4 Indecision
5 distinctive 6 interactive 7 communicator 8 impressive

2 1 was typing, got, had decided, hadn't expected/wasn't expecting, felt, hadn't had/didn't have

2 had known, I'd never realised/I never realised, he'd been (*was* is only possible if Jack is still a footballer), He'd even played/He even played

3 moved, I'd been worried/I'd been worrying, I'd been living/I'd lived, hadn't spent

4 always planned/were always planning, we left/we'd left, didn't manage/hadn't managed, got married, we'd saved

5 was working/worked, qualified

6 had hoped/was hoping, went, said, had sold

3 1 who/that 2 which 3 whose 4 which/that
5 who/that

4 1 monotonous 2 soft 3 husky 4 squeaky
5 warm 6 nasal

ADDITIONAL PRACTICE | **Active Teach** Games: Sheep out!; Stepping stones

3 Ages and stages

Vocabulary and Grammar focus ▶ p.26

Vocabulary

stages of life

Aim

• to expand students' vocabulary related to life stages

Warmer

Focus students' attention on the image on p.26. Ask: *What do you think the image represents?* Elicit some ideas. Direct students to the unit title. Ask: *What do you think is the best age to be? What is the best life stage? Why?*

1 Invite two students to read the quotes aloud. Students discuss each one in pairs and think of examples from their lives or people they know. Conduct whole-class feedback.

2 Look at the first sentence as a class. Ask whether *juvenile* sounds like it is saying something good about a person, or bad. Explain the connotation that *juvenile* has (i.e that it's childish or acting in a silly, irresponsible way). Students complete the activity, then compare their answers in pairs before you check as a class.

3 Students complete the activity and then discuss their answers as a class.

4 Students take turns to practise reading each sentence, and underline the stressed words.

5 In pairs, students brainstorm any other synonyms they know for the words in Activities 2 and 3 and discuss the connotations. Elicit some ideas.

6 Students discuss the questions in pairs. Conduct whole-class feedback.

Alternative

During the class feedback stage, invite a different student to facilitate the feedback on each question by inviting a few responses and responding briefly to each one.

7 Introduce Chris (pictured) and tell the class that he needs some advice about achieving his goals. Give students a few minutes to read the extract to identify his goals (start a family at some point, get promoted or get a new job within two years). Then ask students to discuss in pairs what advice they would give to Chris. Elicit some ideas. Play the recording. Elicit a summary of the life coach's advice.

8 Students discuss the question in pairs. As a follow-up question, ask: *What attributes would a good life coach have?* (e.g. empathy, strong communication skills, being organised).

Answers

2 **1** negative   **2** positive   **3** positive   **4** positive
   5 negative   **6** negative

3 **1** adolescent (negative), childish (negative), infantile (negative)

   2 childish (negative)

   3 boyish (positive)

   4 adult (positive), old (neutral)

   5 aging (neutral), elderly (neutral), old (negative)

   6 old (negative)

4 The underlined words should be stressed.

5 (Suggested answers)

   1 immature (negative)

   2 naïve (neutral)

   3 fresh-faced (positive)

   4 grown-up (positive)

   5 geriatric (negative) ancient (usually neutral, but negative in this context)

   6 past it (negative)

ADDITIONAL PRACTICE | **Maximiser** p.22, Vocabulary | **MEL** Unit 3, Vocabulary | **Active Teach** Game: Pelmanism

Future forms

Aim

- to select appropriate future forms to talk about plans, intentions, predictions and spontaneous decisions

Refer students to the Grammar reference section on future forms on p.152 and ask them to do the exercise on p.153. Check answers as a class.

Grammar reference answers

1 'll cook

2 'll be

3 are we meeting

4 'll get

5 'll be lying

6 will have read

7 will have retired

8 will be doing

Alternative

An alternative to asking students to read the notes then complete the exercise is as follows. Ask students to attempt the exercise in pairs, referring to the notes and examples as required. Go through the answers as a class and elicit a reason for the particular future form in each sentence.

9 Students find an example of each form in the article. Check answers as a class. Emphasise that *will* is not used for intentions or plans unless it is an intention made right at the time of speaking.

10 Emphasise that more than one verb form may be possible in each case and students need to cross out the ones that are not possible. Students complete the exercise then compare in pairs before checking as a class.

11 Read the Language tip with the class and elicit the difference in meaning between *it's only a matter of time before …* (used to say that something will definitely happen in the future) and *it's about time* (used to say strongly that you think something should happen soon or should already have happened).

Ask students to do the activity in pairs. First, they discuss what the sentence is talking about (a completed future action, or an action in progress in the future, etc.), then they identify the tense they ought to use. Check answers as a class.

Additional activity

Ask students to think about some of their own goals for the future. These could be from various areas of their lives such as study, work, fitness, friends or hobbies. Ask students to write down some of these using some of the phrases from Activity 11. For example, *Two years from now I hope I'll be …*; *It's about time I …*; *Within the next six months, I … .*

Put students into small groups to share some of their own ideas.

Answers

9 **1** They're moving to a bigger house soon   **2** We're going to start a family   **3** they think they'll have enough money   **4** I'll get down to some serious planning tomorrow!   **5** I'll have been promoted   **6** I'll be doing exactly the same job

10 **1** I'm starting   **2** I'm doing   **3** I'm achieving   **4** I do   **5** I'll have spent   **6** I see   **7** I'll have stayed   **8** I'm finding

11 **1** will be doing   **2** will have left   **3** will have found   **4** am going to/will pass   **5** meet   **6** find   **7** am living/will live   **8** will learn   **9** got   **10** will be

ADDITIONAL PRACTICE | **Maximiser** p.22, Grammar | **MEL** Unit 3, Grammar | **Active Teach** Extra activity Grammar Focus 1

Reading focus ▶ p.28

1 Students discuss the questions about blogs and diaries in pairs. Conduct whole-class feedback. To extend question 3, ask how many people share things on social media, who might be checking this information and what social media companies do with the information (and also, whether this information is truly private).

Cross-text multiple matching (Part 6)

Aims

* to identify and compare writers' opinions in an article
* to complete an exam-style cross-text multiple matching task (Reading and Use of English Part 6)

Teaching tip: The Reading and Use of English paper

Tell students that Part 6 of the Reading and Use of English paper consists of reading four short texts on a related topic by different writers and answering four multiple matching questions. The questions test their ability to identify where the writers may have similar or different opinions to each other about a specific issue. For more detailed information and strategies, refer students to the Exam focus on p.180.

2 Give students a few minutes to read the extracts, and then elicit which risks are mentioned.

3 Students read the extracts again to complete the table. Check answers as a class.

4 Encourage students to use underlining or highlighting to keep track of where they have located relevant information. For example, in 1, students would need to underline *Giannoni's view on the contents of teenage diaries*, check they understand this view, then scan for a similar view in the other extracts. If they have four different coloured highlighter pens, it's useful to allocate one colour to information relevant to each question 1–4.

Direct students to the Exam tip. Students complete the activity then compare answers in pairs.

5 Ask students to work in pairs to discuss the meaning of each underlined word. Then ask students to complete the sentences. Check answers as a class.

Additional activity

In pairs, students think of …

* *a book / film / TV show they find appalling*
* *a book / film / TV show / podcast they find insightful*
* *a charitable cause they find worthwhile*
* *an online situation where reticence might be wise*

6 In pairs, students discuss which of the opinions in the extracts they agree with.

Answers

2 (suggested answers) rereading diaries as an adult can be embarrassing; it's difficult to completely destroy digital records; social media posts attract unkind comments; people can find your diary and read it; expressing ourselves honestly in a diary can force us to confront uncomfortable truths; what you write online remains there forever.

3 1 A, B 2 B, D 3 B, D 4 A, B, D

4 **1 D** (nothing more than records of childish hopes and ambitions in A; how little space they gave to what really matters and how much time they dedicated to the boy or girl on the bus who might or might not have fancied them in D)

2 B I'm not convinced though that the dangers of expressing ourselves through social media outweigh the benefits.

3 A (though they are in many senses more ephemeral C; can be quickly and completely destroyed, something that can't be said of our digital footprint)

4 D The frequently uncharitable responses to narcissistic display on social media are hardly surprising. If found, a diary too will be read and its contents certainly made fun of in much the same way but the reluctant diarist… in A; the prospect of somebody finding and reading similar outpourings in a secret diary is enough to put many teenagers off the idea of keeping one in B)

5 1 appalling 2 retaliation/retaliating 3 charity 4 justify 5 reticent 6 insightful

ADDITIONAL PRACTICE | **Maximiser** pp.20-21, Reading | **MEL** Unit 3, Reading | **MEL** Extra practice, Reading 5: Scanning for specific information A | **Active Teach** Reading Focus – easily confused words

Grammar focus ▶ p.30

1 Ask students not to open their books yet. Put students into small groups and ask them to make a list of five things (i.e. practical life skills) they think all adults should be able to do by the time they are twenty. Ask a volunteer from each group to share their list with the class. Save these lists for use in Activity 5.

2 Ask students to open their books on p.30 and read the similar list in Activity 2 to see if they mentioned any of the same things. Check students understand *CPR* (cardiopulmonary resuscitation – when you press repeatedly on someone's chest in order to make them breathe again and make their heart start beating again after it has stopped) and *the Heimlich Manoeuvre* (when you help someone who is choking by putting your arms around their waist and jerking upwards strongly). Students tick the things they can already do and choose two more items to add. Ask students to compare their answers in pairs and discuss which of the skills they would most like to learn.

Introductory *it*

- to review the four uses of introductory *it*

3 Read through the four uses of the introductory *it* with the class, then elicit another example for each use from the list in Activity 2. To extend in a strong class, elicit an additional original example for each use. Refer students to the Grammar reference section on introductory *it* on p.153 to read and complete the exercise.

Grammar reference answers

1 It was lovely to visit Lisbon again.
2 It is shocking how many young people drop litter in the street.
3 It is almost inevitable that I will not finish the assignment on time.
4 Fiona made it very clear that she didn't want any birthday presents.
5 It was Eva who made the negotiations run so smoothly.
6 It was on Wednesday that we arranged to meet.

Additional activity

Write the following sentence starters on the board: *I can't stand it when …, I love it when …, I find it important to …, It's always good to …, It's definitely worth …, It's a lot of fun to …, It's astonishing how …* . Ask students to complete the sentences so that they are true for them. Students then take turns to share their ideas with a partner. Monitor to check that students are using the introductory *it* correctly.

4 Focus students' attention on the Language tip and read through it with the class. Students rewrite the sentences while you circulate, providing help as necessary.

Alternative

If students find this too challenging, work with the class to identify the first three words of each rewritten sentence before students complete the sentences individually.

5 Give students a few minutes to write their sentences using *it*. Then ask students to compare their sentences with a partner while you circulate, listening to check the introductory *it* is being used appropriately.

Answers

3 1 It's no fun being in debt. 2 One day it may be your partner or child who needs your help. 3 It's amazing how many people don't know how to find their most beguiling smile. 4 I find it appalling that so many young people live on pot noodles and toast.

4 1 It's sad that we have become so disconnected from the natural environment. 2 It's vital for schoolchildren to learn basic first aid skills. 3 It worries me how dependent people have become on mobile phones. 4 It's you who should get the credit for the work done on the project. 5 It was difficult for me to make new friends. 6 It is vital for people to contact a member of staff first. 7 It makes good sense not to throw away letters with your name and address on them. 8 It was embarrassing telling Charles how I felt.

ADDITIONAL PRACTICE | **Maximiser** p.22, Grammar | **MEL** Unit 3, Grammar | Photocopiable 3A *The it race* | **MEL** Extra practice, Reading 16 Logical and cohesive development A | **Active Teach** Extra activity Grammar Focus 2

Speaking focus ▶ p.31

Collaborative task and discussion (Parts 3 and 4)
responding to and expanding on your partner's ideas

Aim

- to practise responding to and expanding on a partner's ideas in an exam-style collaborative task and discussion (Speaking Parts 3 and 4)

Teaching tip

Find out what students already know about the collaborative task (Part 3) in the Speaking paper. For example, ask: *What are the two parts? What prompts will you be given? How long do you need to talk for?* If students aren't sure, refer them to the Exam focus on p.183 to check.

1 Get students to read the question, then play the recording. Elicit the answer. Read the Exam tip aloud. Point out that knowing strategies for responding will help students in social and work situations, as well as in the exam. Explain that *expanding on your partner's ideas* means to acknowledge something they have said and add more detail, information or another example.

2 Play the recording again and ask students to underline the phrases that Daniela uses to respond to and expand on what Martin says. Check answers as a class.

3 Read the first idea aloud with the class and elicit some possible ways to expand on this. Give students a minute to read the ideas and think about what they are going to say. Then put students in pairs to act out the conversations. Invite a few pairs to share one of their conversations with the class.

4 Ask students to read the questions in Activity 4, then play the recording. Elicit the answers. Refer students to the Exam focus on p.183 and get them to work in pairs to paraphrase the four strategies in their own words.

5 Tell students that they are now going to practise doing Parts 3 and 4 of the Speaking part of the exam in groups of three, with each student taking turns to be the examiner and the two candidates. It would be useful for each group to have a timer for the 'examiner' to use. Students turn to the activity on p.135 to follow the instructions. Encourage the 'candidates' to use the useful phrases from Activity 2 during the task, and the 'examiners' to note how many times the 'candidates' responded to each other or expanded on each other's points.

Answers
1 **1** Daniela responds to and expands on what the other candidate says.

2 <u>You mean,</u> because you're having to ask your parents for money and possibly also having to justify what you spend it on?

<u>There's a lot to be said for that argument. In many cases, I think</u> it does make people less able to take responsibility for their own decisions and it often creates tensions in a family.

<u>Yes,</u> you're forced to be mature by having to make sacrifices and by being responsible for other people, <u>aren't you</u>?

ADDITIONAL PRACTICE | **Maximiser** p.23, Speaking | **MEL** Unit 3, Speaking | Photocopiable 3B *A good answer* | **MEL** Extra practice, Speaking 9 Strategies for dealing with the first part of a Part 3 task

Use of English focus ▶ p.32
Multiple-choice cloze (Part 1)

Aim
- to complete an exam-style multiple-choice cloze task (Reading and Use of English Part 1)

1 Ask students to read the questions, then elicit the difference between *life expectancy* (the length of time a person or animal is expected to live), and *longevity* (a long life). Point out that *life expectancy* refers to animals/people, but *longevity* refers to lots of things (ideas, buildings, food, etc.). Students discuss the questions in pairs. Elicit a few responses to each.

2 Elicit what students remember about the multiple-choice cloze task (Reading and Use of English Part 1) and refer them to the Exam focus on p.178 to check their ideas. Give students one minute to read the article and see if any of their ideas were mentioned.

3 Students complete the sentences individually, then compare answers in pairs.

4 Get students to read the Exam tip and then elicit which item depends on a preposition following a verb (1). Point out that *rely* takes the preposition *on*; *trust* wouldn't take a preposition; *believe* and *confide* take the preposition *in*. Remind students that they should record verbs + prepositions as verb phrases, to help them remember them. Elicit the answer and reason for the second item in Activity 3 (*amount* is the only word that collocates with *of money*).

5 Give students about six minutes to complete the task. Students do the task, then compare their answers in pairs before you check as a class. Elicit the reasons for each answer.

6 Give students a moment to consider their answers. Put students into small groups to compare.

Answers
3 **1** B **2** A
4 **1**
5 **1** D (collocates with *play*)
2 A (collocates with *life/lives*)
3 C (collocates with *at*)
4 C (collocates with *highest*; *amount* not possible with countable noun)

5 D (collocates with *life*)

6 B (followed by dependent preposition *to*)

7 C (followed by dependent preposition *by*)

8 A (only option that can be followed by *in*)

ADDITIONAL PRACTICE | **Maximiser** p.24, Use of English | **MEL** Unit 3, Use of English | **Photocopiable** 3C *Word exchange* | **MEL** Extra practice, Use of English 1 Nouns followed by prepositions | **Active Teach** Game: Sheep out!

Listening focus ▶ p.33

1 Students discuss each statement in pairs. Conduct whole-class feedback. Other life periods for question 2 could include *childhood*, *adolescence*, *young adulthood*, *middle age* and *old age*.

Multiple choice (Part 3)

Aim

- to complete an exam-style multiple-choice listening task (Listening Part 3)

2 Point out that there are two multiple-choice tasks in the Listening paper (Part 1 and Part 3). Read the Exam tip aloud. For more information, students could read the Exam focus on p.182. Give students 45 seconds to quickly skim read the questions (and options if they have time). Play the recording twice. Go through the answers as a class.

Students discuss the questions in pairs. Conduct whole-class feedback.

Answers

2 1 C   2 A   3 D   4 B   5 A   6 C

ADDITIONAL PRACTICE | **Maximiser** p.24, Listening | **MEL** Unit 3, Listening | **MEL** Extra practice, Listening 4: Listening to a longer text

Vocabulary

working out meaning from context

4 Students discuss the meanings of the underlined words in pairs, then check the answers as a class.

Answers

4 1 believing what you want to happen will happen even though it is impossible

2 used when you admit that something is true

3 would definitely prefer

4 relaxed and easy-going

5 change direction suddenly

6 when the situation is the opposite of what it was before

ADDITIONAL PRACTICE | **Active Teach** Game: Noughts and crosses

Writing focus ▶ p.34

Report (Part 2)

dos and don'ts

Aims

- to identify dos and don'ts for writing an exam-style report
- to practise effective planning and writing an exam-style report

1 Remind students that the Writing paper consists of a compulsory essay (Part 1) and a choice of three tasks in Part 2, one of which might be a report.
Students discuss the questions in pairs. Elicit a few ideas for each question.

2 Students read the advice for writing reports and identify which piece of advice should start with *Don't*. Elicit the answer.

3 Students look at the plans and answer the questions. Elicit the answers. Point out that spending time planning is essential in the exam. It will help students get better results because they will be able to save time overall because they can write from their plan, write a better structured answer, and ensure that all aspects of the task are covered.

4 Refer students to the model report on p.174 to read and compare against the advice in Activity 2. Elicit which plan is most similar to the model answer.

5 Tell students that they are going to write a report in response to the task in Activity 2. Ask students to read the useful language on p.175 and select a few expressions to use in their own work.

6 This task could be set for homework or done as timed writing in class. Students will have 45 minutes in the exam to do each writing task. As students have spent time planning, suggest they write their report in 35 minutes to allow five minutes for checking at the end. Suggest students check their work by reviewing the advice in Activity 2.

Answers

2 Item 7 should start with *Don't*.

3 Plans A and B do not include a recommendation section.

4 Plan C is the most similar to the structure of the model report.

6 Model answer

Introduction

The main objectives of this report are to summarise local young people's views about elderly people in their area, and the thought of their own aging. I will present results of a survey I conducted with a random selection of 200 young people at the local high school. I include recommendations as to how attitudes could be improved.

Attitudes to older people

According to my survey, a significant proportion of young people never or hardly ever spend time with someone aged over 65. Reasons that respondents gave for this included: they have nothing in common, the elderly don't like teenagers and lack of time. More promisingly, nearly three quarters of those surveyed (74 percent) agreed that they could probably 'learn something' from older people.

Attitudes to aging

Those responding to the survey were almost equally split between preferring to think about it as little as possible and those who never thought about it. For those who did think about it, the prime concerns were loneliness, poor health and boredom.

Recommendations

Clearly more could be done to bridge the gap between young and old in our community. I would make the following recommendations.

• Set up volunteer tutoring opportunities for elderly citizens to help younger people at the high school with academic work or practical skills.

• Invite young people to tutor old people in technology use, e.g. how to text/send emails in return for a donation to be used for social events.
It is hoped that increased contact between the groups will lead to greater empathy and more positive attitudes.

ADDITIONAL PRACTICE | **Maximiser** p.25, Writing | **MEL** Unit 3, Writing | **MEL** Extra practice, Writing 13: Useful language for reports and proposals

Review ▶ p.35

Aim

• to revise the structures, vocabulary and exam tasks covered in Unit 3

1 – **3** Ask students to complete the activities, monitoring them to provide assistance. Alternatively, set this as a homework activity. Ask students to compare their answers in pairs before doing a class check.

Answers

1 1 F 2 A 3 E 4 C 5 D 6 B

2 1 vital that we learn 2 will still be living 3 the council that should do 4 astonishing how few people 5 find it (really) embarrassing 6 time I got

3 1 C 2 B 3 D 4 A 5 C 6 D 7 A 8 B

ADDITIONAL PRACTICE | **Active Teach** Game: Stepping stones

Progress test 1 ▶ p.36

Aim

• to revise structures, vocabulary and exam tasks covered in Units 1–3

The Progress test gives students an opportunity to revise what has been covered in the module, build confidence in what they know, and to recognise any gaps in their learning. The test may be completed in class or as a homework activity. Set a time limit of 40 minutes, although this may need to be varied according to the ability of the students in your class. Go through the answers as a class, or organise students into small groups to compare and check their answers.

Teaching tip: Checking answers in groups

When students compare and explain answers in groups, it can help the explainer to clarify and consolidate their learning, and is likely to be more memorable and accessible for the listener.

After students have completed the test, organise them into groups of three to compare their answers, and discuss any that they differed on. Then distribute the answer key to the group to check. Circulate, giving students the opportunity to ask you anything they are unsure of.

Answers

1 1 B 2 B 3 C 4 D 5 B 6 C 7 A 8 C

2 1 she 2 out 3 on 4 time 5 have 6 too
7 some 8 what

3 1 amazement 2 imagination(s) 3 unlikely
4 unexpectedly 5 discovery 6 enthusiastic
7 remarkable 8 agencies

4 1 nor is he

2 as yet I haven't

3 is a mystery (to me)

4 who found my (stolen) wallet

5 no idea why she should/might

6 I had already

4 No pain without gain

Listening and Grammar focus ▶ p.38

Sentence completion (Part 2)

Aim

- to complete an exam-style sentence completion task (Listening Part 2)

Warmer

Write *No gain without pain* on the board, and ask students what they think it means. Elicit that any success comes after a lot of hard work or failure.

Elicit some more ideas of things which can only be achieved with a lot of hard work (e.g. getting fit, studying hard to pass an exam, working long hours to launch a business, forgoing small treats to save up for a big purchase, taking a long plane trip to get to an exotic destination).

Point out that the title of the unit is *No pain without gain*, which swaps around the words *pain* and *gain*.

1 Students work in pairs to add three more statements to the questionnaire. Then ask students to interview at least three other students using their questionnaire.

Sentence completion (Part 2)

Teaching tip

Tell students that Part 2 of the Listening paper involves reading eight sentences with gaps, then listening carefully to a monologue to complete the sentences. The word(s) for the gaps will be exactly the same as in the recording. For more detailed information and strategies for Part 2 sentence completion, refer students to the Exam focus on p.181.

2 Give students a minute to read the exam task. Students discuss in pairs what sort of information is missing in each gap, or what type of word (noun, verb, etc.).

3 Play the first part of the talk and elicit the words which could fit grammatically in the gap in question 1. Then elicit the word that makes most sense.

4 Play the whole recording while students complete sentences 2–8. Students compare their answers in pairs, then check as a class.

5 Students discuss the questions in pairs. Conduct whole-class feedback.

Answers

3 pressure, wealth, success, perfectionism

only 'pressure' has increased

4 1 (extreme) pressure

2 frustration

3 mistake(s)

4 negative

5 decision-making

6 confidence

7 substitution

8 ice

ADDITIONAL PRACTICE | **Maximiser** p.26, Listening | **MEL** Unit 4, Listening | **MEL** Extra practice, Listening 5: Understanding specific information

Verb patterns: *-ing*/infinitive

Aim

- to identify which verbs are followed by the *-ing* form, and which are followed by the infinitive form with *to*

Refer students to the Grammar reference on verb patterns on p.153 and ask them to do the exercise on p.154.

Grammar reference answers

1 prevented

2 persuaded

3 intended

4 regretted/suggested

5 forced

6 suggested/regretted

6 Students complete the exercise. Go through the answers. Read the Language tip with the class and share another example, e.g. *I prefer watching / to watch football from the comfort of my own sofa.*

7 Point out that after some verbs, there is a difference in meaning depending on the verb pattern. Students discuss the examples in pairs.

Additional activity

Write the following three sentences on the board and ask students to discuss the difference in meaning between the alternatives.

1 *I'm going to stop to have coffee / having coffee.*

2 *I regret to let you know / letting you know that there will be consequences.*

3 *I remembered to leave / leaving the key.*

Go through the answers:

1 *stop to have coffee* = stop an activity in order to have coffee;

stop having coffee = give up coffee.

2 *regret to let you know* = I am about to tell you something unfortunate;

regret letting you know = I wish I hadn't told you

3 *remembered to leave* = refers to the thought I had before I left the key;

remembered leaving = refers to the memory of leaving the key.

With a stronger class, put students into pairs and ask each one to write a sentence with two alternative versions, using the verbs *stop, regret* or *remember* with *-ing* and the infinitive on a piece of paper. Collect these in and check them for accuracy. Read each pair of sentences aloud and allow students time to discuss the difference with their partner, then elicit the answer.

8 Ask students to identify the collocations in the questions. Encourage students to note these down to learn: *turn your dreams into reality, fulfil your ambitions, leave your comfort zone, make a contribution.* Students discuss the questions in pairs. Conduct whole-class feedback.

9 Students complete the text, then compare answers in pairs before checking as a class.

10 Give students a few minutes to discuss the questions. Conduct whole-class feedback.

Answers

6 1 avoided, attempted, continued, intended, recommended, stopped, suggested, tried

2 attempted, continued, failed, intended, pretended, tried

3 encouraged, persuaded

4 noticed, stopped

5 recommended, suggested

7 1 B   2 A   3 B

8 Students' own answers

9 1 to achieve   2 fulfilling   3 having   4 to make   5 to take on   6 failing   7 (to) leave   8 taking   9 to work   10 doing   11 increasing   12 (to) turn

10 Students' own answers

ADDITIONAL PRACTICE | **Maximiser** p.27, Grammar | **MEL** Unit 4, Grammar | **MEL** Extra practice, Reading 1 Reading for gist: Shooting Scotland | **Active Teach** Extra activity: Grammar Focus 1

Vocabulary focus ▶ p.40

1 Check students understand *entrepreneur* (someone who starts their own business or arranges business deals to make money, often in a way that involves financial risks). Elicit which syllable is stressed in *entrepreneur* (*entrepreneur*; the final underlined syllable). Elicit the adjective form, *entrepreneurial*. Get students to discuss the questions in pairs, then elicit a few ideas for each question.

2 Give students a few minutes to read the article about Levi Roots. Tell them that if they come across unknown vocabulary, they should try to guess the meaning from context rather than using dictionaries. Elicit what is unusual about Levi Roots' success.

3 Students match the words with their meanings, using the context of the article to help them. Check answers as a class.

Answers
1 Students' own answers
2 He went on TV to get funding for his business. He started his business when he was 49. It was successful very quickly.
3 **1** F **2** C **3** D **4** B **5** A **6** E

Additional activity
Ask students to work in pairs to underline the stressed syllable for words 1–5 in Activity 3. Check answers as a class.
Answers: *exposure, envisage, mantra, granted, venture*

ADDITIONAL PRACTICE | **Active Teach** Game: Pelmanism

Verb/Noun collocations

Aim
- to expand students' knowledge of collocations related to success

4 Students work through the questions about the verbs with a partner, then check answers as a class.

Teaching tip
Check students have the correct pronunciation of *seize* by eliciting any rhymes students can think of (e.g. *cheese, please, he's*). Point out that, in English, many different letter combinations can represent the same sound.

5 Look at the first phrase with the class (*encounter a setback*). Elicit which of the verbs in the box can also

collocate with *a setback* (*suffer*). Students complete the activity, then check answers as a class.

6 Read the Exam tip aloud. Students write six sentences using some of the collocations in Activity 6. In pairs, they compare their sentences and check them for meaning. Consider collecting in the sentences to check for appropriate use of the collocations.

7 Students discuss the questions in pairs. Conduct whole-class feedback.

Answers
4 **1** seize **2** grasp, grab, seize **3** Yes
5 **1** suffer, face **2** doubt, follow, rely on **3** gain, receive, win **4** find, gain, receive **5** exceed, fulfil **6** exceed, follow, fulfil, realise **7** receive, win **8** doubt, exceed, fulfil, reach, realise
6–7 Students' own answers

Additional activity
Ask students to look back at the collocations in Activity 5 and use three of them to write a discussion question (e.g. *Where do you get inspiration from? Do you tend to trust your intuition? What advice would you give to a friend who has suffered a setback to starting their own business?*).
Students discuss their questions in small groups.

MyEnglishLab tip
Uploading resources

If you have additional resources you would like to make available for students online, you can add them to the resources folder in MyEnglishLab. Like all MyEnglishLab resources, you have control over whether they are visible or hidden to students at any given time.

ADDITIONAL PRACTICE | **Maximiser** p.27, Vocabulary | **MEL** Unit 4, Vocabulary | Photocopiable 4A *Same word, different sentences* | **Active Teach** Game: Noughts and crosses

Use of English focus ▶ p.41

Key word transformations (Part 4)

Aim
- to complete an exam-style key word transformation task (Reading and Use of English Part 4)

Tell students that in Part 4 of the Reading and Use of English paper, key word transformations involve completing six sentences using three to six words (including a key word given in capitals) so that each sentence has a similar meaning to another sentence given with it. For more detailed information and strategies, refer students to the Exam focus on p.179.

1 Students answer the questions, then compare answers in pairs. Check answers as a class.

2 Students complete the activity, then compare answers in pairs before you check as a class.

3 Focus students' attention on the Exam tip and read it aloud. Students complete questions 1–6, then compare answers in pairs, checking they have not used more than six words in any gap. Point out that contractions (e.g. *isn't*) count as two words. Check answers as a class.

Answers

1 **1** passive **2** negative **3** A
2 **1** B **2** C **3** B
3 **1** isn't expected to do
   2 would have been able
   3 may/might not be realised
   4 is no point (in) learning
   5 whether he/she should take on/whether to take on
   6 prevented me from going

ADDITIONAL PRACTICE | **Maximiser p.28, Use of English** | **MEL Unit 4, Use of English** | **MEL Extra practice, Use of English 16: Key word transformation**

Reading focus ▶ p.42

Warmer

Write the following questions on the board:

1 How important is it to you to have the latest phone, laptop, TV, etc?

2 What are the two best and worst inventions of the 21st century so far?

Students work in pairs to discuss the questions. Elicit a few responses to each question.

Multiple choice (Part 5)

Aim

● to complete an exam-style multiple-choice task (Reading and Use of English Part 5)

Teaching tip: The Reading and Use of English paper

Tell students that Part 5 tests their ability to understand a long text in detail and consists of a text with six multiple-choice questions. For more detailed information and strategies, refer students to the Exam focus on p.179.

1 Give students a couple of minutes to read the article quickly and answer the question. Then elicit how the Museum of Failed Products is similar to and how it is different from a normal museum.

2 Work through this question with the class, eliciting answers as you go.

3 Tell students that the strategy for this type of task is to a) underline key words in the questions, b) identify the part of the text that the question relates to, c) reread that part of the text carefully and d) choose the option that fits. Either display the Exam focus on p.179, which has a similar list of strategies, or write these steps up as prompts for students to refer to during the activity. Refer students to the Exam tip. Students compare their answers in pairs before checking as a class.

4 Ask students to look at the questions in pairs then conduct whole-class feedback.

Answers

1 Supermarket products which are no longer available.
2 **1** Yes
   2 'It takes a few moments for your eyes to adjust to what you're seeing. It appears to be a vast and haphazardly organised supermarket … There is, however, something not quite right about the displays and soon enough you work out the reason.' Option D
3 **1 D** 'There is, however, something not quite right about the displays and soon enough you work out the reason.'
   2 B 'These products may well have been perfectly adequate shampoos let down only by their off-putting names. Whereas some of the other products obviously had more serious flaws.'
   3 B 'It is never far from her mind that real people had their mortgages, their car payments and their family holidays riding on the success of products such as Fortune Snookies.'

4 D 'What McMath hadn't taken into account was the three-word truth that was to prove the making of his career: *most products fail.*'

5 A 'Most surprising of all is that many of the designers who have found their way to the museum have come there to examine – or been surprised to discover – products that their own companies had created.'

6 A 'It isn't hard to imagine how one downside of the positive-thinking culture, an <u>aversion</u> to confronting failure, might have been responsible for the very existence of many of the products lining its shelves … '.

ADDITIONAL PRACTICE | **Maximiser** p.28, Reading | **MEL** Unit 4, Reading | Photocopiable 4B *Get the message?* | **MEL** Extra practice, Reading 6: Scanning for specific information B

Vocabulary
Working out meaning from context

Aim

● to practise working out meaning from context

5 Emphasise that students should use the article to help them choose the correct meanings. Check answers as a class. Demonstrate the pronunciation of *poignant* /'pɔɪnjənt/ and *haphazardly* /ˌhæp'hæzədliː/.

Answers

5 1 A 2 B 3 A 4 B 5 B 6 A

ADDITIONAL PRACTICE | **MEL** Extra practice, Reading 7: Unfamiliar words A | **Active Teach** Reading Focus – meanings in context

Grammar focus ▶ p.44

Warmer:

Write on the board:

Every cloud has a _____ lining.

When one _____ closes, another one opens.

Find out if anyone can complete the sayings (*silver, door*). Ask: *What do these sayings mean? Do you have any similar expressions in other languages you know?* Point out that *Every cloud has a silver lining* is used to say that there is something good, even in a situation that seems very sad or difficult. *When one door closes, another one opens* is used to say that when you miss out on an opportunity, another opportunity will present itself.

1 Give students two minutes to quickly read the article and decide which statements are true or false. Elicit the answers.

2 Students read the article again and choose the correct alternatives. Go through the answers as a class.

3 Students discuss the questions in pairs. Conduct whole-class feedback.

Answers

1 1 T 2 F 3 F

2 1 must 2 had to 3 must have been 4 could
   5 should have listened 6 need 7 could
   8 didn't have to
   9 could have been 10 might not have made
   11 might not have had 12 should

3 Students' own answers

Modal verbs

Aim

● to review different uses of modal verbs in the present, past and future.

Refer students to the Grammar reference section on modal verbs on p.154 and ask them to do the exercise on p.155.

Grammar reference answers

1 might have decided
2 could have been
3 must be
4 needn't have
5 should have
6 mustn't

Teaching tip

You can set Grammar reference exercises for homework and check answers in the next class. Alternatively, you could give the Grammar reference exercises for fast finishers to complete in class if they finish another activity before other students.

4 Students find examples in the article of modals used to express uses 1–7, then compare answers in pairs before you check as a class. Read through the Language tip with the class. Write another example on the board and elicit the difference in meaning: *He didn't need to bring a present.* (It wasn't necessary and it isn't clear whether he brought one or not.) *He needn't have brought a present.* (He did bring a present but it wasn't necessary.)

5 Students complete the questions with the correct form of the verbs in brackets. Check the answers as a class, then put students in pairs to ask and answer the questions.

Alternative activity

If there is room to move around in your classroom, students could ask and answer each of the questions in Activity 5 with a different partner.

Answers

4 2 should have listened (5)

3 must (1)

4 must have been (3)

5 could have (7)

6 could have been (9), might not have made (10), might not have had (11)

7 should (12)

8 didn't have to (8)

5 1 should have achieved 2 did you have to 3 might come 4 didn't need to do/needn't have done 5 could have done 6 must have seen

ADDITIONAL PRACTICE | **Maximiser** p.30, Grammar | **MEL** Unit 4, Grammar | Photocopiable 4C *Modal me* | **MEL** Extra practice, Use of English 13: Modal auxiliary verbs of obligation | **Active Teach** Extra activity Grammar Focus 2

Speaking focus ▶ p.45

Collaborative task and discussion (Parts 3 and 4)

justifying an opinion

Aims

- to use a range of language for justifying an opinion
- to complete an exam-style collaborative task and discussion (Speaking Parts 3 and 4)

Warmer

Working in pairs, ask students to think of at least two hobbies or sports that:

- *cost the earth* (= very expensive)
- *can be done on a shoestring budget* (= very cheap)
- *would appeal to couch potatoes*
- *would be good stress-relief*
- *would be good for all ages*

- *would suit perfectionists*
- *are niche activities* (niche activity = only a select group of people would enjoy it)

Elicit ideas for each category.

1 Students discuss the questions in pairs. Elicit a few examples of hobbies or sports students have given up and why. Then elicit what students remember about Speaking Parts 3 and 4. If necessary, refer students to the Exam focus on p.183 to review the task and strategies in more detail.

2 Give students a moment to read the task and then play the recording. Ask students if they agree with Jan and Marisol's opinions.

3 Students complete the phrases. Play the recording again for them to check. Focus students' attention on the word *demotivated* in sentence 3. Point out that both the prefixes *un-* and *de-* can be added to the adjective *motivated*. Ask students to identify the difference between being *demotivated* and *unmotivated* (*demotivated* conveys lost motivation that you had in the past; *unmotivated* only conveys your lack of motivation at the present time).

4 Students match the phrases in Activity 3 with uses A–D. Check answers as a class. Ask students if they can think of any more phrases that could convey uses A–D. Sample answers could include the following: A *In my view, If you ask me, To my mind*; B *I feel, I am convinced, Personally, I think*; C *In my experience, Speaking from experience*; D *I don't know for sure but, I guess … .*

5 Play the recording and elicit which of the candidates answers the question well and why.

6 Tell students that they are now going to do Part 3 and 4 tasks, taking turns to be the 'candidates' and 'examiner'. Read through the Exam tip with the class. Working in groups of three, students turn to the task on p.135 and follow the instructions. Monitor and note some general areas that students could improve upon.

7 Refer students to the Marking guidelines on p.185. Then give them time to reflect on their performance and decide what the next step to improve is. At this point, you could share some of the feedback you noticed while circulating (without drawing attention to any individual students). If students are keen, give them an opportunity to repeat the task, focusing on the areas which they identified for improvement.

Answers

2 lack of time and money, not making enough progress

3 **1** the reason **2** goes a long way **3** could be wrong
4 my own experience

4 A1 B2 C4 D3

5 Jan gives the best answer because he answers the question and gives both sides of the argument. Marisol gives too much personal information and doesn't really answer the question. She also repeats the wording of the question.

ADDITIONAL PRACTICE | **Maximiser** p.30, Speaking | **MEL** Unit 4, Speaking | **MEL** Extra practice, Speaking 12: Agreeing and disagreeing in Part 3 and Part 4

Writing focus ▶ p.46

1 Put students into small groups and ask them to discuss how useful the tips are for helping people achieve more in their lives. Ask each group to briefly report back to the class.

Essay (Part 1)
effective introductory and concluding paragraphs

Aims
- to identify the features of effective introductory and concluding paragraphs
- to write an exam-style essay (Writing Part 1)

Teaching tip: The Writing Paper

Remind students that the essay in the exam is compulsory. If necessary, refer students to the Exam focus on p.168 to remind them of the two parts of the Writing paper. Tell students that, in the essay, they will always be asked to discuss two or three ideas and then to select one that is most important.

2 Students read the exam task and the two introductions. Elicit which of the introductions is better and why. Read the Exam tip aloud, then ask students to turn to the Writing reference on p.168 for some useful language for outlining issues in the introduction of an essay.

3 Refer students back to Plan A in Unit 1, p.14 for a model of an essay plan. In pairs, students write a plan for the main body of the essay in Activity 2. Monitor, checking students are using a similar model to write their plan.

4 Students decide if the statements are true or false, then compare answers in pairs before you check as a class.

5 Students complete the phrases. Check as a class. Ask students to turn to the Writing reference on p.168 for more useful language for conclusions.

6 Ask students to turn to p.144 and allow them five minutes to plan their introduction in pairs.

7 Give students a time limit of 30 minutes (as homework or in class) to do the task, then suggest spending five minutes using the checklist on p.184 to identify any areas for improvement. Ask students to make the changes they identify.

Answers

2 A

3 Model answer

Benefit 1: reduces stress

+ helps students to put problems into perspective

+ increases general well-being

- positive thinking will not be enough to combat stress for most students

Benefit 2: improves productivity

+ increase achievement

+ more efficient use of time means more time for leisure

- some students might substitute positive thinking for hard work leading to decreased achievement

4 **1** T **2** F **3** F **4** T

5 **1** sum **2** seems/appears **3** all **4** make/emphasise/stress

6–7 Model answer

We often hear about the many benefits of health and fitness. However, less often do we hear concrete suggestions for how to improve participation rates, particularly among young people. In this essay I will discuss two possible actions that governments could take to promote health and fitness to youth today.

The first possible action is to improve physical education teaching in schools. Local students have at times complained that the curriculum is rigid and emphasises repetitive activities instead of team sports and enjoyment. Better role models and more adventurous options could lead to improved attitudes and participation. Naturally, employing specialist sports teachers would incur considerable cost.

A second option would be to attempt to change the overly competitive attitudes that seem ingrained in many of the sports competitions for youngsters. When adults such as parents and teachers focus on winning above having a good time, it puts undue pressure on the participants. They may feel a sense of failure if they lose and also be less inclined to try a new sport.

To sum up, either approach would be a step in the right direction. In my view, it would be wise to prioritise dealing with reducing competitiveness first because I believe it would help young people feel better about the sports they already do. They could then, in turn, influence their friends to join in.

ADDITIONAL PRACTICE | **Maximiser** p.30, Writing | **MEL** Unit 4, Writing | **MEL** Extra practice, Writing 2: Giving an opinion in essays

Review ▶ p.47

Aim

* to revise the structures, vocabulary and exam tasks covered in Unit 4

1 – **4** Ask students to complete the activities, monitoring to provide assistance. Alternatively, set this as a homework activity. Ask students to compare their answers in pairs before doing a class check.

Answers

1 1 could 2 shouldn't 3 didn't need to be 4 must have known 5 would 6 can't

2 1 needn't have booked 2 would have been able to go/ would have gone 3 regretted not applying/(that) she hadn't applied 4 had forgotten to book/make 5 weren't allowed to watch 6 is considering selling

3 1 B 2 B 3 A 4 C 5 C 6 B 7 C 8 A

4 1 helpful 2 characteristics 3 relationships 4 demotivated 5 expectations 6 failure 7 misfortune 8 recognition

ADDITIONAL PRACTICE | **ActiveTeach** Games: Sheep Out!; Stepping Stones

5 The feel-good factor

Use of English and Speaking focus ▶ p.48

Open cloze (Part 2)

Warmer

Focus students on the unit title. Elicit or tell students that a *feel-good factor* means a feeling that everything is going well, e.g. *someone might accept a low-paying job that helps people because of a feel-good factor*. *Feel-good* is also often used to describe films/TV programmes/music, e.g. *His latest film is a feel-good movie* with a *message*. *There are still a few feel-good shows on TV, but most series have a harder edge*.

Ask students to work in pairs to think of a situation, a film, a TV programme and a piece of music that have a feel-good factor, and explain why. Conduct whole-class feedback.

1 Students discuss the questions about happiness in pairs. Elicit a few responses to each question.

Teaching tip: The Reading and Use of English paper

Tell students that Reading and Use of English Part 2 tests their grammar and involves reading a text with eight missing words and putting one word in each gap. For more detailed information and strategies, refer students to the Exam focus on p.178.

2 Focus students' attention on the title of the article. Working in pairs, students predict what the happiness app might be. Then ask students to read the article for general meaning, without worrying about the gaps yet. Elicit how the writer feels about using technology to help people track their thoughts, activities and moods.

3 Read the Exam tip aloud, then ask students to read the article again and fill in the gaps. Students compare their answers in pairs before you check as a class.

Answers

2 He finds it annoying but it has helped him understand that when he's distracted, he's less happy.

3 **1** with/since **2** which **3** how **4** who **5** than **6** less **7** only **8** what

Additional activity

Write the following questions on the board. Ask students to complete them with a preposition, then check answers as a class. Give students a few moments to think about their own answers to each question before discussing them in pairs. Elicit a few ideas for each.

1 *Do you have any particular strategies you rely _____ to put you in a good mood?*

2 *Would you consider signing up _____ a study like the one in the article?*

3 *Do you think you are conscious _____ your feelings most of the time?*

4 *Are you able to focus _____ what you're doing or are you easily distracted?*

Answers: **1** on **2** for **3** of **4** on

ADDITIONAL PRACTICE | **Maximiser** p.34, Use of English | **MEL** Unit 5, Use of English | **MEL** Extra practice, Use of English 2: Singular or plural?

Long turn (Part 2)
speculating (I)

Aim

- to use a range of expressions to speculate in an exam-style speaking task (Speaking Part 2)

4 Ask students what they remember about Speaking Part 2. Refer them to the Exam focus on p.183 to check their ideas. Then read the Exam tip aloud. Read through the expressions in the box with the class. Then ask students to discuss the questions and pictures using the expressions.

5 Play the recording and elicit which things in the list the examiner does *not* ask the candidate to do.

6 Students complete the activity in pairs. After the activity, Student B should tell Student A which phrases they used. Students then swap roles. To extend with strong students, tell Student A to close their book or not look at the phrases during the task.

7 Play the recording and elicit what the candidate has to do. Students discuss the question with their partner.

8 Tell students that they are going to do another exam task. Students work in pairs and do the tasks on p.136 and p.140.

Answers
5 1, 3, 5, 6
7 The candidate needs to answer the question: *Which group of people do you think looks happiest? Why?*

Additional activity

Ask students to look at the pictures on p.21 and p.33. In pairs, they speculate about what the people are talking about using the phrases from Activity 4. Elicit some ideas. Then ask students to select some other pictures of people

from the book and, in their pairs, speculate what the people were thinking about when the picture was taken.

MyEnglishLab tip: Customisable attempt number

The number of attempts students have on each MyEnglishLab exercise is customisable so that you can either set attempts to one or allow unlimited attempts, or anything in between.

ADDITIONAL PRACTICE | **Maximiser** p.35, Speaking | **MEL** Unit 5, Speaking | **MEL** Extra practice, Speaking 6: Giving reasons for speculation in Part 2

Listening focus ▶ p.50

1 Put students into pairs to discuss the questions then conduct whole-class feedback.

Multiple choice (Part 3)

Aim

- to complete an exam-style multiple-choice task (Listening Part 3)

2 Refer students to the Exam focus on p.182 for a review of exam strategies for this task. Ask students to underline the key words in Activity 4, question 1.

3 Play the recording. Elicit the answers to the questions.

4 Give students a minute to underline key words in questions 2–6. Elicit some possible paraphrases for the key words, then play the recording. Read the Exam tip aloud. Play the recording a second time and then elicit the answers.

5 Students complete the activity then compare in pairs before checking as a class.

6 Elicit how much €20 is in your local currency. Give students a few minutes to discuss the questions in pairs then conduct whole-class feedback.

Answers
2 1 What is Donna's <u>attitude</u> towards <u>research</u> into the <u>relationship</u> between <u>money</u> and <u>happiness</u>?

A It has <u>given</u> her a <u>good understanding</u> of the <u>issue</u>.

B It <u>raises more questions</u> than it answers.

C It is <u>not relevant</u> to the <u>questions</u> she wants to <u>address</u>.

D It falls <u>outside</u> her <u>area</u> of <u>expertise</u>.

3 **1** research = studies; given a good understanding = tells me very clearly; money = income

2 A

4 **2** B **3** C **4** B **5** C **6** D

5 **1** A **2** C **3** F **4** D **5** E **6** B

ADDITIONAL PRACTICE | **Maximiser** p.35, Listening | **MEL** Unit 5, Listening | **MEL** Extra practice, Listening 6: Listening for detail

Grammar focus ▶ p.5I

Warmer

Tell students that you have a friend who is feeling a bit stressed and low at the moment. Your friend has asked your advice on what activities to improve well-being. What steps or activities would you recommend?

Students discuss the question in pairs then conduct whole-class feedback.

1 Ask students to read the extract and then elicit the reviewer's impression. Check students understand the meaning of *misanthrope* (someone who does not like other people and prefers to be alone), *cynicism* (not willing to believe that people have good, honest, or sincere reasons for doing something) and *misgiving* (a feeling of doubt or fear about what might happen or about whether something is right.)

2 Students discuss the question in pairs. Elicit a few responses as a class.

Answer

1 very positive

Additional activity

Ask students to discuss these questions in pairs:

• *Have you tried any of these activities from the article? meditation, eating foods high in serotonin, aerobic exercise, sun lamp, pet patting*

• *How effective do you think they would be in improving someone's well-being?*

Substitution and ellipsis

Aim

• to review the use of substitution and ellipsis

Refer students to the Grammar reference section on substitution and ellipsis on p.155. Ask students to read the notes and complete the exercise on p.156.

Grammar reference answers

1 Neither
2 one
3 not
4 so
5 some, it
6 do that
7 there
8 Nor

3 Focus students' attention on the first underlined word in the review (*it*) and elicit what it refers to (reading the book). Tell students that this is called *substitution* and is used to avoid repetition of words. Students work out what each of the other underlined words/phrases refer to. Check answers as a class.

4 Look at the first instance of ↑ in the article. Read the surrounding sentence aloud and elicit which words have been omitted (*it took me*). Tell students that this is called *ellipsis*. Like *substitution*, it is used to avoid repetition. Read the Language tip aloud.

Cultural note

In the UK, a common informal way of saying *How are you?* uses ellipsis:

A: *[Are you] All right?*

B: *[I'm] All right, thanks. [How are] You?*

5 Students work in pairs to complete the activity. Check as a class.

6 Students complete the sentences, then compare answers in pairs before you check as a class.

Additional activity

Write the following sentences on the board or read them aloud one by one. Ask students to discuss in pairs which words or phrases have been left out in these sentences. Then elicit answers as a class.

1 *She was tired but (↑) happy.*

2 *Bring along as many friends as you want (↑).*

3 *Dan can't make it next weekend. He sent me an email explaining why (↑).*

4 *They didn't have any yellow sheets. Only pink (↑).*

5 *That's Bill's bike. This is Kim's (↑).*

6 *She promised she would write but she hasn't (↑).*

Answers: **1** she was **2** to bring **3** he can't make it next weekend **4** sheets **5** bike **6** written

Additional activity

Students work in pairs. They choose one of the pairs of sentences in Activity 6 as the first part of a conversation and try to continue it. Encourage them to use more examples of ellipsis. Invite a few pairs to share one of their conversations with the class.

Answer

3 1 reading the book 5 the book 6 suggestions 7 (really hot) chillies 11 hardened misanthropes 13 it won't make them purr with contentment 14 dogs

4 2 it took me 3 ways 4 I'm 8 Are you having/Do you have 9 it will do it 10 of us/you 12 that it

5 My friend Susan wanted me to buy her a book for her birthday but I couldn't find the one that she wanted in our local bookshop, so I got her another one that I found there instead of the one she had asked for.

6 1 do 2 there 3 so 4 one 5 It 6 not 7 either 8 That

ADDITIONAL PRACTICE | **Maximiser** p.38, Grammar | **MEL** Unit 5, Grammar | **MEL** Extra practice, Use of English 18: Understanding the whole text | **Active Teach** Extra activity Grammar Focus 1

Reading focus ▶ p.52
Multiple matching (Part 8)

Aims

- to complete an exam-style multiple matching task (Reading and Use of English Part 8)
- to practise working out meaning from context

1 Students discuss the questions in pairs. Elicit a few responses for each. Ask students what they remember about Part 8, Multiple matching. Refer them to the Exam focus on p.180 to check their ideas.

2 Give students about three minutes to read the article quickly and match the topics with the sections. Check answers as a class.

3 Focus students' attention on question 1 in the exam task and ask students to find the words/phrases that correspond to the underlined words.

4 Give students about ten minutes to underline key words in questions 2–10 and to choose the sections that correspond to each. Read the Exam tip aloud, then ask students to check their answers to questions 6 and 10. Students compare answers in pairs, then check as a class. When checking answers, elicit the sentences in the text that say the same things in different words for questions 6 and 10.

Answers

2 1 B 2 A 3 D 4 C 5 E

3 1 E 'Find out how things are done. Otherwise you'll be putting yourself under a lot of unnecessary stress. That's what happened to me so I learnt to ask questions – the hard way!'

4 2 D 'To be able to reply to these people individually gives you the sense that you are actually making a difference.'

3 A 'I've been asked to stay on and be paid for it! Had I not been, I would have been a bit surprised ...'

4 B 'It might seem exploitative but, in fashion ..., you have to show your willingness to work hard and for free. If you don't, others will be only too happy to take your place.'

5 A 'To avoid burn out, interns need time off and a bit of work–life balance.'

6 B 'but the build-up to Fashion Week will mean we'll really have our noses to grindstone and will be expected to work much longer hours.'

7 C 'friends are buying houses and have cars and go on holidays. But I never feel I missed out because I'm making a real contribution.'

8 D 'A lot of incredibly able people are closed off from the opportunity of an internship in parliament because they can't afford to travel or live in London.'

9 E 'Contrary to my expectations, luck was on my side and I found a job as a seamstress.'

10 C 'If I was 35 and still working unpaid I would think, 'What am I doing?''

5 Students find the words and phrases that match meanings 1–7, then compare answers in pairs before you check as a class.

6 Students complete the sentences with the correct forms of words and phrases from Activity 5. They then compare answers in pairs before you check as a class.

7 Ask students to find the underlined phrases in the text and deduce the meaning. Elicit the meaning of each. (*Keep your nose to the grindstone* = to work very hard, without stopping to rest; *a real slave driver* = someone who makes people work very hard – used in a disapproving or humorous way; *get a foot on the career ladder* = get your first opportunity in your chosen field.) Give students a moment to consider their answers before sharing in pairs. Conduct whole-class feedback.

Answers

5 1 commute 2 come to terms with came in handy 4 build-up 5 devoting 6 taken on 7 set up

6 1 come to terms with 2 come in handy 3 devotes/devoted 4 Commuting 5 building up 6 Setting up 7 take on

ADDITIONAL PRACTICE | **Maximiser** p.36, Reading | **MEL** Unit 5, Reading | **MEL** Extra practice, Reading 8: Unfamiliar words B | **Active Teach** Reading Focus – matching

Grammar focus ▶ p.54

1 Students discuss the items in pairs. Check they understand *commute* (regularly travel a long distance to get to work) and elicit the word for a person who commutes: *commuter.*

2 Tell students that there is a range of ways to communicate hypothetical meanings in English and in this lesson you are going to review them. Elicit the meaning of *hypothetical* (based on a situation which is not real but might happen or one that didn't happen but potentially could have).

Students choose the correct alternative in each sentence. Ask them to compare their answers in pairs before you check as a class.

Hypothetical meaning

Aim

• to review a range of ways to express hypothetical meaning

Refer students to the Grammar reference section on hypothetical meaning on p.156 and ask them to complete the exercise on p.157.

> **Grammar reference answers**
> 1 would stop
> 2 didn't take
> 3 tidied up
> 4 could turn back
> 5 hadn't spent
> 6 didn't have to

3 Students complete the rules about hypothetical meaning. Check answers as a class.

4 Read the instructions for Activity 4 with the class and point out that this is exam-like practice of Reading and Use of English Part 4. Emphasise the importance of understanding the first sentence before completing the gap. For example, in sentence 1, *wish I had* could fit grammatically, but would not have a similar meaning to the first sentence.

5 Students complete the sentences, then compare with a partner. Encourage them to ask at least one question about each of their partner's answers (e.g. *A: I know my friend wishes that she had studied more before she sat her driving test. B: Why, what happened? Did she have to retake the test?*).

> **Answers**
> 2 1 A 2 C 3 F 4 G 5 B 6 D 7 E
> 3 1 past simple 2 noun/pronoun + *would* + infinitive
> 3 *if only* + noun/pronoun + past simple 4 past perfect
> 5 *could* + infinitive 6 past simple
> 7 *rather* + noun/pronoun + past simple
> 4 1 wish I hadn't 2 would stop borrowing 3 you didn't tell 4 only people learnt/would learn 5 wish I didn't have 6 high time I wrote

ADDITIONAL PRACTICE | **Maximiser** p.38, Grammar | **MEL** Unit 5, Grammar | Photocopiable 5A *You wish!* | **Active Teach** Extra activity Grammar Focus 2

Vocabulary focus ▶ p.55

Prefix *mis-* and false opposites

Aims

• to expand knowledge of words beginning with the prefix *mis-*
• to clarify the meanings of some false opposites

1 Tell students that there are three slightly different but related meanings of the prefix *mis-*. Write the words *misbehaviour, misunderstanding, mistrust* on the board. Elicit the meaning of *mis-* in each case.

1 bad or badly, e.g. misfortune, misbehaviour
2 wrong or wrongly, e.g. miscalculation, misunderstanding
3 used to refer to an opposite or the lack of something, e.g. mistrust

Students complete the sentences, then compare answers in pairs before you check as a class.

2 Focus students' attention on the Language tip and read it aloud. Elicit the meaning of the false opposites *disease* (serious illness) and *ease* (if you do something with ease, it is easy for you; the antonym is *with difficulty*; if you are *at ease*, you feel relaxed; the antonym is *unease*). Students discuss the meanings of the underlined words in pairs. Ask them not to use dictionaries as meanings will be clarified in Activity 3.

Additional activity

Ask students to identify the syllable stress in the underlined words. Demonstrate the pronunciation for students to check. Alternatively, students could look up the words in www.ldoceonline.com and play the sound recording to check.

unassuming /ˌʌnəˈsjuːmɪŋ/
inadvertently /ˌɪnədˈvɜːtəntli/

5

insipid /ɪnˈsɪpɪd/

nondescript /ˈnɒndəˌskrɪpt

nonchalant /ˈnɒnʃələnt $ ˌnɑːnʃəˈlɑːnt/

disgruntled /dɪsˈɡrʌntld/

3 Students match the underlined words from Activity 2 with meanings A–F. Go through the answers with the class and, for each underlined word, elicit whether it has a base form and whether it has an opposite, or is a false opposite.

4 Students answer the questions individually, then share their answers in pairs.

Answers

1 1 misunderstanding 2 misguided 3 misconceptions
4 misleading 5 misgivings 6 misinterpretation
7 misprint 8 mistrustful
3 1 F 2 A 3 B 4 E 5 C 6 D

ADDITIONAL PRACTICE | **Maximiser** p.38, Vocabulary | **MEL** Unit 5, Vocabulary | Photocopiable 5B *Hit and mis-* | **MEL** Extra practice, Use of English 5: Word building in context | **Active Teach** Game: Noughts and crosses

Writing focus ▶ p.56
Review (Part 2)
covering key features

Aim

● to identify the key features of a review

Remind students that for more information on writing reviews, they can read the Writing reference on p.176 for homework.

1 Students work in pairs to discuss the questions. Elicit a few ideas for each question.

2 Tell students to ignore the gaps for now. Ask them to do this exercise in two stages. First, they should identify which extracts include factual information. Then they should decide which extracts include an element of opinion, and whether it is positive or negative.

3 Students match extracts 1–8 with key features A–D. Check answers as a class. Point out that students should make sure to include these key features when writing their reviews.

Answers

2 1 factual information
2 negative opinion
3 factual information
4 factual information
5 negative opinion
6 negative opinion
7 negative opinion
8 negative opinion
3 1 B 2 C 3 A 4 A 5 C 6 C 7 D 8 A

Vocabulary
sentence adverbs

4 Read the Language tip aloud. Focus students on the adverbs in the box, and clarify or elicit the meanings of *hopefully* (a way of saying what you hope will happen) and *ironically* (used when talking about a situation in which the opposite of what you expected happens or is true). Students add the sentence adverbs to the extracts in Activity 2 then compare in pairs before checking as a class.

Additional activity

Check that students understand what a sentence adverb is and how sentence adverbs differ from regular adverbs. Point out that a sentence adverb relates to the whole sentence that contains it and is usually used to describe the speaker's attitude, whereas a regular adverb modifies a verb, adjective or other adverb. Tell students that sentence adverbs are useful for expressing opinions in a review. They are usually placed at the beginning of a sentence. To further illustrate the difference between a regular adverb and a sentence adverb, write the following on the board:

1 Sadly, she left.

2 She left sadly.

Ask students to discuss the difference in meaning between the two sentences, then elicit the answer. The first sentence, where *sadly* is used as a sentence adverb, communicates that the speaker feels sad about the whole sentence (i.e. the fact that she left). In the second sentence, *sadly* modifies the verb *left*, so it communicates that she left in a sad manner.

5 Students look at the exam task and discuss which two films they would like to review.

6 Refer students back to features A–D in Activity 3. Read the Exam tip aloud, then ask students to make notes about the two films they chose under those headings.

7 Suggest a time limit of 30 minutes for writing the review.

8 Give students the opportunity to share drafts in pairs. Students could check that their reviews include the key features from Activity 3. Then allow students some time to improve their reviews before collecting them in.

Teaching tip

Focus your feedback on the lesson aims and grammar covered in the unit. In this case, provide feedback on whether students have included key features, appropriate sentence adverbs, and substitution and ellipsis.

If you don't have time to give individualised feedback, collect the reviews, and skim them quickly so that you can give an overall feedback comment to the whole class about what they did well and what they could improve.

Answers

4 1 Tragically   2 Ironically   3 Curiously   4 Thankfully
   5 Hopefully   6 Unfortunately   7 Happily
   8 Understandably

8 Model answer

In this review I am going to compare two contrasting tales about overcoming adversity. Whereas *The Blind Side* (2009) left me with a huge grin on my face, sadly, *Doctor Zhivago* (1965) left me feeling the weight of the world on my shoulders.

Doctor Zhivago, directed by five-time Oscar winner David Lean, is set in the Bolshevik revolution and follows the title character, who must adapt to the new order while pining for Lara, the beautiful wife of a political campaigner. The director succeeded in creating a film that is thoroughly engaging but full of gritty realism, cruelty and tragic irony. Take the tissues!

The Blind Side, which is based on a true story, is also a bit of a tearjerker, in a completely different way. It stars Sandra

Bullock, who won an Academy Award for her portrayal of a rich white mother in Tennessee who takes a homeless black teenager under her roof. Understandably, the gentle giant thinks he isn't good at anything, but his new mother sees his potential to become a football star and part of the family. The plot is based on a true story, making it all the more touching.

I would strongly recommend *The Blind Side*. It will appeal to a range of people and is a great choice for a movie night. Although *Doctor Zhivago* is a classic, I think it has more of a niche audience and is best saved for when you want a dose of gloom!

ADDITIONAL PRACTICE | **Maximiser** p.39, Writing | **MEL** Unit 5, Writing | **Photocopiable** 5C *Speedy pairs* | **MEL** Extra practice, Writing 16: How to write a good review | **Active Teach** Game: Pelmanism

Review ▶ p.57

Aim

● to revise the structures and vocabulary covered in Unit 5

1 – **4** Ask students to complete the activities, monitoring to provide assistance. Alternatively, set this as a homework activity. Ask students to compare their answers in pairs before doing a class check.

Answers

1 1 would stop   2 started   3 had realised   4 wouldn't rain/didn't rain   5 could get   6 didn't go

2 1 C   2 A   3 B   4 A   5 B   6 A

3 1 then   2 as   3 one   4 them
   5 this/it   6 more   7 so   8 It

4 1 C   2 A   3 A   4 C   5 B   6 C

ADDITIONAL PRACTICE | **ActiveTeach** Games: Sheep Out!; Stepping Stones

6 Living with the past

Use of English and Listening focus ▶ p.58

Word formation (Part 3)

Aim

- to complete an exam-style word formation task (Reading and Use of English Part 3)

1 Students work in pairs to discuss the questions. Elicit a few answers for each. Tell students that sometimes the adjective *stone-age* can refer informally and negatively to something that is crude, basic or outdated, e.g. *They said I'd get a work phone, but it turned out to be a stone-age device.*

2 Elicit what students remember about Reading and Use of English Part 3, Word formation. Refer them to the Exam focus on p.179 to check their ideas. Focus students' attention on the title of the article and check that they understand *mammoth* (noun: an animal like a large hairy elephant that lived on the earth thousands of years ago; adjective: extremely large). Give students a minute to read the article for gist, without worrying about the gaps. Then ask them to close their books and see how many facts they can remember in pairs.

3 Students could cover the text for this activity to focus only on the words with capitals. Elicit the answers.

4 Students complete the activity, then compare their answers in pairs before you check as a class.

5 Students discuss the questions in pairs. Conduct whole-class feedback.

> **Answers**
> 3 **1** extinction, perfection, consideration, confrontation   **2** powerless   **3** imperfect
> 4 **1** perfectly   **2** exciting   **3** analysis   **4** considerably   **5** disability   **6** powerless
>   **7** hunters   **8** confrontation

Multiple choice (Part 1)

Aim

- to complete an exam-style multiple-choice listening task (Listening Part 1)

6 Remind students that Listening Part 1 involves listening twice to three short conversations and answering two multiple-choice questions about each. Give them a minute to read the questions (and underline key words). Read the Exam tip aloud. Play the recording twice. Check answers as a class.

Additional activity

Students discuss the following questions in pairs.

- *What significant archaeological sites are there in your country?*
- *Have you ever been to a dinosaur exhibition? How would you rate it?*
- *Do you think owners of historical buildings should have the freedom to make changes that they want to, or should they have to respect the original character?*

7 Divide the board into two columns headed *in-* and *un-*. Ask students to divide the adjectives in the box into these two groups. Students compare their answers in pairs. To extend with strong students, ask them to think of at least two more words for each column. Finish by checking answers as a class.

Answers

6 1 B 2 A 3 A 4 C 5 A 6 A

7 in-: inaccurate, insignificant

un-: unbelievable, unchanged, unconvincing, uncovered, undiscovered, unfavourable, uninformative, unmodernised

ADDITIONAL PRACTICE | **Maximiser** p.40, Use of English | **MEL** Unit 6, Use of English | Photocopiable 6A *Three in a row* | **MEL** Extra practice, Use of English 20: Spelling practice | **Active Teach** Game: Sheep out!

Grammar focus ▶ p.60

Warmer

Write the following events on the board:

A *Eiffel Tower completed*

B *Marie Curie wins her first Nobel Prize*

C *Michelangelo completes the Sistine Chapel ceiling*

D *Columbus sails to the Americas*

E *Nelson Mandela is elected president of South Africa*

F *Amelia Earhart flies the Atlantic solo*

Ask students to work in pairs to decide on the chronological order of the historical events.

Then write the following years on the board: *1492, 1512, 1889, 1903, 1932, 1994*. Ask students to match each year with an event. Share the answers. The pair with the most correct answers are the winners.

Answers: **A** 1889 **B** 1903 **C** 1512 **D** 1492
E 1994 **F** 1932

1 Students work in pairs and discuss which of the quotes about history they agree with. Elicit a few opinions.

2 Give students time to read and tick the statements that are true for them. Students compare in pairs then conduct whole-class feedback.

Comparing

Aim

- to use a range of language for comparing

Refer students to the Grammar reference section on comparing on p.157 to read the notes and then complete the exercise.

Grammar reference answers

1 by

2 nowhere

3 so/very

4 great

5 not

6 like

3 Direct students to the word *more* in the first sentence in Activity 2. Demonstrate the phrases in the box with *more* to see which fit, e.g. *Older generations are a bit more interested, a great deal more interested, a little more interested* ... Then have students continue the activity themselves. Read the Language tip aloud. Elicit what the speaker thinks about watching cricket (it's boring). Share the examples using *as ... as: He's as tall as his father. Watching cricket is as dull as watching paint dry.*

Additional activity

Write the following prompts using *like/as* on the board and ask students to make sentences that are true for them. Then they share their sentences in pairs.

_____ is like watching paint dry.

I'm _____ like my_____

I'm as _____ as my_____

4 Ask students to read the sentences, then discuss the differences, if any, in pairs. Elicit the answers.

5 Give students a minute to quickly read the article to answer the question. Ask students to underline the words/phrases which helped them to arrive at their conclusions.

6 Students read the article again and choose the correct alternatives. Ask them to compare answers in pairs, then check as a class.

Additional activity

Ask students to find and underline the following phrases in the article: *building boom* (a period when a lot of new construction takes place); *old master* (a famous painter from the 15th to the 18th century or a painting by one of these painters); *open round the clock* (open 24 hours). In pairs, students discuss what each phrase means. Check as a class.

7 Give students about five minutes to discuss the questions, then ask them to present their choice of object to the class. Tell them their presentation should include what the object is and at least three things it would tell future generations about today. If you have a very large class, ask students to present their objects in groups rather than to the whole class.

Alternative

Students prepare a one-minute presentation for homework which they can present in the next class. Students could bring an example of their object or picture of their object to show to the class.

Alternatively, students could write a paragraph about their object and post a picture and paragraph to your class online space.

8 Put students in pairs and ask them to turn to the activity on p.145. Check that they understand the meaning of *posterity* (all the people in the future who will be alive after you are dead). Remind them to use a variety of language to compare the buildings. Students follow the instructions to complete the activity, then swap partners to compare their ideas.

Answers

3 **1** a bit, a great deal, a little, a lot, far, very much **2** almost, just **3** a little, a lot, much **4** by far, much

4 **1** *no more* means the same, *a bit more* means there has been some increase **2** similar meaning **3** *By far* means it has more visitors than any other museum. *One of* means there are other museums which have as many visitors. **4** different – *no better than* means the same, *worse and worse* means it is deteriorating **5** similar meaning

6 **1** never **2** far more **3** the briefest **4** More than ever **5** higher and higher **6** far

ADDITIONAL PRACTICE | **Maximiser** p.41, Grammar | **MEL** Unit 6, Grammar | **Photocopiable** 6B *Opinionated!* | **Active Teach** Extra activity: Grammar Focus 1

Speaking focus ▶ p.61
Long turn (Part 2)
comparing

Aim

● to complete an exam-style long turn task (Speaking Part 2)

Warmer

Write the following words on the board: *ancient past*, *servants*, *school trip*, *guide*, *memories*, *legend*, *granddaughter*. Ask students to discuss in pairs which picture on p.61 they associate each word with.

1 Play the recording and elicit the three things students need to do for this task.

2 Before playing the recording again, focus students on the photos and elicit what they can see in each one. Then play the recording and elicit which two pictures Alessandra is talking about.

3 Go through each of the items, and ask students which information Alessandra included in her long turn.

4 Students discuss Alessandra's answer in pairs. Elicit any points of agreement or disagreement from the class.

5 Read through the expressions in the box with the class, then play the recording while students note down the expressions they hear.

Additional activity

Ask students to use the phrases in the box to make two lists: phrases to introduce a similar idea; and phrases used to present a contrast. Students compare their answers in pairs and see if they can add any additional phrases to the list.

Answers:

Similar: *Similarly, What both photos have in common is …*

Contrasting: *On the other hand, Having said that, Nevertheless, Whilst, Whereas, Although, However, One significant difference is …*

6 Students compare the pictures in pairs, using phrases from Activity 5. Circulate, checking the expressions are being used appropriately.

7 Read the Exam tip aloud. Ask: *What should you do if you can't think of anything else to say?* Elicit some ideas, and point out that it's not a bad idea to paraphrase things you have already said, or go into more detail. Useful phrases like *What I mean is …* and *Let me say more about that* could come in useful. Students complete the tasks on p.136 and p.141, taking turns to be the examiner.

Answers

1 compare two of the pictures, say why the people might be interested in this kind of information about the past, say how easy it might be for them to remember it
2 A and C
3 location, clothes, possible reasons for the visit, the historical significance of the place, and how the people may be feeling
5 One significant difference is, What both these photos have in common is, Whilst

ADDITIONAL PRACTICE | Maximiser p.41, Speaking | **MEL** Unit 6, Speaking | **MEL** Extra practice, Speaking 5: Using linking words in Part 2

Reading focus ▶ p.62
Multiple choice (Part 5)

Aim

● to complete an exam-style multiple-choice task (Reading and Use of English Part 5)

1 Students discuss the questions in pairs. Elicit a few ideas. Elicit the word *descendant* by saying *if someone is your ancestor, you are his or her … .*

Discuss as a class what the best strategy is for approaching Reading and Use of English Part 5, then refer students to the Exam focus on p.179 to check their ideas.

2 Tell students to use the strategies outlined in the Exam focus. Focus students' attention on the Exam tip. Students compare their answers in pairs, then check as a class.

3 Students discuss the question in pairs. Elicit responses from a few students.

Answers

2 **1 B** ('I'd accepted the invitation gladly, not because I had any particular interest in my forebears but because, as a journalist, I thought a story on genealogy would appeal to my readers.')

2 A ('But the name of the programme is a bit of a sham … who we actually are has nothing to do with our ancestors; it's down to our own personality, luck, circumstances, education and that of our parents.')

3 D ('… we should try to make something of ourselves and not dwell on the past.')

4 C ('For them, the fun isn't in the facts, it's in the hunting.')

5 D ('Would I have been able to forgive him for abandoning his family?')

6 B ('I was more interested than I'd expected to be in the fate of Amos'; 'I'm not who I thought I was six months ago'; 'Who I am now is a born-again ancestor bore.')

ADDITIONAL PRACTICE | Active Teach Reading Focus – meanings in context

Vocabulary
adjective/noun collocations

Aim

● to expand students' knowledge of adjective/noun collocations

Teaching tip

Help students make connections between what they are learning and what has already been covered. This helps them recall the prior knowledge and retain the new knowledge. For example, before looking at the compound adjectives in the article, students could briefly review the compound words covered on p.12.

4 Remind students that a *compound word* is one that is made up of two (or more) other words to form a new unit of meaning. Students work out the meanings of the underlined compound adjectives in the article. They then compare answers in pairs.

Background: Tailor-made

Elicit what a *tailor* is (someone whose job is to make clothes which are measured to fit each customer perfectly). A *tailor-made garment* is an item of clothing made to measure by a tailor as opposed to being factory-made. The expression is now applied to other items outside fashion. A synonym is *bespoke*.

5 Students underline the nouns that collocate with the adjectives. Check answers as a class.

6 Students make collocations, then compare answers in pairs before you check as a class. Check students know what is meant by a *nuclear family,* a family unit that consists only of a husband, wife, and children.

7 Tell students a little about your family tree (real or imagined) using the collocations, e.g. *You'd never guess this but apparently, Queen Victoria and I share a common ancestor.* Give students a moment to draw then put them in small groups to discuss their family trees.

Additional activity

Ask students to use some of the collocations in Activity 6 to discuss the following question:

How have family structures or living arrangements changed in your country over the past century?

Answers

4 tailor-made: designed especially for an individual; consumer-driven: focused on material things (in this context); high-minded: having high moral standards

5 **1** trip, course, suit, service **2** fashion, technology, design **3** person, ambition, reason, principle

6 **1** close, distant, immediate **2** common, direct, distant, early **3** close, distant, extended, immediate, nuclear

ADDITIONAL PRACTICE | **Maximiser** p.42, Reading | **MEL** Unit 6, Reading | **MEL Extra practice, Reading 9: Focusing on detail** | **Active Teach** Game: Noughts and crosses

Vocabulary focus ▶ p.64

Warmer

Focus students on the photo and ask them if they know what it shows (a strand of DNA).

Ask students to discuss the following questions in pairs.

1 What do you know about DNA ancestry tests?

2 How do you think the results of an ancestry DNA test might affect someone's sense of identity?

1 Give students a few minutes to read the article without worrying about the gaps at this stage. Elicit an answer to the question.

2 Students discuss the questions in pairs. Elicit a few different opinions.

Answer

1 more international

Prefixes and suffixes

Aim

• to practise word formation with prefixes and suffixes

3 Look at the first gap with the class and elicit the correct adjective form (*unsettling*). Students complete the article with the correct adjective forms, then compare in pairs before you check as a class.

4 Encourage students to make two lists of adjectives. Students discuss the questions in pairs. Check answers as a class.

Additional activity: *-ive or -ing*

Ask students to look again at the adjectives in Activity 4. Ask: *Which words also have an adjective form ending in -ive or -ing?*

-ive: comprehensive, imaginative

-ing: changing, comforting, exciting, moving, reversing

5 Students work in pairs to answer the questions. Check as a class. Focus students' attention on the Language tip and read it aloud.

6 Students choose the correct alternatives, then compare answers in pairs before you check as a class.

7 In pairs, students play the word association game on p.145 and p.147. Encourage them to think of at least five ideas for each word.

Answers

3 **1** unsettling **2** amazed **3** predictable **4** initial **5** understandable **6** unbelievable

4 -able: believable, changeable, comfortable, comparable, considerable, deniable, excitable, identifiable, imaginable, movable, noticeable, profitable, variable

-ible: accessible, comprehensible, resistible, reversible, visible

5 un-: unbelievable, unchangeable, uncomfortable, undeniable, unexcitable, unidentifiable, unimaginable, unmovable, unnoticeable, unprofitable

in-: inaccessible, incomparable, incomprehensible, inconsiderable, invariable, invisible

ir-: irresistible, irreversible

6 **1** imaginable **2** imaginative **3** changeable **4** variable **5** excitable **6** comforting **7** changing **8** comprehensive

imaginable = something which can be imagined

imaginative = creative

changeable = inconstant/capable of being changed

changing = something which is becoming different

variable = something which can vary

varying = different

excitable = easily excited

exciting = something which makes you feel excited

comforting = something which brings comfort

comfortable = something which makes you relaxed or gives physical comfort

comprehensive = complete

comprehensible = something which can be understood

ADDITIONAL PRACTICE | **Maximiser** p.44, Vocabulary | **MEL** Unit 6, Vocabulary | **Active Teach** Game: Pelmanism

Grammar focus ▶ p.65
Modifying adverbs

Aim
• to use a range of adverbs to modify adjectives

Refer students to the Grammar reference section on modifying adverbs on p.157 and ask them to do the exercise on p.158.

Grammar reference answers
1 both
2 seriously
3 really
4 extremely
5 both
6 quite

---

1 Focus students' attention on the examples, then go through the questions with the class, eliciting the answer to each one.

2 Check students understand the meaning of *ungradable* (if an adjective is ungradable, it means that there are no degrees of it. For example, something is either *impossible* or it isn't – it can't be *slightly impossible* or *very impossible*). Students discuss in pairs which of the adjectives are ungradable. Elicit the answers.

3 Use *disappointed* as an example with the class and go through each modifier in the box, eliciting whether it can be used with this word.

Read the Language tip aloud. Write on the board: *quite nice*, *quite perfect*, *quite angry*. Elicit which of these adjectives is ungradable (*perfect*) and elicit the meaning of *quite perfect* (completely perfect). Then elicit the meaning of *quite nice* (fairly nice) and *quite angry* (fairly angry).

Cultural note
Point out that British people are famous for using understatement.

For example, if a speaker says *It's quite good,* that could mean *it's fairly good* or it could mean *it's absolutely amazing!*

In the same way, *It's a little bit disappointing* could mean *it's extremely disappointing.*

---

4 Focus students' attention on the heading and picture and elicit some ideas about what the article might be about. Then ask students to read the article.

5 Ask: *What do you think a false memory is?* Elicit some ideas, then ask students to read the article and check. Elicit how false memories are created.

6 Students choose the correct alternatives, then compare answers in pairs before you check as a class.

7 Students read the questions and may make a few notes if they wish. They then compare their answers in pairs. Ask for a show of hands of whose earliest memory was about a trip to the dentist, a holiday, a birthday party or their first day at school. Elicit what the other first memories were about that weren't mentioned.

8 Students compare their memories.

Answers
1 to give emphasis. Both modifiers intensify the adjective.
2 enormous, awesome, furious, impossible, perfect, terrified
3 extremely, practically (but *practically impossible* is an exception)
5 False memories can be created from TV programmes or books.
6 1 absolutely
  2 pretty
  3 practically
  4 extremely
  5 completely
  6 entirely

Additional activity
In your class online space, ask students to write a short forum post about one of their early memories, how old they were and how reliable it was. Encourage students to include at least three modifying adverbs.

ADDITIONAL PRACTICE | **Maximiser** p.44, Grammar | **MEL** Unit 6, Grammar | Photocopiable 6C *Absolutely right* | **MEL** Extra practice, Reading 1 Reading for gist: Shooting Scotland | **Active Teach** Extra activity Grammar Focus 2

Writing focus ▶ p.66
Essay (Part 1)
structuring an argument

Aim
• to provide well-structured arguments in an exam-style essay (Writing Part 1)

1 Students discuss the task in pairs. Ask a few pairs to share their ideas.

2 Go through the key words with the class.

3 Read the Exam tip aloud. Students read the statements and then discuss their opinions on each one in pairs.

4 Students should write *P* next to the main points and *E* next to supporting evidence. They compare answers in pairs before you check as a class.

5 Ask students to underline useful phrases in Activity 3. Then ask them to turn to the useful language in the Writing reference on p.168 to review more useful phrases for other parts of the essay.

6 Students plan their essays and then share their plans with a partner.

7 Set the writing task as homework and then collect in to provide individual feedback.

Answers

2 Your class has attended a lecture on the <u>action</u> <u>governments</u> can take to make sure <u>cultural heritage</u> is <u>preserved</u> for <u>future generations</u>. You have made the notes below.

<u>Priorities</u> for governments aiming to preserve cultural heritage

- increase <u>funding</u> for <u>museums</u>

- <u>protect old buildings</u>

- <u>teach</u> the importance of <u>cultural heritage</u> in schools

Some <u>opinions</u> expressed in the discussion

- 'Cultural heritage <u>isn't just about buildings</u> – it's about a <u>way</u> <u>of life</u>.'

- 'It's the <u>responsibility</u> of the <u>older generation</u> to <u>pass on</u> <u>cultural heritage</u> to the next generation.'

- '<u>Museums</u> are the <u>best places</u> to keep <u>shared memories</u> of a <u>community</u>.'

Write an <u>essay</u> for your tutor discussing <u>two</u> of the <u>priorities</u> in your notes. You should <u>explain which priority you think</u> <u>is more important</u>, <u>giving reasons</u> to support your opinion. You may, if you wish, make use of the opinions expressed in the discussion but you should <u>use your own words</u> as far as possible.

Write your essay in <u>220–260 words</u> in an <u>appropriate style</u>.

4 **1** P **2** P **3** E **4** E **5** P **6** E

5 Giving main points: I would argue that, The problem is that, It's become necessary to, An urgent priority is

Giving supporting evidence: Perhaps, I'm sure, For example

7 Model answer

Cultural heritage is an invaluable asset for all generations to enjoy. It is about knowing where we have come from and having pride in the place we live. In this essay I will discuss two priorities for the government's support of the cultural heritage in our community.

The first idea is to increase funding to museums. People say that museums are the heart of cultural heritage preservation. Not only do they display objects, they also teach and provide

information about them. Increased funding could attract better care of objects, more specialised staff and more entertaining displays, in turn attracting more people to visit and learn. On the other hand, I would argue that it is unreasonable to expect governments to give more money to museums when they have got more important things to spend people's taxes on.

The second idea is to protect old buildings. It has become clear in recent years that governments can no longer afford to provide generous grants to help people maintain their historically significant houses. I am sure there are many voluntary organisations which would be prepared to work on conservation projects. Nevertheless, the government could provide protection to ensure that old buildings are not demolished or transformed out of character.

In my view, the most pressing priority is to provide protective legislation for old homes and buildings. I'm not alone in my concern about the loss of historical features which take such pride of place in and give character to our communities.

ADDITIONAL PRACTICE | **Maximiser** p.45, Writing | **MEL** Unit 6, Writing | **MEL** Extra practice, Writing 3: Using linkers in an essay

Review ▶ p.67

Aim

● to revise the structures and vocabulary covered in Unit 6

1 – **4** Ask students to complete the activities, monitoring them to provide assistance. Alternatively, set this as a homework activity. Ask students to compare their answers in pairs before doing a class check.

Answers

1 **1** so **2** much **3** nothing **4** great **5** far **6** like **7** ever **8** worse and worse **9** just as **10** simplest

2 **1** B **2** A **3** B **4** C **5** A **6** C **7** B **8** A **9** C **10** A

3 **1** favourable **2** unconvincing **3** misinformed **4** imaginative **5** irreversible **6** inaccessible **7** disbelief **8** inaccurately **9** incomprehensible **10** invisible

4 **1** trip **2** principles **3** design **4** ambition **5** course **6** person **7** service **8** reason

MyEnglishLab tip: Practice tests

The MyEnglishLab Practice tests are an opportunity for students to practise a full exam paper for each of the four papers: Reading and Use of English, Writing, Listening and Speaking. Students are able to re-attempt the questions multiple times for extra practice.

ADDITIONAL PRACTICE | **Active Teach** Game: Stepping stones

Progress Test 2 ▶ p.68

Ask students to complete the Progress Test activities for homework or in class, setting a time limit of 40 minutes. Go through the answers as a class or write the answers on the board for students to check.

Answer

1 1 B 2 D 3 C 4 A 5 B 6 A 7 C 8 D
2 1 More
   2 like
   3 no/never
   4 to
   5 for
   6 much
   7 if/when/should
   8 What
3 1 impressive
   2 considerable
   3 further/farther
   4 believable
   5 invention
   6 curiosity
   7 undeniable
   8 imaginative
4 1 wish they didn't have
   2 were nothing like as
   3 high time they told you
   4 would have been impossible
   5 regretted not having worked/that he hadn't worked
   6 prevented everyone/anyone from entering

7 The hard sell

Grammar and Vocabulary focus ▶ p.70

Review of conditionals

Warmer

Focus students on the unit heading and elicit or share the two meanings of what a *hard sell* is (1 something that is difficult to sell or make popular, e.g. *Cheap solar panels could be the answer to the power shortage, but they are proving to be a hard sell*; 2 when someone uses a lot of pressure to get you to buy something or persuade you to do something, e.g. *Dealers are turning to hard-sell tactics to convince customers to buy now*).

Use the picture on p.70 to introduce *bazaar* /bəˈzɑː/ (a market or area where there are a lot of small shops, especially in India or the Middle East).

Ask: *How do you think this picture relates to the phrase hard sell? Are hard-sell tactics common in your country? Do you think hard-sell techniques are effective? Why / Why not?*

Refer students to the Grammar reference section on conditionals on p.158 and ask them to read the notes. Set the exercise on p.159. Alternatively, refer students to the Grammar reference after Activity 4.

Grammar reference answers
1 If you do that again, I ~~would~~ 'll/will scream.   2 correct   3 correct
4 If I were you, I wouldn't ~~have told~~ tell her what he said.   5 correct   6 correct

1 Organise students into pairs to discuss the questions. Check the meaning of *handicrafts* /ˈhændikrɑːfts/ (something that someone has made in a skilful way using their hands, also *craft*). Conduct whole-class feedback.

2 Ask students to read the questions then play the recording. Elicit the answers.

3 Give students time to read the sentences. Demonstrate the pronunciation and elicit the meaning of *archetypal* /ˌɑːkɪˈtaɪpəl/ (a perfect example of something, because it has all the most important qualities of things that belong to that type). Play the recording for students to complete the sentences. Elicit the answers. Point out that all the sentences are conditional forms.

4 Ask students to match A–D with the sentences in Activity 3, then compare in pairs before checking as a class.

Additional activity

Ask students to match the sentences in Activity 3 to the types of conditionals on p.158.

Answers:

1 First conditional

2 Zero conditional

3 Second conditional

4 Third conditional

5 Students complete the sentences while you circulate and provide help as required. Organise students into groups of four to five to compare their ideas for each sentence. Move between the groups, checking for accurate formation of conditionals and encouraging students to make adjustments as necessary.

Teaching tip: Scaffolding

When necessary, provide scaffolding to bridge the gap between what students can do and what the task requires. For example, if you think your students will struggle to produce accurate conditionals in Activity 5, you could elicit or share a way to complete each sentence before they write their own sentences. An alternative scaffold for Activity 4 would be to ask students to work as a class to identify which kind of conditional from p.158 can be matched with each sentence. Both scaffolds provide assistance for students in selecting the correct form for the second half of their sentences.

6 Read the question with the class. Ask: *Have you ever been to an Apple store? What do you know about the store design?* Play the recording then elicit the answer.

7 Point out that the two sentences are mixed conditionals (i.e. referring to two different time periods). Ask students to read the sentences and identify which parts refer to the present. Elicit the answer. Read through the Language tip with the class.

8 Students complete the sentences as mixed conditionals. Ask fast finishers to write third conditional sentences for the ones that are possible. Go through the answers, eliciting both the mixed conditional and any possible third conditional sentences. Elicit the difference in meaning.

9 Point out that students should use some third conditionals/mixed conditionals in their conversation.

Give a light-hearted example e.g. *I once went to a friend's house and was served a ginger pudding. I actually can't stand ginger but wanted to be polite, so I said it was delicious. After that, they made ginger*

pudding especially for me every time I visited. If I hadn't pretended to like it the first time, I wouldn't have been served it so many times! Then again, if I had been honest about not liking ginger, my friend probably would have felt bad! If only I hadn't been quite so enthusiastic about it!

Answers

2 1 (suggested answer) He doesn't try to force people to buy things/no haggling.

   2 patience, treating customers like kings, teaching them

3 1 ask   2 get   3 would be   4 would, have

4 1 C   2 D   3 C   4 A

6 They are in urban centres and they let people use the products.

7 1 If they could get them into the store, they <u>had a chance of converting them</u>.

   2 If the other companies had moved on from their aggressive shark like approach …, <u>they would probably represent much stronger competition for Apple today.</u>

8 1 had done, would understand

   2 would be, had had

   3 were/was, would have made

   4 hadn't opened, wouldn't be

   5 would have got, were/was

   6 were/was, would have stopped

   Sentences 1, 3, 5 and 6 could be written as third-conditional sentences. Only sentence 6 has no change in meaning. Sentences 2 and 4 both make reference to the present.

ADDITIONAL PRACTICE | **Maximiser** p.48, Grammar | **MEL** Unit 7, Grammar | **Active Teach** Extra activity Grammar Focus 1

Collocations: sales and marketing

Aim

* to introduce collocations related to sales and marketing

10 Take the opportunity to re-use *archetypal* from Activity 3 by rephrasing the question as: *What is the archetypal used car salesperson?* Organise students into pairs to discuss the question, then conduct whole-class feedback.

11 Ask students to read the text to answer the question rather than completing the gaps at this stage. Elicit the answer.

12 Point out that each of the missing words in the article is part of a collocation. Students complete the article then check as a class.

13 Elicit the answers. Demonstrate the pronunciation of *campaign* /kæmˈpeɪn/ and *rapport* /ræˈpɔː/.

14 Organise students into small groups to see how many collocations they can come up with for each word. Conduct whole-class feedback.

Answers

11 He made sure his customers liked him.

12 1 retail 2 marketing 3 campaign 4 product
5 rapport 6 sales 7 mail 8 loyal

13 campaign, rapport

14 (Suggested answers) sales figures, sales conference; product placement, product launch; mail order; business acumen, business partner; customer service, customer complaints, customer relations

ADDITIONAL PRACTICE | **Maximiser** p.48, Vocabulary | **MEL** Unit 7, Vocabulary | Photocopiable 7A *Collocation bingo* | **Active Teach** Game: Noughts and crosses

Listening focus ▶ p.72

1 Students discuss the questions in pairs. If necessary, pre-teach *evoke* (to produce a strong feeling or memory in someone). Share these collocations using *evoke*: *evoke sympathy* and *evoke a response*.

Multiple choice (Part 3)

Aim

- to complete an exam-style multiple-choice listening task (Listening Part 3)

2 Elicit what students remember about Listening Part 3 and the strategies to use. If necessary, refer students to the Exam focus on p.182 to review the strategies. Ask students to underline key words in the questions in Activity 3.

3 Read the Exam tip aloud, then play the recording twice, which is how students would experience the listening tracks in the exam. Go through the answers with the class.

4 Play the recording again while students write expressions that match meanings 1–6. Check answers as a class.

Additional activity

Write the following questions on the board for students to discuss in small groups.

- *Do you think scent marketing would entice you to make a purchase?*
- *What's an interest you were into in the past? What are you into now?*
- *Do you think it's good for people to put their heart and soul into their business? Why / Why not?*

5 Students discuss the questions in pairs. Elicit a few responses from the class.

Answers

2 (Suggested answers)

1 first job
A frustrating, marketing skills
B satisfying, make a contribution
C challenging, work like this
D boring, didn't, design advertisements

2 celebrities used, campaign
A reacted, unreasonable
B old, take part
C shouldn't have allowed, photos
D disliked, poses

3 marketing course
A demanding, limited experience
B potentially useful, sense marketing
C limited relevance, current work
D lasting benefit, herself, clients

4 research, psychological effects, scents
A lost interest, girlfriend
B worried, used inappropriately
C discouraged, not, applied
D justified, interest, generate

5 scent marketing, not attract criticism
A directly connected, product
B not overpowering
C not accentuate, naturally occurring smell
D associated, find attractive

6 object, scent marketing
A aren't justified, undetectable
B don't respond quickly, dangers
C arguments against
D manipulated

3 1 B 2 A 3 D 4 D 5 A 6 C

4 1 B 2 E 3 A 4 C 5 F 6 D

ADDITIONAL PRACTICE | **Maximiser** p.49, Listening | **MEL** Unit 7, Listening | **MEL** Extra practice, Listening 7: identifying opinion | **Active Teach** Game: Sheep out!

Use of English
focus ▶ p.73

Multiple-choice cloze (Part 1)

Aim
- to complete an exam-style multiple-choice cloze task (Reading and Use of English Part 1)

Warmer
Describe asparagus to the class, and get them to guess which food you're talking about, e.g say: *It's a long, thin green vegetable with a point at one end. You usually buy it by the bunch.* Ask students to work in pairs to describe some foods to their partner to guess.

1 Students work in pairs to discuss the four tastes. Elicit them and write them on the board. Elicit three example foods or drinks for each taste (e.g. *sweet: ice cream, fudge, lollipop; salty: soy sauce, crisps, crackers; sour: lemon, lime, sherbet; bitter: coffee, dark chocolate, olives*).

2 Elicit what students remember about the multiple-choice cloze task. If necessary, refer them to the Exam focus on p.178 to review what is required. Students read the article quickly and answer the question without worrying about the gaps yet.

3 Students discuss the example (0) in pairs. Elicit why the other alternatives are not possible. Read the Exam tip with the class.

4 Students fill in the gaps 1–8, then discuss their answers in pairs before you check as a class.

5 Students discuss their answers in pairs. Conduct whole-class feedback.

Answers
1 sweet, sour, salty, bitter

2 Umami. For many years it was thought that people couldn't taste umami.

3 See Exam Tip.

4 **1** B **2** A **3** C **4** C **5** B **6** D **7** B **8** A

ADDITIONAL PRACTICE | **Maximiser** p.49, Use of English | **MEL** Unit 7, Use of English | **MEL** Extra practice, Use of English 17: Agreement

Vocabulary
collocations with *go*

Aim
- to expand students' knowledge of collocations with *go*

6 Start by eliciting the meanings of *bald* (having no hair on your head), *bankrupt* (not having enough money to pay what you owe), *deaf* (unable to hear), *hysterical* (unable to control behaviour or emotion because you are very upset, afraid, excited, etc.; extremely funny) and *mouldy* (covered in mould, a substance that grows on food which has been kept too long or on objects that are in warm, moist places). Students then answer the questions in pairs before checking as a class.

7 Do the first sentence with the class as an example, eliciting the collocation *go downhill*, and the correct form (*gone downhill*). Students complete 2–8, then compare answers in pairs before you check as a class.

Answers
6 **1** bad, bald, bankrupt, deaf, downhill, grey, mad, mouldy, off, sour

  2 become

7 **1** gone downhill **2** go deaf **3** gone mouldy
  4 went bankrupt **5** going grey **6** gone off
  7 gone bald **8** goes mad

Additional activity
Put students in pairs and ask them to write three collocations from the lesson on a piece of paper (e.g. go bald, go downhill, go mouldy). Pairs exchange their lists. Each pair makes up a story using the collocations they have been given. Invite each pair to share their story with the class.

MyEnglishLab tip
Messaging
In MyEnglishLab you can send online messages to individuals or groups of students. Use the 'Message' feature for reminders or encouragement. It can also be a forum for students to ask you a question which you can reply to at a time that suits you.

ADDITIONAL PRACTICE | **Maximiser** p.49, Vocabulary | **MEL** Unit 7, Vocabulary | **Active Teach** Game: Pelmanism

Reading focus ▶ p.74

Warmer

Write these words from the article title on the board: *speedy, creamy, refreshing, comfy*. Point out that *speedy* and *comfy* are informal. Ask students to work in pairs to think of a product or service that could be described with each adjective, e.g. *speedy delivery, creamy dessert, refreshing smoothie, comfy chair*. Conduct whole-class feedback.

1 Students discuss the question in pairs. Elicit some ideas as a class.

2 Give students a few minutes to read the article on p.75 and then elicit any reasons students discussed in Activity 1 that were mentioned in the article. (The article discusses the relationship between sounds, especially vowels, in the brand name, and people's perception of the product.)

Gapped text (Part 7)

Aim

- to identify connections between paragraphs in an exam-style gapped text task (Reading and Use of English Part 7)

3 Elicit what students remember about the task and strategies for Part 7. If necessary, refer students to the Exam focus on p.180 to check their ideas. Give students a few minutes to read the first two paragraphs of the article and the paragraphs A–G which were removed. Then focus students on the reason a student gave for correctly choosing one of the missing paragraphs and read through it with the class. Elicit which paragraph the student is referring to.

4 Read the Exam tip with the class. Students then complete the task.

5 Students compare their answers and reasons in pairs before checking as a class. As you go through the answers with the class, elicit justifications for why each answer is correct.

6 Elicit an overview of the theory put forward in the article (that the sounds in a brand name signal the qualities of a product.) Elicit some ideas from the class.

Answers

3 B

4–5 **2 D** the paragraph before gap 2 gives two important *concerns* – the word that occurs at the beginning of

paragraph D – that have to be balanced; *disastrous consequences* and *demise* in paragraph D are similar in meaning to *debacle* in the paragraph following gap 2.

3 F *single word or a combination of words* connects to *brand names*; *convey* is similar in meaning to *convince us*; *creamier, zippier, more refreshing,* and *more comfortable* are examples of *this kind of information*

4 A *Contemporary* contrasts with *ancient* and *not new*; *apparent connections* is similar in meaning to *correspondence*

5 E If scientists make attempts to *investigate* something they conduct a *study*. *Eighty per cent* is a research finding that can *confirm a hypothesis*.

6 G information about *dogs* connects to *we too use our voices and bodies; ... all this work in linguistics and animal biology* connects to the previous two paragraphs

ADDITIONAL PRACTICE | **Maximiser** p.50, Reading | **MEL** Unit 7, Reading | **MEL** Extra practice, Reading 10: Identifying the writer's attitude A | **Active Teach** Reading Focus – meanings in context

Vocabulary

working out meaning from context

Aim

- to practise working out meaning from context

7 Students choose the correct meaning, then compare answers in pairs before you check as a class. Elicit clues that students used to help them work out the answer.

Answers

7 **1 A** interests (the linguists are not worried about a problem but want an answer to a question)

2 B surfaces (collocates with 'roughest and rockiest')

3 A absolute (a quality such as reliability cannot be transparent)

4 B multitude (the word qualities is a noun in the plural and must be preceded by an adjective)

5 A inherent (the qualities mentioned can be conveyed by the sounds so they are not hidden)

6 A hair (hackles is the name for hair on the back of an animal's neck)

Additional activity

Write up the following prompts and ask students to use them to make sentences that are true for them.

I think there is intrinsic value in …

It always raises my hackles when …

There are a whole host of reasons to perfect one's English, for example …

Something I like to do for the sheer joy of it is …

I think it's sheer stupidity when people …

Speaking focus ▶ p.76

Collaborative task and discussion (Parts 3 and 4)
agreeing and disagreeing

Aims

- to review phrases for agreeing and disagreeing
- to complete an exam-style speaking task (Speaking Parts 3 and 4)

1 Students discuss the questions in pairs. Conduct whole-class feedback.

2 Draw a line on the board with *strong disagreement* at one end and *strong agreement* at the other. Ask students to do the same on a piece of paper and use the tasks 1–5 in Activity 2 to fill out the continuum. Check answers as a class.

3 Play the recording for students to tick the phrases they hear. Play the recording again for students to note the reasons. Conduct whole-class feedback.

4 Put students into pairs. Remind them to use some of the phrases from Activity 2. Play the recording then have students move straight into the task. Time students for two minutes and encourage them to use the whole time.

5 Read the Exam tip aloud, then give students a minute to discuss which would work best.

6 Students change partners and discuss their answers.

7 Tell students that they are going to do another exam task, taking turns to be the examiner and the candidates. In groups of three, they follow the instructions on p.137.

Answers

2 **1** Absolutely!   Indeed it is.   I couldn't agree more.
  2 I'm afraid I just don't see it like that at all.   Surely not!
  3 We'll just have to agree to differ.
  4 I can't argue with that, but …
  5 That's not quite the way I see it.

3 Absolutely! (reason: It's a clever way of warning people not to be taken in);
  I can't argue with that, but …(reason: we are still manipulated by the marketing industry); Indeed it is. (reason: poking fun at advertising robs it of some of its power);

I'm afraid I just don't see it like that at all. (reason: I'd really like to see at least one ad like this outside every shopping mall.);
We'll just have to agree to differ.

ADDITIONAL PRACTICE | **Maximiser** p.52, Speaking | **MEL** Unit 7, Speaking | Photocopiable 7B *Make your pitch* | **MEL** Extra practice, Speaking 10: Using a wide range of vocabulary in Part 3

Grammar focus ▶ p.77

Conditionals: advanced features

Aim

- to review how conditionals are used to sound more formal, polite or hypothetical

Warmer

Ask students to discuss the questions in small groups.

- *Have you ever received something from a company for free as part of a marketing campaign?*
- *Would you accept an offer of free products in exchange for recommending them to friends?*
- *How would you feel if a friend recommended a product, and you found out they were paid or given free stuff in exchange?*
- *Would your feelings change if the recommendation came from a celebrity or online influencer?*

1 Play the recording and elicit what *stealth advertising* is (advertising by getting people to promote products to their friends without them knowing). Elicit the techniques described (paying people to promote products to their friends, giving free samples, then suggesting people recommend them to their friends, using people's blog photos in advertisements without permission). Elicit some opinions about the techniques.

2 Check students understand the explanations. If necessary, clarify *hypothetical* (based on a situation that is not real but that might happen) and *imposition* (something that someone expects or asks you to do for them, which is not convenient for you). Students find the words and phrases. Check answers as a class.

3 Look at the first sentence with the class as an example. Elicit how it would be changed (adding a conditional to make it more hypothetical – *If you were to inherit a lot of money, would you give up working?*).

4 Students cross out the alternative which is *not* possible. They then compare answers in pairs before you check as a class.

5 Students write their dilemmas, then exchange with another pair and discuss. Students can swap two or three more times for extra practice.

Alternative activity

In place of Activity 5, provide some moral or ethical dilemmas related to advertising for students to discuss, e.g.

- *Suppose you saw an online advertisement that you knew was misleading, what would you do?*
- *What would you do if you were offered a voucher for your favourite brand in exchange for sharing a link on social media?*
- *Would you be willing to appear in an advertisement for a product you didn't like if you were paid well?*

Answers

2 1 A If I were to
   2 C Should you
   3 B If you happen to
   4 D Had (inversion)

3 1 If you were to inherit a lot of money, would you give up working?
   2 Should you require assistance, contact a member of staff.
   3 Had we interviewed a larger number of people, we would have obtained more reliable results.
   4 If you happen to see Joe, can you remind him to give me a call?
   5 If your brother were to phone me in the next couple of days, I might be able to arrange an interview.
   6 Had I known working as a journalist was so demanding, I would have done something else.

4 1 If the weather improves
   2 if we won
   3 unless
   4 Provided
   5 supposing
   6 If

ADDITIONAL PRACTICE | **Maximiser** p.52, Grammar | **MEL** Unit 7, Grammar | Photocopiable 7C *Just supposing …* | **Active Teach** Extra activity Grammar Focus 2

Writing focus ▶ p.78

Report (Part 2)

formal language

Aims

- to review features of formal language
- to use these features to write an exam-style report (Writing Part 2)

1 Students respond to the questions, then compare their answers in small groups.

2 Students look at the results on p.145, then read the report to answer the questions. Conduct whole-class feedback.

3 Students underline examples of features 1–4 in the report. Check as a class.

4 Ask students to read the task. Read the Exam tip aloud and elicit possible headings for the exam task.

5 Refer students to the model report on p.174 and the useful language on p.175 of the Writing reference. The writing task could be set in class or for homework. Make sure students understand that they can invent research in their reports. Collect the reports to provide individual feedback.

Teaching tip

Encourage students to write in the same medium that they are going to use in the exam. If they are going to take the online exam, they should practise typing their answers. If they are taking the paper format exam, it is useful to practise writing handwritten answers.

Answers

2 yes

3 1 While …; Strange as it may seem, …; On the one hand, … On the other hand, …; Notwithstanding …
   2 respondents, participants, those surveyed, those whose opinions we sought
   3 regard, considered

5 Model answer

Introduction

In this report I will provide a description of common types of advertising in Australia and present results of consumer responses to these. The final section makes recommendations for possible changes to increase the effectiveness of campaigns.

Common approaches

Television and radio continue to play an important part in advertising campaigns and celebrity endorsements often feature prominently. Print media, including billboards, posters and flyers, are also ubiquitous, especially in large cities. Some companies target consumers by giving away samples in public places and supermarkets, aggressive telemarketing or door-to-door sales. Many companies use social media strategies such as online competitions or special offers for 'likers'.

Consumer responses

I conducted an online survey with 200 Australian contacts. An overwhelming majority cited that they found telemarketing and door-to-door salespeople intrusive, annoying and rude. Nevertheless, over half admitted to buying something from someone through one of these channels. People generally said that they liked advertising when it was suited to their interests or used humour. A number of respondents mentioned that they 'loved free stuff' and would tell others about something they had been given.

Recommendations

In light of the results above, I recommend the following:

• Make sure telemarketers and door-to-door salespeople have adequate customer service training.

• Target young people such as university students for giveaways as this will likely result in positive word-of-mouth advertising and online reviews.

Additional activity

Ask students to find formal words that mean the following in the model report on p.174.

1 *discourage*

2 *unpleasant*

3 *second group*

4 *unreasonably high*

5 *big*

6 *take advantage of*

Answers: **1** deter **2** disagreeable **3** latter **4** inflated **5** major **6** capitalise

ADDITIONAL PRACTICE | **Maximiser** p.53, Writing | **MEL** Unit 7, Writing | **MEL** Extra practice, Writing 15: Report and proposal checklist

Review ▶ p.79

Aim

• to revise the structures, vocabulary and exam tasks covered in Unit 7

1 – **3** Ask students to complete the activities, monitoring them to provide assistance. Alternatively, set this as a homework activity. Ask students to compare their answers in pairs before doing a class check.

Answers

1 **1** I had more money **2** she had got better **3** unless we save **4** I studied the piano for longer **5** you buy one, you can **6** wouldn't be necessary **7** you were to see **8** should you require

2 **1** D **2** C **3** B **4** A **5** B **6** A

3 **1** C **2** A **3** C **4** D **5** B **6** D **7** D **8** C

MyEnglishLab tip: Practice Writing test

For the Practice Writing test, students access the tasks online then write their tasks on separate sheets of paper. Collect these in to provide individual feedback using the Marking guidelines on p.184.

ADDITIONAL PRACTICE | **Active Teach** Game: Stepping stones

8 Passing through

Listening and Grammar focus ▶ p.80

Sentence completion (Part 2)

Aim

• to complete an exam-style sentence completion task (Listening Part 2)

Warmer

Ask students to discuss the following questions in pairs, then conduct whole-class feedback:

• *Do you think travel is about the journey or the destination?*
• *What's the most memorable place you've visited?*
• *What landmarks would you like to see in person?*

1 Students work in pairs to think of reasons. Conduct whole-class feedback.

2 Ask students to look at the exam task in Activity 3 and elicit some possible answers for questions 2 and 4. Read the Exam tip aloud and give students a few minutes to work in pairs to predict the kind of information that would go in the other gaps. Elicit some ideas.

3 Play the recording for students to complete the sentences. Play the recording a second time, then give students a couple of minutes to check that their spelling and grammar are correct and that each sentence makes sense. Go through the answers. Ask: *Were your predictions about the kind of information correct?*

4 The places could be local, national or international. Students discuss the question in pairs.

Additional activity

Write this additional question on the board for students to discuss: *What places have exceeded your expectations?*

Answers

3 **1** comedy club **2** (publication) date **3** restaurant prices/prices in restaurants **4** photos/photographs **5** navigation **6** tailor-made **7** (sportswear) designer **8** (huge) cave

ADDITIONAL PRACTICE | **Maximiser** p.54, Listening | **MEL** Unit 8, Listening | **MEL** Extra practice, Listening 13: Listening for main points and detail

Reported speech

Aim

• to be able to report speech with appropriate changes to verbs and time markers

5 Students choose the correct alternatives, then compare answers in pairs before you check as a class.

6 Tell students that they are going to listen to a conversation between two friends about travel. Play the recording (twice if necessary), then ask students to work in pairs and summarise what each speaker said. Elicit a summary.

7 Students work in pairs to choose the correct alternatives. Check as a class.

8 Students match comments A–E with sentences 1–5 from Activity 7. For more detailed notes, refer students to the Grammar reference on p.160. Point out that in addition to verb changes, time markers also change. Ask students to do the exercise on pp.160-161.

Grammar reference answers

1 Our teacher told us we had to work harder if we wanted to pass the test that Friday.

2 Lily asked the doctor if she could make an appointment for the following/next afternoon.

3 Erica said that she'd made up her mind that she didn't want to go to university.

4 Julie informed everyone that Matt had been living in Athens since the previous/last summer.

9 Read the Language tip aloud. Refer students back to the statements in Activity 7 and elicit where *that* has been omitted: *3 Mia says (that) …; 4 Mia said (that) … .* Students complete the reported statements 1–6, then compare in pairs before checking as a class.

10 Check students understand what a *tourist trap* is (scams that target tourists or overpriced places for tourists that locals never go to) and *get off the beaten track* (visit remote places or places that tourists wouldn't normally see). Give students a few minutes to plan their itinerary in pairs. Suggest that they include four places to visit and at least one recommendation on each of the other listed categories. Students swap partners to give their recommendations. They should make a few notes about what the recommendations were, but shouldn't write down full sentences. Then students work again with their original partner to report what was said. Monitor and make sure students are using correct verb forms for reporting their speech.

Answers

5 1 not to believe   2 don't check   3 wouldn't buy
   4 wouldn't   5 should visit   6 might have missed

7 1 had been/was   2 could   3 she'll   4 is travelling
   5 this/that

8 1 B   2 C   3 E   4 A   5 D

9 1 wishes/wished she had been advised

2 not to visit/(that) they shouldn't visit

3 goes/went again, he will make sure he sees/would make sure he saw

4 had been planning/were planning to be; shouldn't miss

5 if/whether anyone had stayed

6 is/was the most beautiful place in the world; must/had to go there at least once

ADDITIONAL PRACTICE | **Maximiser p.55, Grammar** | **MEL Unit 8, Grammar** | **Active Teach** Extra activity Grammar Focus 1

Use of English focus ▶ p.82

Aim

• to practise selecting correct word forms and identifying other forms of a given word

1 Students complete the activity then compare in pairs. Conduct whole-class feedback.

2 Ask students to work through the list in pairs. Alternatively, divide the class in half, and ask half the class to look at words 1–4 and the other half words 5–8. Conduct whole-class feedback.

Answers

1 1 respectful   2 awareness   3 irresistible   4 symbolic
   5 worthwhile   6 authentic   7 reminder   8 unexpected

2 1 respect (n.v), (dis)respectful (adj)

2 (un)aware (adj) awareness (n)

3 resist (v), resistant (adj), irresistible (adj)

4 symbol (n), symbolism (n)

5 worth (adj), worthwhile (adj), worthless (adj)

6 authenticity (n), (in)authentic (adj)

7 remind (v), reminder (n)

8 expect (v), expectant (adj), (un)expected (adj)

Word formation (Part 3)

Aim

• to complete an exam-style word formation task (Reading and Use of English Part 3)

3 Read the Exam tip aloud, then ask students to read the article quickly. Ask a student to summarise the article, then ask for a show of hands to find out who agrees and who disagrees with the writer's attitude towards souvenirs.

4 Students form a word to fit in each gap, then compare answers in pairs before you check as a class. If students get stuck on one of the gaps, ask: *Does the word in the gap need to be positive or negative? Plural or singular? A noun, verb, adjective or adverb?*

5 Students discuss the questions in pairs. Elicit a few responses for each question.

> **Answers**
> 4 **1** reminders **2** symbolic **3** irresistible
> **4** transportable **5** authenticity **6** worthless
> **7** irrelevant **8** unexpectedly

ADDITIONAL PRACTICE | **Maximiser** p.55, Use of English | **MEL** Unit 8, Use of English | **MEL** Extra practice, Reading 1 Reading for gist: Shooting Scotland | **Active Teach** Game: Sheep out!

Speaking focus ▶ p.83

Long turn (Part 2)
speculating (2)

Aims

- to use a range of language to speculate
- to complete an exam-style speaking task (Speaking Part 2)

1 Students discuss the pictures in pairs.

2 Elicit some possible instructions for the task.

3 Play the recording and elicit what the instructions were. Ask students if they guessed correctly in Activity 2. Point out that the instructions will always involve comparing two of the pictures and 1–2 questions that will require the student to speculate.

4 Ask students to work in pairs to add to the list. Elicit the answers. Read the Exam tip aloud.

Alternative

Instead of Activity 4, students could list what two things they must talk about (why people might want to buy items, usefulness of the items). Then in Activity 5, the question could be: *Does the student answer both questions?*

5 Play the recording for students to check their ideas.

6 Students complete the phrases for speculating, then compare answers in pairs. Play the recording again for students to check.

7 Tell students that they are going to work in pairs and take turns to practise a Speaking Part 2 task. Students follow the instructions on p.137 and p.141.

8 Consider asking students to swap partners to work with someone new. Students complete the communication activity on p.147.

> **Answers**
> 5 She speculates about whether these items were presents and why people are shopping for these items.
> 6 **1** would **2** whether **3** whether **4** couldn't **5** all

ADDITIONAL PRACTICE | **Maximiser** p.56, Speaking | **MEL** Unit 8, Speaking | **MEL** Extra practice, Speaking 8: Comparing Part 2 pictures

Reading focus ▶ p.84

Cross-text multiple matching (Part 6)
identifying attitude and opinion

Aims

- to practise identifying attitude and opinion in a text
- to complete an exam-style cross-text multiple matching task (Reading and Use of English Part 6)

1 Elicit the difference between the terms *expat* and *immigrant* (*expat* is usually used by people to describe themselves when they live abroad temporarily; *immigrant* is usually used to refer to other people who move permanently to a new country). Put students into pairs to discuss the second question. Elicit some of the things they would find most difficult to cope with.

2 Students read the extracts quickly, to decide which issues in Activity 1 are mentioned by each writer. Check answers as a class.

3 Read the Exam Tip aloud. Ask students to match the underlined words and phrases in Text A with uses A–D. Check answers as a class.

4 Ask students to find four examples of adverbs of attitude and two impersonal phrases for making recommendations in Texts B–D. Students could work in pairs for this, then check as a class. Point out to students that there will only be about ten minutes in the exam to complete the cross-text multiple matching activity, so being able to recognise words and phrases that express attitude and opinion will help students identify these quickly in the texts.

5 Before students do the task, refer them to the list of strategies for Part 6 in the Exam focus on p.180.

6 Students work in pairs to find the words and phrases in italics in the texts. Elicit the meaning of each one in context, then ask students to discuss their answers to questions 1–4 with their partner. Suggested meanings: *nurtured* (helped to develop), *daunting prospect* (a possibility that is frightening in a way that makes you feel less confident), *liberating* (freeing someone from feelings or conditions that make their life unhappy or difficult), *blend in* (if someone or something blends in with people or objects, they match them or are similar, and you do not notice them).

7 Students work in pairs and discuss how far they agree with the statements. Elicit some ideas.

Answers

2 all of them except 'being cut off from your roots'

3 1 B 2 A 3 D 4 C

4 adverbs: refreshingly, mistakenly, perversely, understandably; phrases: It's best to …, this is to be welcomed

5 **1 A:** The polite detachment of New Yorkers should be of no consequence because technology has made it possible to maintain ties with friends and family across oceans and time zones.'

D: 'This distance can be hurtful at first. Far from forming lifelong bonds, socialising for most expats is reduced to a series of disappointing casual encounters, compounding a sense of loneliness and isolation'.

2 B: 'It can't be avoided, so it's best to embrace and even celebrate your 'charming' or 'cute' manner of speaking.' (The others talk about the need to lose your accent etc.)

3 D: 'Life becomes routine, yet there's always the comforting thought at the back of their minds that this existence is transient and that one day they'll be able to return home' and 'already dreaming of the warm welcome awaiting them at home.'

B: 'may even come to dread the moment they have to leave.'

4 C: 'mistakenly assume that blending in will be easy'

A: 'Adjusting to life in New York can seem overwhelming for newly arrived expats. Any hopes of fitting in seamlessly are misplaced.'

ADDITIONAL PRACTICE | Maximiser p.56, Reading | **MEL** Unit 8, Reading | Photocopiable 8A *Four texts* | **MEL** Extra practice, Reading 11: Identifying the writer's attitude B | **Active Teach** Reading Focus – matching

Vocabulary focus ▶ p.86

Describing trends

Aim

● to review vocabulary for describing trends

1 In pairs, students check they understand the meaning of the underlined words/phrases. Conduct whole-class feedback.

Alternative

Write the following meanings on the board and ask students to match each one with one of the underlined words/phrases: *A to go down very quickly, B to go down, C to stay the same, D to reach a high point, E was higher than, F a short drop before rising again*

Answers: 1 D 2 C 3 E 4 F 5 B 6 A

2 Play the recording. Students decide if the statements in Activity 1 are true or false. Elicit the answers.

3 Play the recording again for students to note words which match meanings 1–4. Check answers as a class.

Alternative

Write the answers out of order on the board and have students work in pairs to work out which words fit meanings 1–4.

4 Check students understand the difference between *emigrate* (to move permanently *from* a country) and *immigrate* (to move permanently *to* a country). Put students into pairs to discuss the questions, then conduct whole-class feedback.

5 Students complete the text, then compare in pairs before checking as a class.

6 Encourage students to make at least five predictions about future trends where they live. If necessary, revise the use of future forms for predictions (i.e. use *will* + *infinitive* for predicting something based on belief, and *going to* + *infinitive* to talk about things that are certain to happen because of present evidence).

7 Students discuss the question with their partner.

Additional activity

Give students the years listed below and ask them to speculate on what the world's population was. Then ask students to describe the trends using some of the vocabulary from the lesson.

World population estimates:
1 AD: 300 million
1500: 500 million
1900: 1.65 billion
1950: 2.5 billion
2000: 6 billion
2018: 7.5 billion

Answers

2 1 T   2 F   3 T   4 F   5 T   6 F

3 1 substantially, sharp   2 moderate   3 grew, surge, rise, boosted   4 dropped, declines

5 1 risen   2 decline   3 overtaken   4 sudden   5 dropping   6 peak

ADDITIONAL PRACTICE | **Maximiser** p.58, Vocabulary | **MEL** Unit 8, Vocabulary | **Active Teach** Game: Pelmanism

Grammar focus ▶ p.87

Verb patterns with reporting verbs

Aim

- to be able to use a wide range of verbs to report speech with correct verb patterns

Warmer

Write these sentences on the board.
He _discouraged_ me from going to New York.
She _invited_ me to go to New York.
She _denied_ going to New York.
He _persuaded_ me to go to New York.

Point out the underlined reporting verbs. Ask students to work in pairs to work out what the direct speech might have been in each case.

Sample answers:
'Don't go to New York. It's way too crowded and expensive.'
'I'm going to New York for spring break. Care to join me?'
'You couldn't have seen me, I've never even been there!'
'You'll love New York! It'd be the trip of a lifetime!'

Refer students to the Grammar reference section on verb patterns with reporting verbs on p.161.

1 Emphasise that students need to cross out the verbs which are not possible. Check as a class.

2 Students complete the activity. Go through the answers with the class.

3 Ask students to read the statement and match 1 and 2 with endings A–D.

4 Tell students that they are going to hear some statements about emigration of young Irish people. Change the first sentence into direct speech with the class as an example. Read the reported sentence aloud, then elicit what the direct speech might have been. One possible answer is: _There is no alternative to me emigrating._ But a more likely way of saying this directly might be: _I don't have any other choice but to emigrate_ or _I have to emigrate – I don't have a choice._

Ask students to change the statements in Activity 4 into direct speech. Remind them that when they report speech, they move the tenses one step back into the past, but here they will have to do the opposite. Play the recording for students to compare their answers.

Answers

1 1 reminded   2 insisted   3 claimed   4 reminded   5 requested, denied   6 blamed, claimed, denied   7 accused, warned   8 regretted, accepted

2 1 admit, deny, accept, claim, insist
2 admit, regret, deny
3 persuade, warn, urge, advise, encourage
4 accuse
5 object, consent

3 1 B, C, D
2 A

4 1 I hate to admit it but I've got no choice. I have to leave here to find work.
2 Don't worry, Mum, I'm not lonely. I've made loads of friends here already.
3 I wish I hadn't left. I think I would have had a better chance of starting my own business at home.
4 The government hasn't done enough to create jobs – that's why so many people are leaving.
5 Listen, Son, I really think you should stay in Australia. You've got lots more opportunities there.
6 I don't regret emigrating for one minute. It's the best decision I've ever made.

ADDITIONAL PRACTICE | **Maximiser** p.58, Grammar | **MEL** Unit 8, Grammar | Photocopiable 8B _Interviews with the famous_ | **MEL** Extra practice, Use of English 10: Verb tenses | **Active Teach** Extra activity Grammar Focus 2

Impersonal reporting verbs

Aim
* to practise using impersonal reporting verbs to sound more formal

Refer students to the Grammar reference section on impersonal reporting verbs on p.161 and ask students to do the exercise.

Grammar reference answers
1 My mum reminded me to phone her as soon as I arrived.
2 My brother accused me of taking his keys.
3 Kerry blamed Dan for them missing the plane.
4 Rob regretted having emigrated to Australia.
5 Ella discouraged me from going to the party.
6 Jon objected to having to work long hours.

5 Invite a student to read the two sentences aloud. Then ask students the questions. Tell them that *It is believed (that)* is a common impersonal reporting phrase. Elicit other similar phrases that students can think of that use a similar passive structure (e.g. *It is thought, It is said, It is accepted*).

6 Ask students to tick the statements they agree with and discuss with a partner. Then rewrite the first sentence with students as an example. Read the sentence aloud, then focus on the verb in brackets (*accepted*). Elicit how this could be changed to an impersonal reporting form (*It is accepted*). Students rewrite the other sentences. Check answers as a class.

7 Share an example with the class (e.g. *It is said that the more languages you know, the easier it is to pick up another one*). Put students into pairs and ask them to think of at least three other facts to present to the class. Students could research some facts, e.g. on their mobile phones or for homework.

Answers
5 2 (found in formal written texts)
6 1 It is accepted   2 It is suggested/It's been suggested
3 It is claimed   4 It is expected   5 It was assumed
6 It has been argued

ADDITIONAL PRACTICE | **Active Teach** Game: Noughts and crosses

Writing focus ▶p.88
Proposal (Part 2)
using an appropriate style

Aim
* to write an exam-style proposal using an appropriate style (Writing Part 2)

Warmer
Ask students to discuss these questions in pairs:
* *What benefits are there for students participating in exchange programmes with other countries?*
* *Have you ever been on an exchange?*
* *If you went on an(other) exchange, where would you like to go?*

1 Students read the task and discuss the questions in pairs. Ask students to underline the information they need to include in the task question to make sure they don't miss anything.

2 Students make a plan using the headings given. Suggest they include three benefits, three ways to promote the exchange programme and three recommendations.

3 Elicit what style a proposal should be written in (relatively formal and impersonal). Invite six students to read each of the recommendations aloud. After each one, elicit whether it is in an appropriate style for a proposal.

4 Students discuss in pairs. Check as a class. Refer students to the Writing reference on p.175 for more useful language for proposals. It is also a good time to remind students of the Marking guidelines on p.184.

5 Students complete one of the tasks in class or for homework.

6 Students swap their proposal with a partner and make suggestions on ways it could be improved. They should make the suggested changes before handing in their proposals for individual feedback.

Answers
3 2, 3, 4, 6
4 2, 3, 4

5 Model answer

Introduction

This proposal is intended to outline common issues students have when studying abroad, and suggest ways that a course could help them to deal with these. The final section makes recommendations about what should be included in the course curriculum.

Problems when studying abroad

Interviews were conducted with 20 students who have recently completed a student exchange programme. The majority of students were of the opinion that overcoming the language barrier in their new country was the biggest challenge and nearly half also said that they experienced culture shock. Other problems cited included unrealistic expectations, loneliness and packing the wrong things – particularly being unprepared for a different climate.

Ways a course could address these

A course could prepare students for culture shock by raising awareness of the phenomenon and describing cultural differences that students may encounter in their host country. To aid participants with language, a course could include some useful phrases for the first days after arrival, in addition to some resources for language learning. The course could also include a discussion about combating isolation and adjusting expectations.

Recommendations

I would like to make the following recommendations:

Invite students who have previously studied abroad to share aspects of the culture they found surprising and give advice on what to take.

Provide a list of useful phrases, together with suggestions of useful resources for language learning such as websites, blogs or e-books.

Facilitate a discussion about engaging with people to avoid loneliness and isolation.

If these recommendations are implemented, young people are bound to feel more prepared for their experience.

ADDITIONAL PRACTICE | **Maximiser** p.59, Writing | **MEL** Unit 8, Writing | Photocopiable 8C *City of the year* | **MEL** Extra practice, Writing 14: Choosing appropriate headings in a proposal

Review ▶ p.89

Aim

● to revise the structures and vocabulary covered in Unit 8

1 – **4** Ask students to complete the activities, monitoring them to provide assistance. Alternatively, set this as a homework activity. Ask students to compare their answers in pairs before doing a class check.

Answers

1 1 B 2 C 3 B 4 A 5 A 6 C 7 B 8 C

2 1 recommended Sam travel/that Sam should travel 2 will remain stable 3 reached a peak in 4 was a drop in demand 5 is/was/has been accused of not building 6 have to be so knowledgeable about

3 1 increasing 2 steadily 3 rise 4 growth 5 lower 6 overtaken 7 expected 8 drop

4 1 off 2 maintain 3 shock 4 belonging 5 barrier 6 assimilate

ADDITIONAL PRACTICE | **Active Teach** Game: Stepping stones

9 Reading the mind

Use of English and Vocabulary focus ▶ p.90

Open cloze (Part 2)

Aim

- to complete an exam-style open cloze task (Reading and Use of English Part 2)

Warmer

Focus on the title *Reading the mind*. Elicit what it means to read somebody's mind (to guess what someone else is thinking).

Students work in pairs. They choose any word and then say it aloud at the same time. They repeat to see if they can get the same word by finding common ground between the words. An alternative (easier) version can be played by students writing down words at the same time. An example is below.

A: Coffee

B: Umbrella

A: Wet

B: Water

A: Splash

B: Rain

A: Puddle!

B: Puddle!

For a recap of the open cloze task requirements and strategies, refer students to the Exam focus on p.178 to review the task and the strategies.

1 Elicit what is meant by *nature or nurture* in the first question (*nature* means the genetic disposition you inherit), *nuture* means the education and care that you are given as a child, and the way it affects your later development and attitudes). Allow students time to answer the questions, then put them into pairs to discuss their answers. Elicit a few answers for each question.

2 Students read the article quickly, without worrying about the gaps. Elicit the answer to the question. Elicit what students know about Reading and Use of English Part 2 and how to approach the task.

3 Read the Exam tip aloud. Focus students' attention on gap 1, where they might expect *stared* to be followed by the preposition *at*. However, the word in the gap (*in*) combines with the words *apparent disbelief* to form an adverbial phrase. Ask students to complete the remaining gaps and then compare answers in pairs before you check as a class.

Answers

2 Because the babies seemed surprised when they were shown images that appeared to defy the laws of physics.

3 **1** in **2** out **3** but **4** same **5** anything
  6 for **7** no **8** nothing

ADDITIONAL PRACTICE | **Maximiser** p.62, Use of English | **MEL** Unit 9, Use of English | **MEL** Extra practice, Use of English 3: Articles

Expressions with *brain* and *mind*

Aim

● to understand and use a range of expressions with *brain* and *mind*

4 Students work in pairs to put the developmental milestones in order. Play the recording for them to check their answers.

Background: *Milestone*

A milestone is a very important event in the development of something. This word comes from its other meaning: a stone next to a road that shows the distance in miles to the next town. Romans used milestones along roads, including in Britain.

5 Play the recording again for students to note down the phrases. Students compare answers in pairs before you check as a class.

6 Students answer the questions. Check as a class, then read the Language tip aloud.

7 Elicit whether each expression in Activity 6 is two separate words, a hyphenated two-word compound or one word (see answers to Activity 6).

Students complete the sentences with compound nouns or verbs from Activity 6. Remind them to check that their compound words are correctly written and hyphenated. Students compare answers in pairs before you check as a class.

8 Invite a student to read the first question aloud. Elicit from the class some things that might have happened beforehand (e.g. *You might have broken or lost something of theirs. You might have had to cancel plans.*). Students discuss the questions in pairs. Finish by eliciting a few ideas for each question.

Answers

4 **1** return a smile **2** recognise familiar faces **3** know her own name and respond to it **4** enjoy hiding games **5** try to be a help **6** learn to put on her own clothes

5 recognise familiar faces – know who's who

learn to put on her own clothes – get the hang of dressing herself

know her own name and respond to it – recognise her own name and react to it

enjoy hiding games – get a real kick out of the game of *peekaboo*

try to be a help – display helpful behaviour

return a smile – smile back

6 **1** brainchild, brain damage, brain drain, brain scan, brainstorm, brain teaser, brainwash, brainwave

2 **A** mind-boggling, **B** mind reader

1 brain drain **2** brainchild **3** brain damage **4** brainstorm **5** brainwave **6** brain teasers **7** brainwashing **8** brain scan

8 (Suggested answers)

1 something disappointing or upsetting

2 No, she'll just think about it.

3 They want one.

4 Because another person has used a taboo word in front of a child or someone who might find it offensive.

5 Because you are about to say something that partially contradicts something you or another speaker has previously said.

6 a question that might cause embarrassment or be understood as an invasion of privacy

Additional activity

In pairs, students make up a short conversation for one of the scenarios they thought of in Activity 8. It should include the relevant phrase using *mind*. Invite pairs to share their conversations with the class.

ADDITIONAL PRACTICE | **Maximiser** p.62, Vocabulary | **MEL** Unit 9, Vocabulary | Photocopiable 9A *As quickly as you can* | **Active Teach** Game: Noughts and crosses

Grammar focus ▶ p.92

Warmer

Tell the following joke to the class:

Q: What did the doctor say to the man who had an elephant sitting on his brain?

A: I think you have a lot on your mind.

Elicit what the 'joke' is. It uses a pun (an amusing use of a word or phrase that has two meanings, or of words that have the same sound but different meanings). The man literally has a lot on his mind because he has an elephant sitting on it, but he also has a lot on his mind in the sense that he has a big problem to worry about.

Point out that puns are sometimes used in titles for effect. Direct students to the title of the article on p.92 and ask them to work in pairs to discuss what the pun is. (*Crest* literally means the top or highest point of something such as a hill or a wave. If you're *on the crest of a wave* it means you're very successful. In this case, the wave is a *brainwave* which refers to the subject of the article. It refers to how the work on brainwaves has been very successful.)

1 Time students for two minutes as they quickly read the article to find the uses. Elicit these.

2 Put students into pairs to discuss the questions. Elicit the meaning of *envisage* /ɪnˈvɪzɪdʒ/ (to think that something is likely to happen in the future). Conduct whole-class feedback.

Answers
1 to control electronic devices, to direct musicians to play music

Future in the past

Aim
- to use appropriate forms to talk about future in the past

Refer students to the Grammar reference section on future in the past on p.161 and the exercise on p.162. Alternatively, do this after Activity 4.

Grammar reference answers
1 were
2 was
3 had
4 have
5 going
6 would

Teaching tip: Diagrams

Many students find visual diagrams helpful for understanding concepts. To illustrate the concept of the future in the past, draw a timeline. Point out that the future in the past is used when we are talking about the past, and events that were in the future at that time but may be in the past now. For example, last month, you might have been writing an essay for submission last week. At the first point in time (last month), last week was in the future, even though it's now in the past.

3 Direct students to the underlined verbs and elicit what each refers to.

4 Ask students to read the instructions and example. Circulate while students rewrite the paragraph.

Conduct whole-class feedback. Go through the Language tip and point out that the options given in the example are all possible.

5 Students work through the activity, then compare answers in pairs before checking as a class.

6 Put students into A/B pairs, and ask them to turn to the relevant page. Give students a few minutes to plan their answer individually before role-playing the situation.

Alternative
Get students to work in pairs of two As, and two Bs to plan their answers, before they swap partners and role-play the situations.

Additional activity
Use the additional scenarios below for fast finishers to have extra practice after Activity 6.
1 *Student B was going to meet Student A for a coffee yesterday, but didn't show up.*
2 *Student A promised to lend Student B an English novel, but no longer can.*

Answers
3 All the underlined forms are predictions made in the past about the future.

4 Psychologists <u>are aiming</u> to find out how acquiring new skills, such as speaking a foreign language, <u>can affect</u> the structure of the brain. They <u>think</u> that these <u>changes will not take place</u> at the same rate in older people and <u>want</u> to find out if there <u>is</u> an optimal age for learning a language.

Changes from future in the past to present: past continuous – present continuous, *would – will, could – can, would have been – would be*

5 **1** was considering **2** was going to be **3** would win
   4 were hoping **5** would have been **6** was going to take

ADDITIONAL PRACTICE | **Maximiser** p.63, Grammar | **MEL** Unit 9, Grammar | Photocopiable 9B *I was going to, but …* | **MEL** Extra practice, Use of English 11: Past tenses with future meaning | **Active Teach** Extra activity Grammar Focus 1

Speaking focus ▶ p.93

Long turn (Part 2)
paraphrasing

Aim
- to practise following examiner instructions and using paraphrasing to avoid repetition in a long turn task (Speaking Part 2)

1 Put students into pairs to look at the pictures and discuss the questions.

2 Elicit what students remember about Speaking Part 2. If necessary, refer students to the Exam focus on p.183 to review the task and strategies. Play the recording, then elicit the instructions. Write these on the board for students to refer to in Activity 3.

3 Students work in pairs, following the examiner's instructions from Activity 2.

4 Play the recording. Elicit which pictures the candidate compared and whether she followed the instructions.

5 Allow students time to read the gapped sentences, then play the recording again for students to fill in the gaps. Check answers as a class.

6 Play the recording once for students to listen to the question and answer. Discuss as a class whether the candidate responds effectively.

Teaching tip: Marking guidelines

Reminding students of the marking criteria can help focus their performance. Take the opportunity to refer students to the Marking guidelines for speaking on p.185 so they can reacquaint themselves with what is required for a high scoring (Band 5) answer.

7 Tell students that they are going to try a long turn task and take turns to be the candidate and the examiner. Read the Exam tip aloud. Point out that a key purpose of paraphrasing the instructions is for students to show they can use a varied range of vocabulary (Band 5 lexical resource). Students work in pairs and follow the instructions for the activities on p.138 and p.142.

Answers

2 The examiner asks the candidates to compare two of the pictures and say why people might be doing these things on their own and what reactions they might get from other people.

4 Yes. She compares two of the pictures, says why people might be doing these things and suggests possible reactions people might have.

5 **1** by himself **2** without anyone else **3** all to himself **4** solitary **5** lone **6** unaccompanied

6 The examiner asks who is happiest doing these things on their own and why. The candidate responds effectively.

MyEnglishLab tip: Practice Speaking test activities

Students will need a partner for the MyEnglishLab Practice Speaking test activities and someone to act

as 'examiner'. You can print the tasks for use in class if necessary. Before students do the task, ask them to reread the Marking guidelines for speaking on p.185. Students could do the practice test in groups of four, with one pair completing Parts 1–4 as candidates while the other pair act as examiners, time-keeping and noting down any good vocabulary/phrases the candidates use. After pairs swap roles, give them time to discuss the feedback and what they need to improve on.

ADDITIONAL PRACTICE | **Maximiser** p.63, Speaking | **MEL** Unit 9, Speaking | **MEL** Extra practice, Speaking 8: Comparing Part 2 pictures | **Active Teach** Game: Pelmanism

Reading focus ▶ p.94

1 Give students time to think about what they remember about their first day at primary school and their first teacher, then organise students into pairs. Conduct whole-class feedback.

2 Allow students time to read the list of comments. Check students understand *analogue clock* (a clock that uses pointers, not changing numbers, i.e. not a digital clock). Students discuss the comments in pairs then as a class.

Gapped text (Part 7)

Aim

- to complete a gapped text task (Reading and Use of English Part 7)

3 Elicit what students remember about Reading and Use of English Part 7. If necessary, refer them to the Exam focus on p.180 to review the task and strategies. Give students about five minutes to read the article quickly and find out which of the difficulties in Activity 2 are mentioned.

4 Read the Exam tip aloud. Point out that this first reading should be quick. Remind students to look for links between the main text and paragraphs. Go through the answers and reasons as a class.

Answers

3 Points 1 and 4: 'It took me ages to be able to tell the time on an analogue clock. I don't know why but I sometimes couldn't understand what I read or what the teacher explained to us.'

4 **1 B** (Paragraph B provides further evidence and examples of the last statement in the first paragraph: *She didn't know what was wrong.*)

2 F (*somebody*, *His* and *he* in the third paragraph refer to 'the injured man' in paragraph F)

3 G (*an area of my brain wasn't working* in the third paragraph is a paraphrase of *The bullet had lodged in a part of the Russian's brain where information from sight, sound, language and touch is synthesised, analysed and made sense of*)

4 A (*this* in the fifth paragraph refers to the clock face exercise described in paragraph A)

5 D (*It* in the sixth paragraph refers to the *exercises* she developed)

6 E (*So many children get written off* in the final paragraph is a paraphrase of *Thousands of children dismissed as impossible to teach*)

ADDITIONAL PRACTICE | **Maximiser** p.64, Reading | **MEL** Unit 9, Reading | **MEL** Extra practice, Reading 17 Logical and cohesive development B

Vocabulary
working out meaning from context

Aim
- to practise working out meaning from context

5 Focus students' attention on the underlined words in the text and ask them to discuss in pairs the meaning of each one. Emphasise that students will need to change some of the forms to fit the gapped sentences. Check answers as a class.

Additional activity

Ask students to reflect on the following questions, then discuss their answers in small groups.
1 *Do you remember a moment when you had a breakthrough in learning English? When?*
2 *What strategies do you use if you don't get something in class?*
3 *Have you devised any methods for improving retention of what you learn in class?*

6 Students share experiences in pairs.

Answers
5 1 dismal 2 breakthrough 3 devised 4 got
   5 premise 6 written off

ADDITIONAL PRACTICE | Photocopiable 9C *Invented words* | **MEL** Extra practice, Reading 12: Inferring meaning A | **Active Teach** Reading Focus – meanings in context

Listening focus ▶ p.96

Warmer

Focus students on the title of the article on p.92. Point out that *crest* means the top or highest point of something such as a hill or a wave. If, for example, a surfer is on *the crest of a wave* it means they are surfing very well.

Ask students to discuss in pairs what *On the crest of a brainwave* might mean. Encourage them to think about the meaning of *brainwave* (when someone has a very good idea). Check answers and elicit that the article is about being on the highest point of a very good idea. Point out that the titles of articles often use language in creative ways like this.

1 Read through the comments with the class. Check students know the literal meaning of *sieve* (a round wire kitchen tool with a lot of small holes, used for separating small pieces of food from large pieces). Elicit the meaning of the expression *have a memory like a sieve* (forget things easily) and elicit whether there are any similar expressions in the students' own languages. Ask students what *absent-minded* means (likely to forget things, especially because you are thinking about something else). In pairs, students discuss which of the comments apply to them.

Teaching tip: Image search
Some words are quicker to teach with a picture. For a word like *sieve*, show an online picture. You may also be able to find a memorable image for the idiom *memory like a sieve*.

Multiple matching (Part 4)

Aim
- to complete an exam-style listening task (Listening Part 4)

2 Elicit what students know about Listening Part 4 and how to approach the task. If necessary, refer students to the Exam focus on p.182 to review the task and strategies. Then students look at Task 1 and discuss the question. Elicit some ideas.

3 Focus students' attention on Task 2 for pair discussion. Conduct whole-class feedback.

4 Read the rubric and Exam tip aloud. Play the recording twice for students to complete the tasks. Check answers as a class.

5 Organise students into pairs of A and B. Students turn to p.145 and p.147 respectively. Students need to work together to make six complete sentences using parts from both students' lists (without looking at the other student's page). Conduct whole-class feedback.

6 Encourage students to use phrases from Activity 5 and remind them to use a range of narrative tenses when they tell their story. Give students a moment to think about what they are going to share, then put them in pairs to talk about their experiences.

Answers
4 Task 1: 1 C   2 G   3 A   4 F   5 H
  Task 2: 6 D   7 C   8 G   9 H   10 E
5 1 F   2 D   3 E   4 B   5 C   6 A

ADDITIONAL PRACTICE | **Maximiser** p.66, Listening | **MEL** Unit 9, Listening | **MEL** Extra practice, Listening 11: Identifying the main point

Grammar focus ▶ p.97

Future in the past: advanced features

Aims
- to use future in the past to describe actions which were interrupted
- to use a range of ways to refer to unfulfilled intentions or events that didn't happen

Warmer
Write the following in speech bubbles on the board:
I know I was meant to call you last night but …
I know I was supposed to submit the report today but …
I know I was due to start my shift at 4 pm but …
Ask students to work in pairs to think of some different ways to complete the excuse in each situation. Conduct whole-class feedback to find out who has thought up the most plausible and the most original excuses for each scenario.

1 Focus students' attention on the first sentence as an example. Look at each phrase in the box in turn, eliciting whether it could replace the underlined phrase, and any changes that would need to be made. Students work through the remaining sentences, then compare answers in pairs before you check as a class.

2 Go through the examples with the class, getting a student to read each one, and eliciting the answers as you go.

3 Students complete the sentences and then discuss their answers as a class.

4 Students complete the activity, then compare answers in pairs before you check as a class. Read the Language tip aloud to the class.

Answers
1 1 was about to   2 weren't meant to   3 was meant to/ due to leave (verb form changes here)   4 were thinking of inviting (verb form changes here)   5 was about to
6 was about to
2 1 no   2 yes   3 yes   4 yes
3 1 were to have left   2 was to go on   3 was to have been published   4 were to be informed   5 were to sign   6 was to have become
4 1 was supposed to be/have been finished   2 were due to publish   3 were to have been told   4 was thinking of asking (for)   5 was about to close   6 would have invited Sarah

Additional activity
Ask students to think of a time when their plans changed because something unexpected happened. Students share their experience with a partner using future in the past. As a prompt, you could share a brief anecdote of your own or share the following for times when plans may change: *unseasonable weather, a delayed connection, an unexpected phone call/visit, winning something, losing something.*

ADDITIONAL PRACTICE | **Maximiser** p.66, Grammar | **MEL** Unit 9, Grammar | **Active Teach** Extra activity Grammar Focus 2

Writing focus ▶ p.98

Email (Part 2)
adopting the right tone

Aim
- to write an email using an informal tone

Warmer
Ask students to discuss these questions in pairs:
1 How helpful do you think reading books are in learning a language?
2 Do you ever read books in English?

1 Students read the blog entry and discuss the question in pairs. Elicit a few ideas.

2 Give students time to read the blog again. Elicit answers to the question, asking students to justify them with examples from the blog.

3 Working in pairs, students decide if each piece of advice is formal or informal. Check as a class.

4 Point out the importance of adopting the right tone in communication depending on the situation. Ask students to work with their partner to rewrite the formal items in a less formal tone. Check as a class. In pairs, students decide whether they agree with each piece of advice.

5 Students read the exam task and points for inclusion. They put them in order to make a coherent plan. Elicit the correct order.

6 Refer students to the Writing reference on p.172 for useful language for informal emails. Set the writing task for homework.

7 Students share their writing in groups of three and make any improvements suggested. Collect the emails to provide individual feedback.

Answers

2   The text is informal. The following features tell us this: contractions (e.g. *I'd read*); *and* is used frequently as a linker; simple vocabulary (e.g. *got it wrong*) and phrasal verbs (e.g. *work out, end up*).

3   1 F   2 I   3 F   4 F   5 I   6 I   7 F   8 I

4   (Suggested answers)

   1 It wouldn't be a bad idea to get yourself a dictionary.

   3 If I was thinking of learning a language, I'd most probably do a course.

   4 Reading as widely as you can could help.

   7 I wouldn't try learning a language by yourself.

5   **1** Acknowledge receipt of the message and apologise for not writing before.

   2 Express pleasure about friend's plans to relocate and reiterate the question in the email.

   3 Comment briefly on my experience of learning English.

   4 Make a series of suggestions about learning my language drawing on my own and others' experience.

   5 Express the hope of having been of some assistance.

   6 Conclude with the wish to receive a reply and the usual salutation.

6   Model answer

   Hi Emma,

   So good to hear from you. I'm sorry for not getting back to you earlier, I was snowed under with exams. Thankfully, I've now got them done and dusted for another year.

   What great news that you're finally coming to Spain – and you're going to learn Spanish too – even better! Seeing as you ask, I do have a few suggestions that might help you pick it up more quickly.

   I guess it's been ten years since I had my first English lesson, and it's been an incredible journey with only a few hiccups along the way. By far the most useful experience was when I got to do that immersion course in Brighton. I think you'll find that the more you can immerse yourself, the quicker you'll progress.

Before you arrive, you could start off with some apps. I'm a bit sceptical about their claims that they'll make you fluent but they're great for learning some of the building blocks. I'd suggest enrolling in a course in your first weeks here to get the basics down. Read as widely as possible, online newspapers, blogs, books, the back of a cereal packet – anything, really! What's also crucial is that you get exposure to real Spanish. A part-time job with locals could be just the ticket, I'd be happy to help you with the job search.

Anyway, I hope that's helped give you a few ideas. Do write back as soon as you can so we can pencil in a catch up!

Cheers,

Ana

ADDITIONAL PRACTICE | Maximiser p.67, Writing | MEL Unit 9, Writing | MEL Extra practice, Writing 8: Planning a letter or email

Review ▶ p.99

Aim

• to revise the structures, vocabulary and exam tasks covered in Unit 9

1 – 3 Ask students to complete the activities, monitoring them to provide assistance. Alternatively, set this as a homework activity. Ask students to compare their answers in pairs before doing a class check.

Answers

1   **1** was planning   **2** was meant to be coming   **3** was going to ask   **4** would be   **5** were babysitting   **6** was supposed to   **7** were due to play   **8** would have been

2   **1** brainstorming   **2** wave   **3** brain   **4** Brainteaser   **5** brain   **6** damage

3   **1** leadership   **2** unemployed   **3** uneasy   **4** registration   **5** solution   **6** unoccupied   **7** collaboratively   **8** confusion

ADDITIONAL PRACTICE | ActiveTeach Games: Sheep Out!; Stepping Stones

Progress test 3 ▶ p.100

Answers

1   **1** C   **2** A   **3** B   **4** A   **5** B   **6** D   **7** D   **8** B

2   **1** own   **2** was   **3** up   **4** along   **5** well   **6** less   **7** to   **8** by

3   **1** unemployment   **2** shortage   **3** perceptions   **4** prospective   **5** assumptions   **6** recruitment   **7** openings   **8** exceptional

4   **1** if I had waited   **2** you happen to pass/be passing   **3** quite impossible for me to attend   **4** if any of us/them/you had   **5** regretted having told/telling Angela   **6** for as long as (is)

10 A perfect match

Vocabulary and Grammar focus ▶ p.102

Expressions for describing compatibility

Aim

- to introduce a range of expressions for describing compatibility

1 Check students understand the meaning of *compatibility* (the ability to have a good relationship with someone because you have similar interests, ideas, etc.). Elicit the negative form, *incompatibility* and the adjective form *compatible*. In pairs, students discuss the question. Conduct whole-class feedback. Elicit a few answers and if students answer *no*, then elicit what elements they consider more important (e.g. loyalty, honesty).

2 Students complete the questions, then check answers as a class. Elicit the meaning of the idioms *be on the same wavelength* (think in a similar way and understand each other well), *be as different as chalk and cheese* (be very different) and *get on like a house on fire* (get on very well). Then get students to discuss the questions with a partner. Conduct whole-class feedback.

3 Students complete the sentences, then check answers as a class. Focus students' attention on the Language tip and read it aloud.

4 Students discuss the questions in pairs or small groups. Conduct whole-class feedback.

5 Give students time to consider the questions individually before comparing in pairs.

6 Ask students to read the advice and tick the items they agree with, making any changes they want to. Then students compare in pairs.

Answers
2 **2** from **3** on **4** as, as, on **5** to/with **6** with
3 **1** fitted **2** matched **3** matches/matched **4** fitting

ADDITIONAL PRACTICE | Maximiser p.70, Vocabulary | **MEL** Unit 10, Vocabulary | **Active Teach** Game: Noughts and crosses

whoever, whatever, etc.

Aim

- to review the use of *whoever, whatever,* etc.

Refer students to the Grammar reference section on *whoever, whatever,* etc. on p.162 and set the exercise on p.163.

Grammar reference answers
1 however   2 Whenever   3 Wherever
4 Whoever   5 whatever

7 Direct students to the first sentence and elicit what phrase could be used to replace *However* (It doesn't matter how / No matter how). Students rewrite the remaining sentences then check as a class.

Alternative
Ask students to find and underline the words with *-ever* in Activity 6. While they do that, write up the answers to Activity 7 out of order on the board. Ask students to select the correct meaning for the *-ever* word in each sentence.

8 Students complete the sentences, then compare answers in pairs before you check as a class.

9 Rewrite the first piece of advice with the class. Students then rewrite the rest, comparing answers in pairs before you check as a class.

10 Students discuss the advice in pairs, then write two more pieces of advice using an *-ever* word. Elicit some of the students' additional advice.

Answers
7 (Suggested answers)

 1 It doesn't matter how   2 Any time   3 Anything
 4 Even if it may be tempting   5 no matter who
 6 it makes no difference how

8 1 Whatever   2 However   3 whenever
 4 whichever   5 wherever   6 whoever

9 1 However well you know and trust the person – never share your log-in details.

 2 Set your notifications to tell you whenever someone tags you in a photo.

 3 However much you enjoy spending time on social media, try to limit yourself to two hours a day.

 4 Wherever you're going on holiday – don't broadcast the fact. You might not want everyone to know you're away.

ADDITIONAL PRACTICE | Maximiser p.70, Grammar | **MEL** Unit 10, Grammar | Photocopiable 10A *Perfect advice* | **Active Teach** Extra activity Grammar Focus 1

Reading focus ▶ p.104

1 Elicit the meaning of *match-make* (try and find a suitable partner for someone else) and elicit the noun forms *match-maker* and *match-making*. Students discuss the statement in pairs. Conduct whole-class feedback.

2 Students read the article and choose the best title. Elicit the answer.

Answer
2 1

Multiple choice (Part 5)

Aim
● to complete an exam-style multiple-choice reading task (Reading and Use of English Part 5)

3 Focus students' attention on the underlined word *dozen*. Even if students know what it means (twelve), ask them to find the information later in the paragraph that would help (*the eleventh*). Read the Exam tip aloud and elicit what students remember about the strategies for tackling Reading and Use of English Part 5. If necessary, review the strategies in the Exam focus on p.179.

4 Give students ten minutes to complete the activity.

5 Ask students to underline or highlight phrasal verbs in the article. Then ask students to replace the underlined verbs with an appropriate phrasal verb. Elicit the answers.

Answers
3 twelve

4 1 D 'Although he had met lots of girls during his first semester at college, he just hadn't clicked with any of them.'

 2 C '... supposedly designed to match clients with the man or woman of their dreams. But can they?'

 3 B '... none of these matching services have ever subjected their secret algorithms ... to any kind of objective analysis or independent scrutiny.'

 4 D 'In fact, a 'selection bias' – a statistical bias that occurs when a sample population is different from the norm – may be at work.'; 'The claimed success of matching services may have more to do with narrowing the pool of eligible daters ...'

 5 B '... online matching services may work because the couple believe their compatibility has been validated by relationship experts using complex computer science.'

 6 D 'He has abandoned algorithm-assisted online dating in favour of online chat rooms and forums ... Matching software, it seems, is no match for a good chat-up line.'

5 1 signing up   2 turned him down   3 cut back
 4 back up   5 weed out   6 chatting up

ADDITIONAL PRACTICE | Maximiser p.68, Reading | **MEL** Unit 10, Reading | Photocopiable 10B *Compatibility* | **MEL** Extra practice, Reading 13: Inferring meaning B | **Active Teach** Reading Focus – meanings in context; Game: Pelmanism

Use of English focus ▶p.106

Open cloze (Part 2)

Aim

• to complete an exam-style open cloze task (Reading and Use of English Part 2)

1 Students discuss the questions in pairs. Conduct whole-class feedback.

2 Elicit what students remember about the strategies for tackling Reading and Use of English Part 2 and, if necessary, review them in the Exam focus on p.178. Ask students to read the title and the article quickly, then elicit the answer to the question.

3 Read the Exam tip aloud, then give students about seven minutes to fill the gaps. Check as a class, eliciting reasons for the choice for each gap.

4 Students work in pairs to choose the correct alternatives, discussing in each case why the other alternative is not possible.

5 Students answer the questions. They may make a few notes but should not write full sentences. Then they compare their responses in pairs. Conduct whole-class feedback. Use the opportunity to recycle *outweigh: Do the advantages outweigh the disadvantages?*

Answers

2 It involves developing professional relationships and can be used to share ideas

3 **1** one **2** further **3** of **4** way **5** as **6** few **7** next/close/near **8** Although/While

4 **1** few (a couple of) **2** does (make something = create) **3** out (set up = establish) **4** Rather (*Instead* is followed by *of* not *than*) **5** up (*out* not followed by *on* and different meaning) **6** all (some of)

Additional activity

Tell students that they are going to do some speed revision. First, give students a few minutes to look back through the coursebook and their notes and choose a few words, phrases, tips or concepts that have been useful during the course. If possible, set up your classroom like the photo on p.106 so that there is a long table with chairs for pairs of students facing each other on either side. Give students one minute to share which items they chose and why with each other before getting students to move down one place or swap partners,

either by one side of the table moving down one place or by students walking around to find a new partner.

ADDITIONAL PRACTICE | **Maximiser** p.70, Use of English | MEL Unit 10, Use of English

Listening focus ▶p.107

Multiple matching (Part 4)

Aim

• to complete an exam-style multiple matching task (Listening, Part 4)

Warmer

Write the following short personality test on the board:
I am a person who
1 never gives _____, even if things get really tough.
2 is always coming _____ with great ideas.
3 works well _____ pressure.
4 works best _____ collaboration with others.
5 gets anxious _____ disruptions to my routine.
Ask students to work in pairs to complete the gaps, then check as a class. Students then grade each statement so that it is true for them on a scale of 1–5, where 1 represents 'strongly disagree' and 5 represents 'agree completely'. Students compare their answers with their partner. Invite each person to share something they learnt about their partner's personality.
Answers: 1 up **2** up **3** under **4** in **5** about

1 Elicit what students can remember about the strategies for tackling Listening Part 4 and, if necessary, review them in the Exam focus on p.182. Then ask students to look at the exam tasks in Activity 3 and discuss the questions in Activity 1 in pairs.

2 Read the Exam tip aloud, then give students time to underline key words in the tasks. Play the recording and elicit whether the information comes in the same order as the two tasks.

3 Play the recording for students to complete the tasks. Play the recording a second time for students to complete and check their answers, then go through the answers as a class.

4 Put students into small groups to discuss the questions about personality tests. Point out that *bend the truth* means to say something that is not completely true as opposed to an outright lie. Elicit some ideas from each of the groups.

ADDITIONAL PRACTICE | **Maximiser** p.71, Listening | **MEL** Unit 10, Listening | **MEL** Extra practice, Listening 14: Identifying attitudes and feelings

Grammar focus ▶ p.108

1 Put students into pairs to discuss the question. Conduct whole-class feedback.

2 Give students a couple of minutes to read the article then elicit some opinions.

Participle clauses

Aim
- to review the structure and use of participle clauses

Refer students to the Grammar reference section on participle clauses on p.163 and set the exercise. Alternatively, do this after Activity 4.

Grammar reference answers
1 ~~Having been b~~Brought up in several countries, he could speak five languages fluently.
2 ~~After we had~~ Having seen the film, we wanted to read the book. / Seeing the film made us want to read the book.
3 There were hundreds of people ~~who were~~ waiting in the queue for tickets to the show.
4 The machine, ~~which was~~ invented at the end of the 19th century, still works today.
5 ~~Once I had understood~~ Understanding the problem, made it much easier to find a solution. / Having understood the problem, it was much easier to find a solution.

3 Focus students' attention on the underlined sentences in the article in Activity 2. Give students a moment to consider the questions then elicit the answers.

4 Ask students to underline four more participle clauses in the article. Elicit the answers. Point out that participle clauses would be an example of a complex grammatical form they could use in the exam (see Marking guidelines, Band 5, pages 184–185).

5 Focus students' attention on the example. Students match 1–6 with A–F, then rewrite the sentences using participle clauses. Students may work in pairs for this

activity. Check as a class, then read the Language tip aloud. Elicit how the example could be changed so that the subject of both clauses is the same (e.g. *Picking up the phone, I heard an unfamiliar voice greet me.*).

6 Students work in pairs. They should decide who is A and B before turning to p.144 and p.146 because they are going to do an activity individually and then check each other's work. When students are ready to do the checking, make sure they do it verbally rather than looking at their partner's work.

Answers
3 1 living (that/who live), envisaged (which was envisaged)
   2 Having reached (Because we have reached)
4 Having developed (Because/After they have developed), looking and behaving (who/which that look and behave), adapted (which was adapted), Having discovered (After he has discovered)
5 1 D Realising I was going to be late, I tried to find a taxi.
   2 E Having not/Not having slept a wink the night before, I was really tired.
   3 B I was worried about finding myself in another tense situation with Andrea having not/not having actually spoken to her since our last disastrous encounter.
   4 F Not wanting to have to be responsible for running the meeting, I asked Victoria if she would chair it for me.
   5 C Convinced everyone knew about the situation with Andrea, I decided it was pointless to behave as if nothing had happened.
   6 A Feeling very nervous as I walked into the room, I tried not to look anybody in the eye.

ADDITIONAL PRACTICE | **Maximiser** p.72, Grammar | **MEL** Unit 10, Grammar | Photocopiable 10C *Participle clause match* | **Active Teach** Extra activity Grammar Focus 2

Speaking focus ▶ p.109

Collaborative task and discussion (Parts 3 and 4)
negotiating and co-operating

Aim
- to use a variety of language to negotiate and cooperate in collaborative tasks and discussion tasks (Speaking Parts 3 and 4)

Warmer
Put students into pairs and ask them to think of three jobs that machines or robots can do now that they wouldn't have done one hundred years ago, and three

jobs that we do now that might be taken over by artificial intelligence in the future. Conduct whole-class feedback. Then ask: *Which jobs do you think are safest from being threatened by robots? Why?*

1 Direct students to read the task and questions 1–3. Play the recording for students to select the correct option.

Additional activity

Play the recording again and ask students to notice the questions and phrases that Adam and Nadia use to negotiate and cooperate. Ask students to turn to the audioscript on p.218 and underline the questions and phrases. Elicit these.

Suggested answers:

Would you go along with that?

I would, up to a point.

Sure. But, don't you think ...

I suppose so. I hadn't thought of that. How would you feel about ... ?

Mmmm. Maybe – as long as ...

So we're saying that ...

Right.

2 Read the Exam tip aloud. Tell students that using phrases to negotiate and co-operate can help them sound confident without being too direct. Give students time to discuss the prompts Adam and Nadia didn't talk about, i.e. they should discuss the prompts 'teach in a school' and 'design clothes'. Then give students one minute to do the negotiation phase (i.e. decide which of the tasks a robot would perform best). Ask each pair to briefly report back what they decided, with a reason.

Alternative

Time students for two minutes for the discussion phase as if it is a real exam task. Allow students to choose which prompts to talk about, including the ones that Adam and Nadia have talked about if they wish. Then time them for one minute for the negotiation phase.

3 Encourage students to make their own chart with the headings, and write the phrases under each one.

Additional activity

While students are completing Activity 3, write up the following phrases on the board for students to add under each heading.

7 That may well be so, but ...
8 Might it not be the case that ...
9 I have no hard and fast view on this, really, but ...
10 Have you considered the possibility that ...
Answers: A 9, C 7, 8, 10

4 Students should take turns to ask and answer questions from the list out of order. Encourage them to use the phrases from Activity 3. Conduct whole-class feedback.

5 Tell students that they will be doing a Part 3 task. After they turn to p.138, give them one minute to look at the prompts then time them for two minutes as they discuss the prompts, then one minute for the negotiation.

6 Students take turns to ask and answer the questions.

Answers
1 **1** Adam. Because he thinks passengers feel more comfortable with a human pilot and humans are better at making decisions in an emergency.

2 could. Robots could help with practical tasks such as washing and dressing as long as the person also had some human contact.

3 would. Because they could do simple tasks like putting toppings on pizzas.

3 **A** 3, 5 **B** 1, 6 **C** 2, 4

ADDITIONAL PRACTICE | **Maximiser** p.72, Speaking | **MEL** Unit 10, Speaking | **MEL** Extra practice, Speaking 13: Managing a Part 3 and Part 4 discussion

Writing focus ▶ p.110

Formal letter (Part 2)
including relevant information

Aim
- to practise selecting relevant information to include in a formal letter (Writing, Part 2)

Warmer

Ask students if they every had to write a formal letter or email, either in English or their own language. Put them into pairs to discuss who they were writing to, what the purpose was, and the effect they wanted to have on the reader.

Elicit some ideas, and point out that we often write formal letters when we don't know who it is we are writing to, and when we expect a serious outcome or result.

1 Students read the task and discuss the question in pairs. Elicit the answers.

2 Students read the letter and underline the irrelevant information. They discuss their answers in pairs before you check as a class. Read the Exam tip aloud. As the tasks will always require 220–260 words, it is a good idea for students to get used to writing to this length.

3 Put students into pairs of A and B. Give students five minutes to read the exam task on p.146 and plan their allocated section. Students share their plans in pairs. Remind them about the useful language for formal letters in the Writing reference on p.170. Then students write their letters.

Alternative

Have students plan and write this exam task individually as a timed practice for 40 minutes in class or at home. Encourage them to avoid looking at the task before the time starts.

Answers

1 points not to be included: your opinion about these students, what is not taught at the school, other subjects you would like to see introduced, why you can't offer some courses at the moment, what you've heard people say about your school

2 paragraph 2: Apparently, there is some discussion about offering Chinese at some time in the future but it is not currently available. (too vague and negative)

paragraph 3: It can be very difficult to find accommodation here, so it is a good thing that the school provides such a service. (too negative)

paragraph 4: The oldest student we've ever had was seventy-eight years old. (too specific)

3 Model answer

Dear Dr Hill,

I am writing to apply for the summer exchange programme at Dublin College.

I am currently in my penultimate year at your sister institution, Fredrikson College, where I have been studying a broad curriculum. My programme includes compulsory courses in mathematics, science, economics and history. As electives, I have been taking classes in three foreign languages, including English. I recently sat my mid-year exams and achieved excellent results.

Aside from my excellent academic results, there are many other reasons I believe I would prove an ideal exchange candidate. I am open-minded, have a friendly disposition and enjoy being exposed to new experiences. Having regularly befriended exchange students at my own school,

I feel I have a realistic understanding of what an exchange involves, including the more challenging aspects of possible homesickness and culture shock.

In addition to improving my English, I hope to gain a deeper understanding of Irish cultural traditions. It would also be a valuable opportunity for me to grow in confidence and independence. I hope to work abroad in the future, and this experience would be the first stepping stone towards realising this long-held dream.

I very much hope you will consider my application favourably and I look forward to receiving your response in due course. If you require any further information, please do not hesitate to contact me.

Yours sincerely,

Jana Novic

ADDITIONAL PRACTICE | **Maximiser** p.73, Writing | **MEL** Unit 10, Writing | **MEL** Extra practice, Writing 9: Useful language for formal letters

Review ▶ p.111

Aim

• to revise the structures, vocabulary and exam tasks covered in Unit 10

1 – **3** Ask students to complete the activities, monitoring them to provide assistance. Alternatively, set this as a homework activity. Ask students to compare their answers in pairs before doing a class check.

Answers

1 1 doesn't matter what 2 makes no difference how
3 having heard it was going 4 how much you like
them 5 regardless of what 6 wherever I happen
7 don't mind what we 8 you would like to come around

2 1 with 2 from 3 on fire 4 on 5 to 6 do with

3 1 C 2 D 3 A 4 C 5 B 6 B 7 C 8 A

MyEnglishLab tip: Mock Reading and Use of English paper

The mock tests are complete papers for exam practice. Suggest to students that they allow 90 minutes to complete the mock Reading and Use of English paper Parts 1–8 as a block, to get a feel for the progression in the exam.

ADDITIONAL PRACTICE | **ActiveTeach** Games: Sheep Out!; Stepping Stones

11 Face value

Vocabulary and Use of English focus ▶ p.112

1 Students work in pairs to decide if the statements are true or false. If necessary, pre-teach *frown* (a facial expression used to indicate displeasure). Ask for a show of hands for who thinks each statement is true or false, then ask students to turn to p.147 to check their answers.

Words to describe emotions

Aim

- to expand students' knowledge of vocabulary for describing emotions

2 Ask students to work in pairs or small groups to discuss the questions. Conduct whole-class feedback.

Additional activity

Ask students to underline the syllables which are stressed in each word in the box.

Answers: a<u>muse</u>ment, a<u>ston</u>ishment, <u>bitter</u>ness, con<u>fu</u>sion, con<u>tent</u>ment, de<u>light</u>, em<u>barr</u>assment, exhila<u>ra</u>tion, frus<u>tra</u>tion, hys<u>te</u>ria, in<u>diff</u>erence.

Answers

2 **3** amusement – amused; astonishment – astonished; bitterness – bitter; confusion – confused; contentment – content/contented; delight – delighted; embarrassment – embarrassed; exhilaration – exhilarated; frustration – frustrated; hysteria – hysterical; indifference – indifferent

ADDITIONAL PRACTICE | **Maximiser** p.76, Vocabulary | **MEL** Unit 11, Vocabulary | Photocopiable 11A *The right word, the right form* | **Active Teach** Game: Pelmanism

Open cloze (Part 2)

Aim

- to complete an exam-style open cloze task (Reading and Use of English Part 2)

3 Students discuss the questions in pairs, then conduct whole-class feedback.

4 Give students one minute to read the article. Ask students to decide how to summarise the article in no more than a few sentences, then compare answers in pairs.

5 Students complete the article, but don't check the answers yet.

6 Read the Language tip aloud, then ask students to work in pairs to compare their Activity 5 answers, and discuss questions 1–3.

7 Encourage students to share information about the context of the meal, the food itself, and the emotions associated with it. Prompt them to use some of the words from Activity 2, if possible.

Answers

5 **1** until **2** why/how **3** with **4** as/like **5** only
6 whether **7** more **8** hardly/scarcely
6 **1** not, but also **2** in addition to **3** not much

ADDITIONAL PRACTICE | **Maximiser** p76, Use of English | **MEL** Unit 11, Use of English | **MEL** Extra practice, Use of English 6: Reflexive and personal pronouns

Listening focus ▶ p.114

Warmer

Tell students that they are going to play a quick game where the point is not to laugh. If you laugh, you lose.

Put students into pairs. Tell them that they can take turns to ask their partner a question or say something and see if they can get their partner to laugh. The last person not to laugh is the winner. Play the game briefly for about two minutes.

Conduct whole-class feedback with some of the following questions:

- *Who laughed?*
- *What was funny about it?*
- *Was it harder to supress your laughter because you knew you weren't supposed to laugh?*

1 Students discuss the question in pairs. Elicit some ideas.

Multiple choice (Part 3)

Aim
- to complete an exam-style multiple choice listening task (Listening Part 3)

2 Give students two minutes to underline key words in the questions. Read the Exam tip aloud, then play the recording twice, pausing for a minute in between to help students complete the task. Then check answers as a class.

3 Students discuss the questions in pairs. Conduct whole-class feedback.

4 Students choose the correct alternatives to complete the sentences from the recording. Play the recording again for students to check, or refer students to the audioscript on p. 218.

Answers

2 **1** A **2** D **3** A **4** B **5** B **6** C
4 **1** advocating **2** lighten **3** impulses **4** anecdotes
5 contagious

Additional activity

Ask students to find and write down three adjectives ending in -ous in Activity 4 (*spontaneous, contagious, dangerous*). Ask students to discuss in pairs the number of syllables in each word and to underline the stress.

Answers: spon<u>ta</u>neous (4), con<u>ta</u>gious (3), <u>dan</u>gerous (3)

ADDITIONAL PRACTICE | **Maximiser** p.77, Listening | **MEL** Unit 11, Listening | **MEL** Extra practice, Listening 18: Listening for stated opinions, attitudes and inferring ideas

Grammar focus ▶ p.115

1 Start by getting students to see if they can describe what the dog is doing in each picture using some of the expressions in the box. Then students work in pairs to speculate on what a dog would be expressing by each action. Conduct whole-class feedback.

2 Give students a chance to read the statements, then play the recording. Elicit which one is true.

Answer

2 Only 2 is true.

Passive forms

Aim
- to review the forms and uses of the passive

Refer students to the Grammar reference section on passive forms on p.163 and set the exercise. Alternatively, do this after Activity 3.

Grammar reference answers

1 Identity cards must be shown when entering the building.

2 The form needs to be sent by next week.

3 The job will be finished today.

4 She wasn't expected to win the election.

5 Tom should have been invited to the party.

6 It was agreed that the meeting should be cancelled.

3 Direct students to A–C, which compare what the woman says with what the researchers had written (in italics). Ask students to discuss the questions in pairs. Conduct whole-class feedback.

4 Rewrite the first sentence as a class. Elicit the object in the sentence (*the dogs*) and write this first. Then elicit how the sentence should be completed. Students rewrite the remaining sentences.

Alternative

Provide scaffolding for the exercise by getting students to identify and underline the object in each sentence first. Elicit these and write them on the board as the sentence starters, then get students to complete each sentence. For example:

1 *The dogs …*

2 *The results …*

3 *Dog owners …*

4 *A dog's emotions …*

5 Before students read the text, invite students to speculate on some ways that dogs are similar to young children. Then ask students to read the text to see if any of their ideas were mentioned.

6 Students complete the text then compare their answers in pairs before checking as a class. Ask students to read the Language tip. Point out that there are two passives in the examples, the passive in the reporting verb structure, and the passive that follows it.

Answers

3 **1** The passive is used because it is more formal and sounds more objective. Impersonal passive structures are used with reporting verbs because the agent is unknown or unimportant, e.g. *it is thought*.

2 Other changes – more formal verbs are used, e.g. *carry out, conduct, establish, interpret; Further* is used instead of *more, able to* is used instead of *can*.

4 **1** The dogs may have been confused by the test.

2 The results must have been a surprise for the researchers.

3 Dog owners should be believed when they say they understand how their dog feels.

4 A dog's emotions can be interpreted by most people.

6 **1** had been/was predicted

2 was not supported

3 were considered

4 have always been disputed

5 being displayed

6 has generally been accepted

7 can be experienced

8 has always been associated

9 may be forced

10 is now believed

ADDITIONAL PRACTICE | **Maximiser** p.77, Grammar | **MEL** Unit 11, Grammar | Photocopiable 11B *A myth or not?* | **MEL** Extra practice, Use of English 14: Active or passive voice | **Active Teach** Game: Noughts and crosses; Extra activity Grammar Focus 1

Reading focus ▶ p.116

Cross-text multiple matching (Part 6)

Aim

• to practise identifying differences of writer opinion in an exam-style cross-text multiple matching task (Reading and Use of English Part 6)

1 Students work in pairs to discuss the questions. Elicit a few responses to each.

2 Elicit what students remember about Reading and Use of English Part 6 and how to approach the task. If necessary, refer students to the Exam focus on p.180 to review the task and strategies.

Give students three minutes to quickly read the text for gist, then elicit the answers to the questions.

3 Ask students to answer the questions individually, then compare answers in pairs before you check as a class.

4 Read the Exam tip aloud. Give students time to complete the questions, then go through the answers as a class.

5 Students discuss the questions in pairs. Elicit a few responses from the class.

Additional activity

Write on the board the verbs: *portray, display, depict, expose, highlight, reveal*. Ask students to find and underline examples of these words in the text and notice how they are used.

6 Point out that in each sentence, only one verb sounds right. Students choose the best verb to complete each sentence, then compare answers in pairs before you check as a class.

7 Elicit the noun forms of the verbs in Activity 6 and write them on the board.

8 Students discuss the questions in pairs. Ask each pair to share something interesting from their discussion.

Additional activity

Select three photographic portraits from the internet, including one by Irving Penn. Ask students to compare the styles and discuss their own opinion of the work in pairs.

Answers

3 **1** His work continues to be very influential, 'is and will continue to be a giant in the world of photographic portraiture' and 'his relevance also endures as a fashion photographer'.

2 B 'These all demonstrate that Penn's technical mastery is without equal. He undoubtedly created a style that later generations of photographers have found impossible not to imitate.'

3 D 'As Penn's reputation inevitably begins to fade'

4 **1 B** (C: 'Penn is and will continue to be a giant in the world of photographic portraiture'; B: 'He undoubtedly created a style that later generations of photographers have found impossible not to imitate.')

2 D (A: 'From the 1940s until his last work in 2007, he remained constant in his approach, never failing to deliver anything less than utter perfection.'; D: 'Only in the last decade of his life does his work lose some of its magic.')

3 A (B: 'In showing the sitters without any of the trappings of celebrity, Penn successfully reveals qualities not seen in other portraits.'; A: 'The simplicity of the sets he used in all his portraits cleverly leaves his subjects nowhere to hide, exposing the individual behind the icon.')

4 C (C: 'the omission from this exhibition of some of his most iconic images for *Vogue* results in an incomplete portrayal of his achievements')

6 **1** portrays   **2** exposed   **3** displayed   **4** highlights
   5 reveals   **6** depict

7 portrayal, exposure/exposé, display, highlight, revelation, depiction

ADDITIONAL PRACTICE | **Maximiser** p.78, Reading | **MEL** Unit 11, Reading | **MEL** Extra practice, Reading 18: Understanding text development | **Active Teach** Reading Focus – easily confused words

Speaking focus ▶ p.118
Long turn (Part 2)

Aim

• to practise using a range of language to express certainty and uncertainty in an exam-style long turn task (Speaking Part 2)

1 Put students into pairs to discuss the questions. Conduct whole-class feedback.

expressing certainty and uncertainty

2 Play the recording and elicit what the examiner asked.

3 Ask students to read the sentences and tick the ones they agree with. Then ask them to underline the phrases that express certainty or uncertainty within the sentences. Students discuss in pairs then conduct whole-class feedback.

4 Remind students that after the other candidate has completed the long turn about a set of pictures, the listening candidate will be asked a follow-up question about the same pictures. Play the recording of the follow-up question. Read the Exam tip.

5 Students read the questions, then play the recording again for students to note the phrases. Check as a class.

6 Write the task from Activity 2 on the board (compare two of the pictures and say how successful the people are at creating the image and how people might react to them). Encourage students to time their partner for one minute.

7 Students do the tasks on p.139 and p.142, taking turns to be the answering candidate and the listening candidate. Remind them to try to use some of the phrases from Activity 3.

Answers

2 I'd like you to compare two of the pictures and say how successful the people are at creating the image and how people might react to them.

3 **1** There's no doubt that   **2** I'm convinced that
   3 undoubtedly   **4** It's an undeniable fact that

   5 1 it's quite hard to say   **2** I suppose   **3** extremely influential

ADDITIONAL PRACTICE | **Maximiser** p.80, Speaking | **MEL** Unit 11, Speaking | **MEL** Extra practice, Speaking 7: Answering the listening candidate's question | **Active Teach** Game: Sheep out!

Grammar focus ▶ p.119

1 Put students into pairs to discuss the questions, then conduct whole-class feedback.

2 Students quickly read the text without worrying about the gaps, then discuss questions 1–4 with a partner. Elicit some responses to each question.

3 Elicit the answer and evidence as a class.

Answers

2   2 C

3 advantages mentioned: gain respect and credibility in public life, sign of affluence and good taste, wear a suit and you display discipline, commitment and ambition, the most effective way to win instant acceptance

3 evidence of formal written style: passive forms, no contractions, long complex sentences, abstract academic lexis (e.g. *universally recognised, attire, credibility, donning, impeccably, utter, signify, be well advised, win instant acceptance*)

Linking adverbials

Aim

• to use a range of linking adverbials to introduce reasons, information or a contrast.

Refer students to the Grammar reference section on linking adverbials on p.164 and set the exercise.

Grammar reference answers

1   On the other hand
2   As well as
3   What's more
4   Even so
5   For this reason

4 Students complete the activity then compare in pairs before checking as a class. Read through the Language tip. Tell students that other cohesive devices will be covered in Unit 12.

5 Students answer the questions, referring to the Grammar reference if necessary. Then check answers as a class.

6 Working in pairs, students complete the activity. Monitor, checking that the linking adverbials are being used correctly. Conduct whole-class feedback.

Alternative

Divide the class into an equal number of pairs or groups of three. Assign half of the pairs to write three reasons why suits should be required at work and assign the other half of the pairs to write three reasons why suits shouldn't be required. Combine pairs to form groups of four to take turns to give their reasons for and against wearing a suit at work.

Answers

4   1 B   2 C   3 C   4 C   5 A   6 B

5   1 additionally, moreover, furthermore, what's more, besides this, as well as this

2 in view of, given, for this reason, consequently

3 apart from, in contrast, even so, on the other hand, alternatively, on the contrary

ADDITIONAL PRACTICE | **Maximiser** p.79, Grammar | **MEL** Unit 11, Grammar | Photocopiable 11C *Can you continue?* | **Active Teach** Extra activity Grammar Focus 2

Writing focus ▶ p.120

1 Focus students on the pictures and put students into pairs to discuss the questions. Conduct whole-class feedback.

Essay (Part 1)
planning your essay

Aim

• to develop a process for planning a well-structured essay (Writing Part 1)

2 Ask students to read the exam task and then ask them to make a plan including points 1–4. Students could do this in pairs if they wish. Elicit a model plan and write it on the board.

3 Set the writing task in class or for homework. Allow students 30 minutes for the writing, as some of the allocated exam time would be used up with the planning, and then checking the work. Remind students of the useful language for essays in the Writing reference on p.168. Read the Exam tip with students and remind them of the linking adverbials covered earlier.

4 Refer students to the checklist on p.166, and encourage them to make any relevant changes. Collect the essays to provide individual feedback.

Teaching tip

Ask students to ensure their essay meets the required word count. Tell students they should practise estimating the length of their writing, to avoid wasting time counting individual words in the exam.

In the Writing paper, candidates have 90 minutes to complete both Parts 1 and 2, with 220–260 words required for each part.

Answers

2   Model plan

Introduction: current situation: no clothing guidelines, currently considering dress code due to safety and image concerns

Advantage 1: improve safety – students wearing unsafe footwear has caused and will cause accidents

Advantage 2: improve image – scruffiness and offensive T-shirts have led to complaints from community

Conclusion: safety is most important reason because student safety is college's responsibility

3   Model answer

It is often said that young people should have the freedom to express themselves through clothes. However, at our college, the lack of guidelines has led some students to dress in a way that compromises both safety and our reputation in the community. In this essay, I will discuss two advantages of introducing a dress code at our college.

Firstly, a dress code is crucial for promoting health and safety. There have been a number of incidents at the school that could have been prevented by a more stringent dress code. For example, a student recently sustained an injury after tripping on the stairs while wearing platform shoes. Were there to be sensible limits placed on footwear choices, fewer such accidents would occur in the future.

Secondly, putting a dress code in place is likely to improve how other people view our institution. With more and more students turning to ripped jeans and outrageous slogans, our image is gradually becoming tarnished. This month alone, the college received five phone calls complaining about students' scruffy appearance during work placements.

In addition, requiring a higher standard of dress may lead to an enhanced self-image for students and a sense of pride in the college.

In my view, the most persuasive reason for a dress code is safety. Keeping students from harm is a key responsibility of the college, and it's time to act in students' best interests, even if it is an unpopular move among the student body.

ADDITIONAL PRACTICE | Maximiser p.81, Writing | **MEL** Unit 11, Writing | **MEL** Extra practice, Writing 4: Useful language for essay writing

Review ▶ p.121

Aim

- to revise the structures, vocabulary and exam tasks covered in Unit 11

1 – 4 Ask students to complete the activities, monitoring them to provide assistance. Alternatively, set this as a homework activity. Ask students to compare their answers in pairs before doing a class check.

Answers

1   **1** is **2** for **3** were **4** without **5** before **6** A **7** only **8** ourselves

2   **1** indifferent **2** discontented **3** astonishment **4** frustrating **5** relieved **6** nervousness **7** delightful **8** amusing

3   **1** was to have been banned **2** is considered to have been **3** was/had been thought to have been **4** is nothing to be done/is nothing that can be done/isn't anything to be done **5** want to be seen (by others) (to be) **6** caused/provoked confusion among/in/amongst/to

4   **1** Given **2** Even so **3** Despite **4** What's more

ADDITIONAL PRACTICE | Active Teach Game: Stepping stones

12 Brilliant ideas

Listening and Vocabulary focus ▶ p.122

Sentence completion (Part 2)

Aim

- to complete an exam-style sentence completion task (Listening Part 2)

Warmer

Write the title *Brilliant ideas* on the board.

Ask students to work in pairs to discuss these questions.

1 What do you think have been the most brilliant ideas in human history?

2 Have you ever had an idea that you think is brilliant?

1–**2** Ask students to discuss the questions in pairs. Conduct whole-class feedback.

3 Play the recording and elicit which things were mentioned.

4 Give students one minute to skim the text. Play the recording again for students to complete the text.

5 Ask students to discuss the question in pairs then conduct whole-class feedback.

Answers

2 jokes and laughter, listening to music at the end

3 everything except 'taking notes'

4 1 radio producer   2 performances by musicians   3 experiments   4 black holes
   5 questions   6 to network   7 Britain and France   8 inclusive

ADDITIONAL PRACTICE | **Maximiser** p.82, Listening | **MEL** Unit 12, Listening | Photocopiable 12A
That's what you need | **MEL** Extra practice, Listening 19: Listening for examples | **Active Teach**
Game: Noughts and crosses

Multi-part verbs

science and research

Aim

- to expand students' vocabulary related to science and research

6 Students discuss the question in pairs. Elicit some ideas from a few students.

7 Tell students that they are going to read a scientific article about designing a study for paper planes. Elicit whether it should use formal or informal language (formal). Tell them that there is also some more specific vocabulary used for academic writing. Look at the first item with the class and elicit the answer (*determine*). Point out that although all the alternatives fit grammatically, *determine* is a more scientific alternative than *find out* and *know*. Ask students to read the rest of the article and choose the most appropriate alternative in each case.

Additional activity

For a brief change of pace, give students a piece of paper and invite them to make a paper plane, but not to fly it yet.

Ask students to compare their paper plane designs in small groups and hypothesise which will go furthest and why. Give students the chance to fly their planes to see if they were right, and report back to the class about whether their initial hypothesis was confirmed.

8 Students replace the underlined verbs with the correct form of the multi-part verbs then check as a class.

9 Go through the example with the class. Students work in pairs to decide which other patterns can be used with the multi-part verbs, then check as a class.

10 Students write sentences using the multi-part verbs and nouns. Conduct whole-class feedback.

11 Ask students to discuss the steps they would take in a study using some of the multi-part verbs.

Answers

7   **1** determine   **2** observed   **3** arrive at   **4** validate
    5 varying   **6** plot   **7** findings   **8** initial

8   **1** carried out   **2** looking into   **3** make clear
    4 put forward   **5** take into account   **6** point out
    7 set out   **8** take issue with

9   **1** A ✗, B ✗, C ✓   **2** A ✓, B ✓, C ✗   **3** A ✓, B ✓, C ✗

10 (suggested answers)
    We took into account certain factors.
    We took certain factors into account.
    We took them into account.
    (Not possible: We took into account them.)
    We were counting on getting a grant.
    We were counting on it.
    (Not possible: We were counting it on. We were counting getting a grant on.)
    He turned down a job offer.
    He turned a job offer down.
    He turned it down.
    (Not possible: He turned down it.)
    Both *take into account* and *turn down* are 'separable' multi-part verbs. This means the object can go between the main verb and the second part(s) which is an adverb / are adverbs.
    Count on is an 'inseparable' multi-part verb. The second part (*on*) is a preposition and it is not possible to put the object between the main verb and the second part.

ADDITIONAL PRACTICE | **Maximiser** p.82, Vocabulary | **MEL** Unit 12, Vocabulary | Photocopiable 12B *Crossword links* | **MEL** Extra practice, Use of English 8: Phrasal verbs and common expressions

Grammar focus ▶ p.124

1 Give students a minute to think about their answers to the questions. Then put students into pairs to discuss their answers. Elicit a few responses for each.

2 Students read the article, then discuss the answer to the question in pairs. Elicit the answer.

Cohesion

Aim

● to identify ways to make a text cohesive

Read the Language tip with the class. Refer students to the Grammar reference section on cohesion on p.164 and set the exercise on p.165.

Grammar reference answers

1 it
2 they
3 do
4 won't
5 not
6 So

3 Students underline the different ways the scientists are referred to in the article. Elicit the answers from the class.

4–**6** Students work through the activities at their own pace while you monitor and provide assistance as required. Check answers as a class.

7 Students discuss the questions in pairs. Conduct whole-class feedback.

Answers

3 Otto Loewi: one scientist, his, Loewi, he, him
   John Eccles: the other, he, his, him, Eccles, himself
   Loewi and Eccles: their, Both, they
4 nap: siesta, full night's sleep
   question: problem, challenges
   wrote: jotted ... down
5 the other (scientist), Both (scientists)
6 **1** Like **2** while **3** so **4** until **5** but
   6 however/though

Additional activity

Ask students to choose a reading text that they enjoyed from an earlier unit. Can they find an example of the following cohesive devices in the text?

1 Reference

2 Substitution

3 Ellipsis

4 Conjunction

5 Lexical cohesion e.g. collocations, reptitions or use of synonyms/antonyms

6 Linking adverbial

Students share their findings in pairs or small groups.

ADDITIONAL PRACTICE | Maximiser p.83, Grammar | MEL Unit 12, Grammar | **MEL** Extra practice, Reading 19: Understanding text development | **Active Teach** Extra activity Grammar Focus 1

Speaking focus ▶ p.125

All parts

improving your performance

Aim

* to identify strategies to improve performance in the Speaking paper

1 Tell students that in this lesson they are going to review all four parts of the Speaking test. Get students to read the questions, then play the recording. Elicit the answers.

2 Ask students to read the questions then play the recording. Elicit the answers.

3 In pairs, students turn to p.139 and p.143 to practise a Long turn task.

4 Direct students to the task and list of strategies. Play the recording and elicit the strategies they have used at the end of the discussion.

5 Students do the collaborative task on p.139. Time them for two minutes for the discussion phase and one minute for the negotiation phase. Students evaluate their performance against the list.

6 Play the recording, then elicit the answers.

Additional activity

Students work in groups of three. Students take turns to be the examiner and ask the other students one or two of the Part 4 questions from Activity 6.

Answers

1 Gustave. He should give longer, more communicative answers.

2 Maria doesn't answer the second question (why people choose to do research like this). Gustave's answer is long enough but only after the examiner prompts him.

4 Both candidates fail to respond to one another's comments. Gustave is less inclined to involve or encourage Maria and less willing to compromise at the end of their discussion.

6 Maria performs well. Gustave should give longer, more communicative answers without having to be prompted by the examiner. He should also respond more to Maria's comments.

MyEnglishLab tip: Mock Speaking paper

Students will need a partner for these activities and someone to act as 'examiner'. You can print the tasks for use in class if necessary.

Students could do the mock paper in groups of four, with one pair completing Parts 1–4 as candidates while the other pair act as examiners, checking the time and noting down any good vocabulary or grammar structures that the 'candidates' use.

After pairs swap roles, give them time to give each other feedback and discuss what they need to improve on.

ADDITIONAL PRACTICE | Maximiser p.86, Speaking | MEL Unit 12, Speaking | **MEL** Extra practice, Speaking 19: Using discourse markers

Grammar focus ▶ p.126

1 Put students into pairs to discuss the questions, then conduct whole-class feedback.

2 Focus students on the photograph. Emphasise that students shouldn't read the text before they write their three things. Students write their list then compare with a partner. Then students read the text. Ask: *What new things did you learn about Marie Curie's life?*

Emphasis with inversion

Aim

* to be able to recognise and use inversion for emphasis

Refer students to the Grammar reference section on emphasis with inversion on p.165 and set the exercise. Alternatively, do this after Activity 4.

Grammar reference answers

1 Seldom have I been so angry.

2 Hardly had I got into bed when the neighbours started playing loud music.

3 Only when she told me how she felt did I understand what had gone wrong.

4 At no time did he attempt to discuss it with us.

5 No sooner had we put our towels down/put down our towels than the sun went behind a cloud.

6 Under no circumstances should you say anything to Gary about this.

3 Ask two students to read 1A and 1B. Elicit the difference in impact. Do the same with 2A and 2B.

4 Elicit the answer. Go through the Language tip with the class.

5 Students rewrite the sentences individually then compare in pairs before checking as a class.

6 Elicit a possible situation for the first sentence, then have students discuss the remining ones in pairs.

Answers

3 The two 'A' sentences make the surprising information more prominent by placing it at the beginning.

4 In the sentences from the text, the subject and verb are inverted as in question forms. These sentences begin with an adverb. The alternative sentences have a different sentence word order. The adverbs are in the middle of these sentences.

5 1 Seldom has this city been in greater need of energy-efficient public transport than it is today.

2 Scarcely had we ordered our meal when the waiter rudely asked us if we would mind paying the bill.

3 Rarely have I seen such a brilliant display of artistry and expertise.

4 Not only have you failed to hand in your essay on time, you have also copied several paragraphs directly from the internet.

5 Under no circumstances should you let people who don't respect the dress code into the club.

6 No sooner had she posted the letter than she began to regret what she had said.

7 At no time has my client ever revealed the contents of this document to the media.

8 Hardly had I finished the assignment when my boss asked me to do something else for her.

6 (Suggested answers)

1 editorial in a newspaper or political speech   2 letter of complaint or post on travellers' advice website   3 review of a performance or exhibition   4 teacher's comment on a student's essay   5 instructions given to bouncers at a club   6 story   7 lawyer giving evidence in court   8 letter to a friend

ADDITIONAL PRACTICE | **Maximiser** p.83, Grammar | **MEL** Unit 12, Grammar | Photocopiable 12C *Inversion chat* | **MEL** Extra practice, Use of English 7: Word order | **Active Teach** Extra activity Grammar Focus 2

Use of English focus ▶ p.127

Key word transformation (Part 4)

Aim

* to practise strategies for the exam-style key word transformation task (Reading and Use of English Part 4)

Warmer

Write the following sentences on the board and ask students to work in pairs to discuss what words could go in the gaps (using the key word in capitals).

1 *Marie Curie was a Polish-born physicist.*

Marie Curie was a _____ Poland. WHO

2 *She rose from obscurity to discover a new element, radium.*

She _____ after she discovered a new element, radium. WELL-KNOWN

Elicit the answers. Invite students to compare the strategies they used to work out the missing words.

Answers:

1 physicist who was born in

2 wasn't well-known until

1 If necessary, refer students to the Exam focus on p.179 to review the task and strategies. Students complete the activity, then discuss their answers in pairs before checking as a class.

2 Students match the grammatical points with the sentences. If students are unsure of any of the grammatical points, refer them to the relevant Grammar reference section.

Additional activity

Ask students to work in pairs and choose an adjective + noun, and write it down before you explain the activity.

Tell students that they need to work with their partner to write an example for each of the grammatical points in Activity 2 which includes their adjective + noun combination. For a greater challenge, they can make their examples related as in the sample answer below.

Sample answers using *brilliant idea*:

- *No sooner had I shared my brilliant idea than my colleague stole it.* (emphasis with inversion)
- *It is said that she has made millions from my brilliant idea.* (introductory *it*)
- *After she stole my brilliant idea, I decided I wouldn't take people at face value any more.* (future in the past)
- *If only I hadn't shared that brilliant idea with her, I would have been rich by now!* (hypothetical meaning)
- *I might have another brilliant idea in the future, who knows?* (modal verbs)

3 Point out that it is a common mistake to get most of the answer right, but just miss out one word. Each question has two marks available and, to get full marks, students need to include all the words. Students work in pairs to discuss what the missing word is in each sentence. Read the Exam tip with the class. Remind students that contractions count as two words.

4 Explain that in this exercise, the current answers make sense grammatically but do not convey the same meaning as the first sentence. Students make the necessary changes, then compare answers in pairs before you check as a class.

5 Do the final exercise as timed exam practice. Give students eight minutes to complete the exercise and check their answers individually. Then check answers as a class.

Answers

1–2 **1** only I had written down (hypothetical meaning)
  2 must have been (modal verbs)
  3 was only by going (introductory *it*)
  4 was to (later) change (future in the past)
3 **1** sooner had I arrived than
  2 no recollection of ever
  3 on behalf of my daughter
  4 you are determined to remember
4 **1** it is less difficult to forget
  2 take back the dress to/take the dress back to
  3 never struck me that
  4 it when people give me
5 **1** wish I hadn't sent
  2 must have happened
  3 I succeeded in getting
  4 did to resolve the problem was
  5 rumoured/said to be retiring
  6 no circumstances should you say anything

ADDITIONAL PRACTICE | **Maximiser** p.83, Use of English | **MEL** Unit 12, Use of English | **MEL** Extra practice, Use of English 19: Using the key word | **Active Teach** Game: Sheep out!

Reading focus ▶ p.128

1 Ask students to quickly complete the quiz on p.148 individually, then compare answers in pairs. Tell students that they will find out some of the answers when they read the article.

Gapped text (Part 7)

Aim

- to complete an exam-style gapped text task (Reading and Use of English Part 7)

2 If necessary, refer them to the Exam focus on p.180 to review the task and strategies. Read the Exam tip with the class. Students read the article and answer the questions in the quiz that they couldn't answer.

3 Remind students that clues to the correct answers often take the form of cohesive devices that were covered in the lesson on p.124, especially reference, substitution and lexical cohesion. Students choose paragraphs for each gap, then compare answers in pairs. Elicit the answers and justifications for each one.

4 Students choose the correct meanings, then compare answers in pairs before you check as a class.

Answers

1–2 **1** Guglielmo Marconi
  2 Thomas Edison
  3 alternating current and direct current
  4 alternating current
  5 direct current
  6 Heinrich Hertz, James Clerk Maxwell and Christian Hülsmeyer are all credited with the invention of radar.
3 **1** G (The 'people who so rapidly answered the call' in the first paragraph were 'Tesla's hugely loyal fan-base' referred to in paragraph G.)
  2 D (*one of these* (line 1, paragraph D) refers to a 'Tesla coil' mentioned in the second paragraph.)
  3 A (*It*, the first word in paragraph A, refers to Marconi beating him to the radio, mentioned in the third paragraph; *this*, in the fourth paragraph, refers to the electric light bulb.)
  4 F (*also*, in paragraph F, links Tesla's contribution to making the light bulb workable, in the fourth paragraph, with his making enough electricity come out of sockets in paragraph F.)
  5 C (*great rival*, in paragraph C, refers to Edison and their intense antipathy, mentioned in the fifth paragraph; *though*, in the sixth paragraph, concedes that Tesla was a man of exceptional talents despite fans tending to exaggerate Tesla's inventive genius, as mentioned in paragraph C.)

6 E (*strange habits*, in the seventh paragraph, refers to sleeping only two to three hours a night and obsessions such as a loathing for round objects, as referred to in paragraph E.)

4 1 B   2 A   3 B   4 A   5 A   6 A

ADDITIONAL PRACTICE | **Maximiser** p.84, Reading | **MEL** Unit 12, Reading | **MEL** Extra practice, Reading 19: Recognising paraphrase A; Reading 20: Recognising paraphrase B | **Active Teach** Reading Focus – matching

Vocabulary
expressions with *matter*

Aim
* to review expressions with *matter*

5 Students choose the correct alternative in each sentence. Check answers as a class.

6 Ask students to discuss the questions in small groups. If they can't think of an actual situation, they can speak hypothetically about how they would feel in that kind of situation.

Answers
5 1 dark   2 fact   3 principle   4 time   5 interest
6 life and death

ADDITIONAL PRACTICE | **Maximiser** p.85, Vocabulary | **MEL** Unit 12, Vocabulary | **Active Teach** Game: Pelmanism

Writing focus ▶ p.130
Essay (Part 1)
using linking phrases and conjunctions

Aims
* to review features of a good essay
* to use a range of linking devices in an essay (Writing, Part 1)

1 Students complete the sentences, then compare answers in pairs before you check as a class.

2 Give students time to read the task and essay and find examples of the good pieces of advice. Elicit the answers from the class.

3 Ask students to find the four linking words and match them to uses 1–4. Check as a class. Read the Exam tip with the class. Remind students to include other cohesive devices as covered on p.124.

4 Refer students to the writing task on p.148 and put them into pairs to spend five minutes planning and 35 minutes writing. Put students into small groups to share their work and assist each other with editing.

Alternative
Instead of sharing their work in small groups, get students to read over their work carefully using the checklist on p.166.

Answers
1 1 Don't   2 Do   3 Do   4 Do   5 Do   6 Do   7 Do
8 Don't

2 (Suggested answers)
2 'While this would almost certainly give scientific research a more positive image, it implies placing restrictions on the freedom of the press.' (paragraph 2)
3 'In my view, the second of these two approaches should be implemented.' (paragraph 4)
4 'Nevertheless, any resistance might be overcome by' (paragraph 3)
5 'A potential difficulty here is that some adults' (paragraph 3)
6 'But how might this be achieved?' (paragraph 1)
7 (many examples) 'This lack of appreciation is the result of insufficient information about scientists and the work they do.' (paragraph 1)

3 1 One possible approach   2 While   3 In my view   4 thus

4 Model answer

People owe much to scientific breakthroughs, yet many young people seem to eschew science in favour of other more glamourous-sounding professions. In this essay I will discuss two possible methods that governments could employ to help persuade more teenagers to consider pursuing studies in science.

Given that careers advisors play an influential role in students' lives, one possible approach would be to target careers advisors within schools. For example, they could be provided with regular up-to-date course advice, or be invited to attend science experience days. If they are exposed to modern problem-solving approaches, it seems far more likely that they will on-sell scientific careers to students with the requisite enthusiasm.

A second tactic that the government could employ would be to invite scientists to share their work in schools. This would be a golden opportunity to shatter lingering stereotypes about scientists, which in turn may encourage a more diverse cross-section of students to consider entering the field. Realistically, there would be some challenges to secure the time of high profile scientists. Yet, this could be overcome with creative solutions such as having scientists doing a five-minute virtual visit from their laboratory.

Overall, I would say that the most effective measure would be to have guest speakers. Hearing real tales of satisfaction and innovation from real scientists is much more likely to influence career choice than some second-hand advice.

ADDITIONAL PRACTICE | **Maximiser** p.87, Writing | **MEL** Unit 12, Writing | **MEL** Extra practice, Use of English 7: Essay writing

Review ▶ p.131

Aim

- to revise the structures and vocabulary covered in Unit 12

1 – **3** Ask students to complete the activities, monitoring them to provide assistance. Alternatively, set this as a homework activity. Ask students to compare their answers in pairs before doing a class check.

Answers

1   1 carried   2 forward   3 took   4 into   5 at   6 down

2   1 did I manage to buy

2 only are the neighbours

3 no time should you

4 have been living here for

5 no circumstances should you

6 sooner had I closed

3   1 She   2 they   3 both/the   4 Although/Though
5 none   6 one   7 would   8 to   9 so   10 had

ADDITIONAL PRACTICE | **Active Teach** Game: Stepping stones

Progress test 4 ▶ p.132

Answers

1   1 B   2 A   3 C   4 D   5 A   6 B   7 A   8 C

2   1 around   2 out   3 according   4 made   5 which
6 this   7 where   8 without

3   1 indignantly   2 abilities/ability   3 criticism
4 demanding   5 suspicious   6 mismatches
7 untrustworthy   8 responses

4   1 suggest (that) you talk   2 only does Michael   3 are
sometimes prevented from entering   4 despite being worth
5 had I got to the theatre   6 is thought to have invented

Practice Test ▶ p.186

To give students experience in doing a mock exam at the end of the course, you could ask students to do the Practice test, which starts on page 186 of the Student's Book. You could also do the Practice test at the beginning of the course, to assess students' abilities, and how ready they are for the real exam. To do the exam under timed conditions, use the following time limits.

- **Reading and Use of English:** 1 hour 30 minutes
- **Writing:** 1 hour 30 minutes

Make sure that students are in a quiet area when you play the recordings for the Listening part of the exam.

For the Speaking part of the exam, you will need to put students into pairs. Play the recording for students to hear an authentic examiner asking questions. You could ask students to speak directly to you, or to another pair of students.

Reading and Use of English

Part 1

1 C   2 B   3 D   4 B   5 A   6 C   7 A   8 D

Part 2

9 Not   10 Yet/But   11 in/during   12 more
13 all   14 would   15 of   16 on

Part 3

17 provision   18 maintenance   19 distribution
20 negotiations   21 collaboratively   22 participants
23 effectiveness   24 prestigious

Part 4

25 threw herself into her new role

26 the aid of

27 put him in the picture

28 the event of (it) being postponed/the event of a postponing/
postponement/the event that it is postponed

29 under no circumstances should they

30 were the chances of (her) winning/the chances were of (her)
winning/her chances were of winning

Part 5

31 B   32 D   33 C   34 B   35 A   36 D

Part 6

37 D   38 A   39 C   40 A

Part 7

41 E   42 C   43 G   44 A   45 F   46 B

Part 8

47 D   48 A   49 B   50 D   51 A   52 D
53 C   54 B   55 A   56 C

Writing

Model answers

Part 1: Essay

A country's government should definitely play an active role in keeping its citizens healthy. Otherwise, it may cost them more in the long run as they will have to deal with increased levels of illness among the population.

One action the government can take is to educate the public better about the dangers of sugar and junk food. This could easily be achieved by using effective advertising campaigns in the various media. They should also promote the benefits of exercise for all children and adults. If people are more knowledgeable about the benefits of being physically fit, they're more likely to engage in exercise at least a few times a week. Such educational campaigns have been very successful in other countries, so perhaps it's time our government took a similar approach.

The government could also control people's diets better by introducing taxes on food items like sugary drinks or junk food. If the prices increase, this should mean that fewer people would buy them. Currently, many people opt for snacks which are high in fat and sugar content because they don't cost very much. The cost of fruit and vegetables needs to be lower and unhealthy food should be less appealing to people on low budgets.

Personally, I believe that regulating the cost of food would be the most effective approach to take. I've seen the results of increased taxes on unhealthy food in other countries, where sales dropped significantly. This is what our government needs to do as soon as possible for the sake of our country's citizens.

Part 2

2: Review

The one modern-day gadget that I couldn't live without is my mobile phone. The phone I'm currently using is an iPhone 8, which I've had for just over six months now.

I find the phone useful in so many ways. Firstly, I use it for phone calls obviously, to keep in touch with family and friends. Not only can I get in touch with people whenever I need to, but they can also contact me 24/7. This is especially useful in the case of an emergency.

I also use my phone for receiving and replying to emails when I'm on the go. I run a business, so it's really important that I reply to my clients as quickly as possible. It's also useful to be able to use search engines to find any information I need, whether for the purposes of work or entertainment.

Many people use apps nowadays, and I'm no different. At the moment, I have at least thirty apps on my phone, ranging from things like an app to track calories to a music shop app to an app which monitors traffic on the roads around where I live. These apps help me manage so many aspects of my everyday life that I can't imagine doing without them.

All in all, I consider my smartphone to be part of me now and I need to have it within arm's reach at all times. And I guess I'm not alone in that!

3: Report

Introduction

The purpose of this report is to provide general feedback on this year's Cambridge Music Festival, which took place on August 10. The report will also make some recommendations for next year's festival.

Parking facilities

The general feeling is that the parking facilities for this year's festival were inadequate. Visitors complained about the queues to enter and exit the car park and also about the potholes in the ground there. Comments were also made about the low number of parking marshals on hand to give people directions.

Variety and quality of food

The usual types of food stalls were available: burgers, pizza, etc., but long queues at each stall meant that some people decided to walk away rather than waste time queuing.

Position of the stage

The stage this year was in the northwest of the field and this seems to have been a popular decision with most festival goers.

Recommendations for next year's music festival

I strongly recommend that multiple car parks are used for next year's festival, and that these sites are carefully chosen to prevent damage to people's cars. I also recommend significantly increasing the number of marshals to direct traffic on the day. A final recommendation is to increase the number of food stalls within the festival grounds. As well as having more of the usual fast food, we could consider inviting some luxury food stalls too and therefore cater for all types of festival goer. As the weather is usually hot in August, we could have more drink and ice-cream sellers across the grounds.

4: Email

Hi Alex!

Thanks for your email. Wow! What an opportunity! I think you should definitely accept their offer and move here for a year. It would be so great to have you here for all that time instead of just your usual two-week holiday.

Life in England's pretty good actually and, if you're based in London, which I imagine you will be, then it doesn't get any better. London's an amazing city. It's really cosmopolitan, and you'll see people of all nationalities here. That means there's also a great variety of exotic food to try. Life in the cities, like anywhere, is fast paced, but things are a little slower out in the countryside. And basically people everywhere are friendly and polite.

In terms of things to do here, you're spoilt for choice. London's a very cultural city: there are lots of museums, galleries and theatres and there's always some event or other happening. I know you love going to markets, and there are all sorts here from farmer's food markets to antique markets to markets selling quirky clothes. Of course there are plenty of coffee shops and restaurants everywhere too – eating out's a thing now! And if you fancy getting away from the hustle and bustle of urban life, the beautiful English countryside's only a short drive away. You can also get to the coast within an hour. Here you can pretty much do any sport or activity that you like – no problem there.

Anyway, write soon and let me know what you decide. I can't wait to hear!

Listening

Part 1

1 B 2 B 3 C 4 B 5 A 6 C

Part 2

7 wildlife capture 8 bottle(-)feeding
9 enclosures 10 rating system
11 sleeping patterns 12 (wooden) huts / accommodation
13 chemistry 14 veterinary medicine

Part 3

15 C 16 C 17 A 18 C 19 D 20 B

Part 4

Task 1

21 E 22 B 23 H 24 G 25 D

Task 2

26 E 27 H 28 C 29 D 30 F

Audio scripts

Unit 1

▶ 01

Ex = Examiner K = Karl El = Elena

Ex: Good morning. My name is Irene and this is my colleague, Deborah. And your names are?

K: Karl Weber.

El: Elena Calvi.

Ex: Can I have your mark sheets, please? Thank you. First of all, we'd like to know something about you. Where are you from, Karl?

K: I'm German. I live just outside Berlin now but I grew up in the centre of the city.

Ex: And Elena?

El: Italy.

Ex: What do you do there, Elena?

El: I work in a hotel.

Ex: Karl, what do you like most about the area where you grew up?

K: Well, there are so many things, really, but I suppose the one that really stands out for me is living so close to a great city like Berlin.

Ex: Elena, who has more influence on your life: your friends or your family?

El: My family.

Ex: Why?

El: I don't know, really. They just do.

▶ 02

For years I'd been telling all my friends that I wanted to get away from the hustle and bustle of London to somewhere quiet and peaceful. What I had in mind was a little cottage near the sea. Well, they say you shouldn't wish too hard or your wish just might come true and that's exactly what happened. Out of the blue, I was offered a job managing a hotel in a remote part of Ireland. Suddenly, it seemed to me that I had, in fact, always been a real city person who could negotiate the complexities of urban life, the crowded underground trains, the roar of traffic, the millions of people – all of it – and without blinking. But the job offer was too good to turn down and a few weeks later I found myself in Castletownbere. In less than 24 hours I'd gone from a huge metropolis with a population of over 8 million to a quaint fishing village with barely 800 inhabitants. It was a huge change.

By the beginning of next month I will have been living here for exactly a year. I've been looking back, retracing my steps and coming to understand just how great a change it

has been. I've got to know almost all of those 800 people and found a real sense of belonging, though I've also occasionally longed for the anonymity of city life. I've spent hours exploring the glorious countryside by bicycle and on foot, and have discovered a taste for silence and solitude I didn't know I had. I've also had great fun managing the hotel and getting to know some of its rather eccentric regular guests. I'm learning all the time. It seems as if every day presents a new challenge. By the time the first year comes to an end almost all my London friends will have been here to stay and they love it almost as much as I do. Of course, there are many things I miss, though in the end the crowded underground trains and the noisy London traffic I can easily do without.

▶ 03

1

I seemed to be always giving or throwing away things I'd bought but wasn't using. The only way to stop the cycle was to move into a much smaller place and really take downsizing and simplifying my life more seriously. It's going well so far though it's also been a challenge. There's less and less clutter and I now feel that my thinking is much clearer too. I spend more time outside, of course, because you can feel pretty hemmed in in such a small space. But there are some great places to walk literally outside my back door and I can even see the sea through my kitchen window, which is a real bonus. I don't think I could live here without that.

2

As soon as the prize money was in the bank I went out and bought this extraordinary 17th-century mansion. It was supposed to be my dream home but in some ways it's turned out to be a complete nightmare. I had no idea how edgy I was going to feel in a large and very ancient house. I have to be careful not to watch horror films on TV because I start to imagine every creak and groan from the rafters is actually someone lurking in one of the other rooms. Of course, it's glorious to have so much space. I've been able to accept my grandfather's gift of a grand piano because I've actually got somewhere to put it. Next step will be learning to play it.

3

I came to live in this part of town almost twenty years ago when I started university. My first home, if you can call it that, was a hall of residence just round the corner and then I lived in a series of shared flats. Finally I had enough money in the bank to get a mortgage and buy this place. I couldn't be happier living right in the centre of the city like this. Apart from the usual shops, there's a cinema, some rather pleasant cafés and even a really great arts centre round the corner. If I lived out of town, I know I'd really miss all that. I must admit I'm walled in by other buildings on all sides and that gets to me sometimes but it really doesn't outweigh the many advantages of inner-city living.

4

I tried to find something a bit bigger but everything I looked at was way outside my price range so I had to take this. I've had to leave a lot of my stuff at my parents' place. Perhaps one day I'll have enough room for more than a sofa bed and a desk! I tend to go out to eat – even for breakfast. The kitchenette is so tiny there's barely room to chop a carrot and it's difficult to get rid of the cooking smells afterwards. There are loads of cafés on this street and a lot of the people from round here hang out there in the mornings, so I've got to know them and find it to be a really vibrant neighbourhood. That's a real plus for someone living alone like me.

5

Where my partner and I lived before there were rooms we barely used, particularly after the children had all left home. That's one of the reasons I wanted to move. It's not at all cramped here but there's no excess either. I'm in and out of all the rooms every day. We both work from home and so we've each claimed one of the spare bedrooms as an office. It's great to have an office of my own, though it's right next to the room our neighbour, Tom, has set up as a gym and I can hear him working out. It reminds me that I'm living in close proximity to other people but it's sometimes a bit irritating.

▶ 04

I like to think I know most of my neighbours but perhaps I could get to know more of them or get to know the ones I do know a bit better. There is a neighbourhood association and they hold all sorts of social events, like barbecues and picnics and even run courses of various kinds, like yoga and language classes, but I somehow haven't managed to get involved in anything they offer apart from the annual street party, which is really great.

I read something interesting the other day that made me think. I read that the average American moves more than ten times in a lifetime. That sounds like a lot to me, but I bet if you move so often, you don't have much of a chance to get to know your neighbours at all. Apparently, that's the case, so someone has come up with the bright idea of creating an online forum so that neighbours can get to know each other. The publicity says it's like a town square where people can go to voice opinions and needs and even offer things for sale. If it sounds a bit far-fetched to you for people to have to go online to get to know their neighbours, you might be surprised to hear how successful it has been. Apparently, in one small town where the forum was launched, almost two-thirds of the town's inhabitants had posted after the end of the first year. Perhaps if there was a forum like this for my neighbourhood, more busy people like me might get involved.

Personally, I'd like to see a local market place with stalls offering goods and services. I love markets and the idea of seeing what my neighbours have to offer really appeals to me.

Unit 2

▶ 05

1

I'm not saying I'm completely addicted but I would feel anxious if I didn't get a message every couple of minutes. I'm just used to talking to my friends pretty much all the time. I mean, obviously, there are exceptions – I do turn my phone off when I'm in class and I don't text when I'm having dinner with my family. But generally speaking, I like to be in contact twenty-four seven.

2

That totally depends on the situation – I'm sure some people would argue that not replying immediately shows a lack of interest or respect but the way I see it, there's more to life than texting. And I don't have a problem if my texts go unanswered for hours or even days.

3

I think that goes without saying. We all know people who've been dumped by text and that's a really mean and cowardly thing to do. Only the most insensitive person would even consider doing that.

4

I wouldn't go that far but yes, sometimes texting is preferable because you've got a bit more time to respond. I think it's fair to say that a lot of people are more outgoing and funny in their text messages than they are in a group situation.

▶ 06

This picture shows four friends sitting outside a café. They aren't talking to one another; instead they're all preoccupied with their phones. It could be that this photo captures a moment when they're all looking at the same message they've all just been sent and a few seconds before this was taken they'd all been chatting – but I imagine it's more likely that they're all looking at different messages because one of the boys looks very serious and one girl is laughing. I think this behaviour is quite typical among teenagers but it's not a good thing. People should really focus on the people they're with and ignore phone messages. There's no point going to a café with friends if you're just going to ignore them. This picture also shows two friends. They're taking a selfie. It looks like they're on holiday somewhere cold. They're both wearing similar outfits – I don't know for sure but maybe they're wearing some sort of costume for a special event. They seem to be having a good time anyway.

▶ 07

1

A: I really related to the ideas on certain personality types in the book. I found it quite reassuring. Before I read this, I just thought I was weird because I didn't enjoy meeting new people or going to parties. I didn't realise I was an introvert and that there was actually absolutely nothing wrong with that at all.

B: Of course there isn't! In fact, I actually prefer introverts to extroverts. Extroverts are so attention-seeking and are only really interested in themselves. Introverts are much nicer people. Reading this book confirmed that for me.

A: The ideas were great but sometimes I found reading it a bit of a slog – especially all those long descriptions of studies on the brain and how that accounts for the way we behave. I found it all a bit boring, to be honest. A quick summary would have been enough. And, anyway, some of the results seemed to come to opposite conclusions.

B: Yeah, I'm always quite sceptical about that kind of thing. Most of those case studies are probably unreliable, so not worth devoting so many pages to them. It's a pity because she's good at making complicated scientific information quite accessible, which is a real achievement.

2

A: I'm not saying people shouldn't use social networking sites. It's just the online relationships with casual acquaintances I have a problem with – I mean, everyone presents a certain cultivated image of themselves online, which isn't always totally accurate. You know, the way people might admit to having a bad day in private, even if they'd never do so publicly online.

B: Exactly. And you can't blame them for that. I wouldn't dream of mentioning any of my insecurities online. The problem is that if all you see of someone is endless photos of parties and exciting holidays, it can be a bit annoying. It's the same as reading about celebrity lifestyles – all you see is a carefully edited version of their lives, which gives a totally false picture.

A: Absolutely. What gets me is people who insist on going on and on about their perfect life when they know you're going through a bad time.

B: Well, I suppose no one has to read anything they find boring or upsetting.

A: But we just can't resist. Everyone, including me, is so obsessed about staying in contact. I know I'd hate not to know what people are up to more than I hate all their shameless self-promotion!

3

A: I decided to see what it would be like to stay offline for a month, with no internet access at all, because I thought I was becoming too dependent on the internet.

B: Yeah, that was my motivation too. And how did you feel after the first week?

A: Well, I was finding it easier to distract myself with other activities, like phoning older relatives and reading. The problem was not that I was waiting to hear from anyone in particular – rather the feeling of being connected and available to the world. It was weird – almost like being invisible. I expect you'd get used to it eventually, though. But I think it's something everyone should consider trying.

B: Yes. Actually, I'd recommend it because it made me realise how easy it is to waste time doing basically nothing. So now I limit my internet time to an hour each day. I've had to learn to be strict with myself because I do really enjoy chatting online. It's interesting because I've still managed to maintain the online relationships I care about, without having to feel I need to be available to chat twenty-four seven.

▶ 08

Research has shown that it's possible to identify a lot of information, such as people's socio-economic status and their emotional state, from their voice alone. It's also claimed that someone's age, height and weight can also be estimated just by listening to the way they speak.

Unit 3

▶ 09

Chris should start planning his future right now. There's no sense in putting it off. First he needs to prioritise his career goals. He should picture what job within his current company he'd like to aim for and he should also consider any other companies he'd ideally like to work for in the longer term and in what capacity. He should think about how it feels to be doing that job. Then he should think about the steps he needs to take in order to get there. For example, are there any training courses he needs to do? Are there any extra responsibilities he could take on now? He should set monthly targets on the road to getting promoted and achieving his goals.

Deciding when to start a family is a big decision and isn't something you should take on lightly. Chris and his wife need to have a serious discussion about this. Money is an important factor, so it makes sense to plan ahead and start saving so that one or other of them can afford to stay at home and look after the baby if they want to. Finally, I think Chris needs to dream a little. His plans for the future aren't that well defined and are a little unambitious.

▶ 10

E = Examiner D = Daniela M = Martin

E: Now I'd like you to talk about something together for about two minutes. Here are some things that we often think make people mature and a question for you to discuss. First you have some time to look at the task. Now talk to each other about the extent to which these things make people consider themselves to be mature.

D: Shall we make a start?

M: OK.

D: Hmm … well, first of all, I really don't consider that we ever complete our education. What I mean is, it may be the case that you finish a university degree but nowadays a lot of people go on to do postgraduate courses or vocational training of some kind, even when they're quite old. It's more and more common for people to return to study throughout their lives.

M: I think that being financially independent is the key. If you are still reliant on your parents for money, you are never entirely free to make your own decisions, so in some senses you remain in the position that you were in when you were a child.

D: You mean, because you're having to ask your parents for money and possibly also having to justify what you spend it on?

M: Yes.

D: There's a lot to be said for that argument. In many cases I think it does make people less able to take responsibility for their own decisions and it often creates tensions in a family but it doesn't necessarily have to be like that. I read recently about someone who was over 40 and had to go back to live with his elderly parents. He was actually doing all sorts of things for them they needed done and couldn't do themselves, so there was a kind of balance in that case. And that brings me to another point. I don't think moving into your own flat or house necessarily makes you an adult either. A lot of people move out when they start university – I did, but although I probably thought of myself as very grown up, I wasn't, really.

M: Apart from earning your own living, I think the thing that really gives you adult status is having your own family. With children of your own, you grow up fast.

D: Yes, you're forced to mature by having to make sacrifices and by being responsible for other people, aren't you? For me that's the crucial thing: taking responsibility or being treated as if you are capable of taking responsibility. That's why the real transition from childhood to adulthood is being treated as an adult. Do you see what I mean?

M: Yes.

D: So, having your opinion sought by other adults is a real marker of maturity as I see it. It may be as a parent, as someone with professional skills and expertise or simply as someone who has accumulated enough knowledge of the world to justify their opinions.

E: Thank you. Now you have about a minute to decide which experience has the most effect on a person's maturity.

M: Well, for me it's being a parent.

D: I can't argue with the fact that people who are parents grow up fast – my older sister and brother-in-law certainly did – but I think having your opinions sought and respected is important too.

M: So which one shall we choose?

D: Mmm … being a parent, I suppose, because children often seek their parents' opinions. We'll settle for that.

 11

E = Examiner M = Martin D = Daniela

E: Thank you. Can I have the booklet, please? How important is it to continue to seek advice from older people throughout our lives?

M: Very. I think older people have a lot to offer, particularly on family matters.

D: Yes, indeed. All those years of experience of bringing up children are invaluable. But I think that there are a whole range of issues on which older people can offer advice and guidance.

M: Such as?

D: Well, I certainly wouldn't ask my grandmother how to delete an app from my phone but I do go to her for all sorts of other practical advice. She's a wonderful cook and she knows how to make things you don't find in recipe books, for example, but I also just consider her to be a wise person in general, with insights that I perhaps don't have.

E: Some people say we have stopped respecting older people. What do you think?

M: I think we have a bit because the world has changed so quickly and they haven't always been able to keep up with the changes – in technology, for example. This means we sometimes even make fun of them, something that certainly wouldn't have happened when they themselves were young.

D: No, it wouldn't – and it doesn't happen in traditional societies even today. The idea of older people as a source of wisdom is still very strong in those contexts.

E: Thank you. That is the end of the test.

12

I = Interviewer D = Dan

I: My guest today is Dan Johnson, a scientist who does research into longevity – why some types of people tend to live longer than others. Thank you for joining us this morning, Dan. I'm going to start with a question about my own family background. Both my grandfather and great-grandfather were in their 90s when they died and I like to think I've inherited their long-life genes. What are my chances of making a century?

D: I wish I could look into a crystal ball and tell you the answer to that question. Sure, if I had a grandfather and a father who'd lived into their nineties, I'd be hoping science would tell me that I had a good chance of doing as well or better, but in fact that's just wishful thinking. Sometimes I think that the appeal of the genetic explanation lies in our desire to see matters taken out of our hands. I'd go even further and say that many people use it as an excuse not to make basic lifestyle changes, preferring to rely on the belief that because they have family members who've lived into their 80s and 90s, they will too. Regardless of whatever harmful habits they might have, such as smoking or not getting enough exercise, they live in the false hope that their genes will protect them. I hate to say it, but having family members who've lived long lives doesn't mean that you will too.

I: OK but my great grandfather is unusual, don't you think? Or am I wrong about that too?

D: Sorry but yes you are. I always tell people to take a good look at photographs from the late nineteenth and early twentieth centuries. There are plenty of elderly people in them so it really wasn't so very unusual to live a long life.

I think I know where the confusion comes from because if we look at the average age at death it's much lower than it is today but that's because without antibiotics, everyone was more vulnerable to diseases, particularly babies and children. But if you did happen to make it into adulthood, you had almost as good a chance of living a long life as we do today.

I: And life was a lot less stressful then, so that would have helped too.

D: Do you think so? Granted, a miserable job you dislike causes the wrong kind of stress. Even those of us who have jobs we enjoy, comfortable homes and families who care about us, experience stress but much of that stress we experience comes from our own minds. As I see it, to a large extent, it's under our control. In the past, external factors were far more important. Think about all the wars, famines and epidemics. And the backbreaking work people had to do. An ordinary soldier in the First World War, or a young woman working as a maid in one of those big houses would have suffered far greater levels of stress than most of us do. Given the choice between the stresses of the past and contemporary stresses, I can tell you that I'd take the boring office job any day.

I: OK, but there's a common belief that stress is a factor and that laid-back people live longer. Is that true?

D: I wouldn't even go so far as to say that. What if you like your job, even if it is tough, and enjoy the challenges it presents? That's more likely to lead to a longer life than sitting round doing nothing and getting incredibly bored. But don't get me wrong, I'm not talking about being a success rather than being a loser. People who work hard tend to live longer but it's not because they are hugely successful and making a lot of money. What we've found is that there's a relationship between being hard-working and conscientious and being cautious and sensible about health. If you're responsible and reliable in your professional life, you'll have the same attitude to your health. For example, you'll probably avoid eating a lot of junk food and opt for healthier choices but you won't veer to the other extreme of starving yourself either. And that's another important part of the record that needs to be set straight: just because animals on a very low-calorie diet live longer, it doesn't necessarily mean that we do. Starvation dieting is disastrous for your health.

I: I seem to be getting all the factors wrong but, surely, being happily married does lead to a longer life, doesn't it?

D: It depends. Our research shows that for men, being married is closely related to being happy and healthy and if a man is happy with the relationship and healthy, his partner tends to be as well. I know I was more than a little disconcerted to discover that when the boot is on the other foot – that is, if a woman is happily married and her partner is not so happy – then it won't have such a positive impact on the length of her life. This strikes me as rather unfair – it doesn't matter how close they are in age, a woman always worries about her partner and feels responsible for him. The results of our study are really making me reassess my own relationships and behaviour.

I: What about widows? I've read they often live longer than women whose partners are still alive.

D: Yes, that's true. But the big question is why this should be the case. Let me tell you what I think could be an explanation. Women are fortunate in that they're often better at establishing and maintaining strong friendship networks than men are. Once women are on their own, they can enjoy and find support in these networks more than they could when their partners were still alive. This is just a theory, of course, but it's one that seems to make a lot of sense. I was in Japan last year and almost every tourist site I visited was full of happy groups of elderly women, who I assumed were widows. I saw men with their wives but I didn't see any groups of elderly men doing this kind of thing, I mean going on day trips together. This is just anecdotal evidence of course, but I think it does give credence to my theory that women's friendships contribute to them living longer once they are widows.

I: Indeed! Well, thank you very much for joining us, Dan. I've been keeping track of all the beneficial factors and I don't think I'm doing too badly!

D: That's good to hear. Thank you for having me on the programme.

Unit 4

▶ 14

Good morning. I'm Jon Hayes and for the last twenty years I've worked as a sports psychologist with top football teams, helping to prepare players mentally for important matches. People assume top footballers must be happy because of all their wealth and success. But they often forget that as well as all the benefits, the players are also under extreme pressure, and this is something that I think's got much worse in recent years. They're expected to perform at the highest level week after week. Of course, managers and fans always expect a lot from their team, which is OK, but a big problem for some players is that they expect perfection from themselves all the time.

A big part of my job is to help players cope when they don't perform their best. Players find being able to manage their frustration can make a big difference to their behaviour on the pitch and their enjoyment of the game.

I think sports psychology training is particularly helpful for the young players, many of whom are still teenagers. When they make mistakes, like missing a goal for example, they can sometimes get a lot of negative publicity and even abuse. So we also work on not taking criticism personally.

Sports psychologists like me give players a range of mental tools and techniques to help develop mental resilience. For example, footballers are taught to get rid of overly negative feelings through symbolic actions, such as wiping their hands on the grass or on their shirt to erase anything which might distract them from the game.

Many of the techniques we use are grounded in cutting edge science, and all are designed to keep the mind clear and focused. Owing to improvements in neuroscience, we now know which area of the brain is used for decision making – which is vital for improving performance. What we aim to do is to get the brain to release chemicals such as dopamine, which have a positive effect and can increase our confidence. Just as nutritionists advise players not to eat junk food before matches, we help players to develop positive thinking skills to control their brains.

Even body language can be manipulated to project a positive frame of mind. If you have your head down and shoulders slumped, your brain chemistry changes for the worse. It's why I advise managers to look at players' body language to decide when to make a substitution. If they see a player with their head down and their eyes fixed on their feet, they'll know it's time for this player to come off the pitch.

I teach footballers to use memorised keywords to trigger appropriate mindsets or responses to certain situations. For example, a player might be trained to say 'ice' to remind him to stay cool when things get heated on the pitch. These keywords need to be simple, visual triggers that the brain can process quickly. Basically, all this training is aiming to give players more control and focus to enhance their performance on the pitch. But many of these techniques would work equally well in daily life.

▶ 15

J = Jan M = Marisol

J: In my opinion, the reason many people give up a sport or hobby is because of the costs involved.

M: I agree. It can be very expensive to join a gym, for instance. The monthly costs can be as high as 100 euros per month, which is too much.

J: Yes, and then what tends to happen is that people often join with the best of intentions but then find they don't have time to go often enough to justify the membership fee.

M: So you're saying lack of time and money are very significant reasons for people giving up sport?

J: Yes. I believe that goes a long way to explaining why people have to give up.

M: What about hobbies? Playing an instrument, for example?

J: I could be wrong but I imagine many people get demotivated because they realise they're never going to be an amazing pianist or guitar player.

M: Mmm … I know from my own experience that that's quite common. I gave up the piano after two years because I wasn't making enough progress, despite practising fairly often.

▶ 16

1

I think there is a lot of value in having a hobby. I used to play the piano and now I've stopped, and I regret that. I used to hate practising for piano exams but, at the same time, I felt a sense of achievement. Perhaps I'll take it up again one day.

2

There's a lot of criticism of computer games but I think the people that criticise them have never played them. They're often criticised for being too violent and for stopping boys especially from doing other things, like going outside and playing football. But I'd argue they can also develop your imagination and even social skills because often playing them is a shared experience.

Unit 5

▶ 17

In this part of the test I'm going to give each of you three pictures. I'd like you to talk about two of them on your own for about a minute, and also to answer a question briefly about your partner's pictures.

It's your turn first. Here are your pictures. They show people who are very involved in what they're doing. I'd like you to compare two of the pictures and say why the people might be so involved in what they're doing, and how they might be feeling.

▶ 18

Which group of people do you think looks happiest? Why?

▶ 20

I = Interviewer D = Donna G = Graham

I: Good morning. In the studio this morning we're joined by Donna Marchant and Graham Donovan, two psychologists who've undertaken studies looking into some important questions: What makes us happy and does money have anything to do with it? Well, let's start with the second question. Donna?

D: The answer I get from reading other psychologists' research is a clear yes, though only to a limited extent. Other people's research tells me very clearly that if your income meets your basic needs, it will make you relatively happy, but – and it's a big but – if you have more than you need to make ends meet, you won't necessarily be any happier. The really interesting question is if you've reached that point, what should you do with the excess and how does that affect your happiness levels? That's what I've been looking into in my most recent research.

I: But how do we determine what excess income is? Is it everything that's left after we've covered basic needs like food, shelter, warmth? What do you think, Graham?

G: As I understand it, what Donna is saying – and she should know, she's the expert – is that without food and shelter, no one feels happy. But you also need safety. After that comes the need for relationships, a feeling of being appreciated and valued. In fact, as it's often said, without being able to achieve your full potential, you won't be completely happy.

I: So Donna, there's a kind of hierarchy of needs, is there?

D: Yes. Graham is drawing on a classic model or hierarchy developed by the American psychologist Abraham Maslow. I think I'm right in saying that this is where your research interests lie, don't they, Graham? But going back to your question, let me just say that fulfilling these higher-order needs takes money. And I would agree with Graham that none of the levels in the hierarchy are really extras. Money spent on your professional and personal development is money very well spent.

G: That's not my point, actually. Maslow's model is about the psychological development of the individual over time rather than what a person needs to be happy overall. The emphasis changes over different stages in a person's life. I'd add to that that after you've got food, shelter and safety, money doesn't really come into it so much. You can't buy friendship, self-esteem or fulfilment.

I: No, that's certainly not my experience. So Donna, what would you say is wrong with the way people spend their excess income?

D: There's a tragic paradox about money and happiness such that people often squander their wealth on the very things that are least likely to make them feel good, namely, consumer goods. What's more, the more they indulge in consumer goods, the more inclined they are to obsess about money and the less willing they'll be to use that money to help others. Obviously the implications of this are very serious indeed. Using money to help others – that's the key to happiness.

I: Graham, do you think the research on happiness supports Donna's position?

G: It's not quite that straightforward. There's a research study that tried to establish a link between altruistic spending and happiness but it's come in for quite a bit of criticism, much of which I would go along with. For what it's worth, the researchers got people to tell them how much they earned, how happy they felt, how much money they spent on themselves and how much went on 'social spending'; by that they meant gifts for others and donations to charity. They then looked at the relationship between income, happiness and the two types of spending. Because of the way they'd designed the study they couldn't prove it was the type

of spending that made people happy or not but it was clear that spending seems to have more to do with happiness than income alone. I'm beginning to wonder if it's possible to look into this and come up with a definitive finding.

I: Donna, could you tell us more about the study you and your team conducted recently?

D: We took up the challenge. The more we know about the relationship between spending and happiness, the better able we will be to teach people the facts and perhaps change the emphasis on acquiring things in a vain attempt to make ourselves feel happier. I think that's a very important goal and one we've partially met in a paper the members of my team and I have just published. We're proud of having come up with a design that gets over the problems Graham mentioned. What we did, actually, was to ask people how happy they were before and after receiving a bonus at work. The bonuses varied in amount, I should add. After a few weeks we asked them how they had spent the money and how happy they felt. This time the relationship between social spending and happiness was much more clear-cut, so much so, in fact, that we feel confident in stating that the way people spent the bonus played more of a role in their happiness than the size of the bonus itself.

G: I don't want to quibble but how do you know that there were no other factors that might have intervened to make these people feel happy or unhappy? That said, rabid consumerism and fear about sharing our resources with others are social evils research needs to address and that's something you do seem to be doing. People should hear about your work.

I: I think so too and I hope that today's programme has helped in that regard but I'm afraid that's all we'll have time for. Thank you both, Donna and Graham, for being with us today.

Unit 6

▶ 21

1

A: Have you been down to the archaeological site recently?

B: Yes, the other day. It was really fascinating to see how much the archaeologists have unearthed already. I was amazed by it, really. I mean, it's a huge site and even with a sizeable team in place, they've only uncovered a fraction of it. It's going to be absolutely enormous when they've finished. I just can't believe that something like this can remain undiscovered for hundreds of years and only now come to light. And all of us locals virtually living on top of an important ancient settlement without having a clue that it's there!

A: I know. It makes you look at Saxton differently, doesn't it? I don't know about you but even though there are lots of more famous sites around, this feels more significant to me somehow.

B: I know what you mean. We're all familiar with the history of the town over the last few hundred years but this takes us back much further in time.

A: It's like the layers of centuries have been removed and I can actually understand much better how people lived over a thousand years ago.

B: And in some ways our lives haven't changed that much.

2

A: What did you think of the dinosaur exhibition then, James?

B: You know, I'd get more out of playing a computer game about dinosaurs than this exhibition.

A: Really? All the kids around us were absolutely loving it.

B: I know, but they were only young. Teenagers wouldn't be so impressed. You'd spend less on a computer game and could then relive the experience again and again. And the special effects would be far superior.

A: But I think you get more of an idea of the scale of dinosaurs from this exhibition and what the environment was really like.

B: I suppose so, and the other thing is I'm not sure how historically accurate games generally are.

A: Well, that's quite a big consideration! The museum obviously tried hard to recreate a real dinosaur experience and some of the dinosaurs were pretty terrifying but I felt I didn't really learn enough. I gave up trying to read those little information signs because there was always a large group of people around and I couldn't see them properly.

B: I just came away feeling confused about when the different dinosaur periods were and which dinosaurs were which.

3

A: That really old house in Wales is for sale – where we had that holiday – do you remember? It looks exactly the same.

B: Yes, of course. It was such a weird place, wasn't it? Great for playing hide-and-seek, though.

A: Yes. Brilliant, but freezing cold and Mum was always complaining there was never any hot water. But what I mainly remember is being fascinated by its history and its occupants, wishing I could go back in time. I liked it when Dad used to make up creepy stories about the people in the old paintings.

B: Which we never believed!

A: No – wouldn't it be awful if the person who buys it tries to update it unsympathetically – like get rid of all the original windows?

B: Mmm. I shouldn't think they'd be allowed to – it's bound to have a preservation order on it so they won't be able to turn it into flats or a hotel.

A: I expect you're right. I can't imagine all the furniture and paintings being auctioned off or ending up in a museum. I wish we could afford to buy it.

B: And take our kids there on holiday? Dream on!

▶ 22

Here are your pictures. They show people finding out about the past. I'd like you to compare two of the pictures and say why the people might be interested in this kind of information about the past, and how easy it might be for them to remember it.

▶ 23

What both these photos have in common is that they are of guided tours of historical places. The first picture looks as if it could be in a palace in Europe – possibly in the bedroom of a king or other important historical figure. The other picture is of an ancient monument in Egypt maybe. Whilst the people in the first picture look as if they live locally, the other group of tourists may have travelled a long way to get there and could be visiting many ancient sites. Neither of the groups looks as if they're very serious about remembering the information as they're not taking any notes. It may be a place they feel they should visit rather than having a particular interest in that period of history.

One significant difference in the pictures is the approach taken by the guides. The guide in the bedroom is wearing a period costume and could possibly be an actor. I think the aim of this is to make history come alive, which of course, makes it more memorable. Perhaps this is a more interesting approach as some of the people in the other picture look a bit bored – I doubt whether the tourists will remember very much about the talk given by the guide if they're just visiting the site for a few hours. Unless they've done a lot of reading beforehand and already know quite a lot about this site, it can be hard to imagine what the lives of the people who lived there thousands of years ago might have been like.

Unit 7
▶ 24

If you ask people to describe the archetypal salesperson, chances are the rug seller will come near the top of many lists. The pushy souk merchants tugging at every passing tourist begging, charming and then bullying customers to buy. Abdelmajid Rais El Fenni, known as Majid, is different. He runs one of the most successful boutiques in the Kasbah of Tangiers, selling rugs, lamps, silverware and embroidery to clients from all over the world. He used to claw for business like his neighbours, who sell identical trinkets and rugs. But he soon realised that if he wanted to succeed, haggling would not get him anywhere. Instead he learnt to create value around his products, telling stories and selling the very best things he could find. 'You are like a beggar in sales, asking again and again all day,' he explains. 'My father used to say if you get upset, you lose the customer.' Businesspeople often talk about the importance of humility, of serving your customers and acknowledging the fickleness of the markets. For salespeople, humility is not an option but something that can be turned to their advantage. 'You look at everyone,' he says. 'You pay attention. Often customers don't even look at salespeople. They treat them like dirt. If I were a customer in someone else's shop, I would be friendly and polite. I tend to leave people alone to look at things. I turn the lights on, pay attention to what they're looking at, but I don't hassle them. If I see a salesman who interrupts and waves his hands about, I know he has another 20 years of learning to do.' Majid is a master at categorising the people who walk through his door and tailoring his approach. Majid explains his strategy after dealing with a tricky customer. 'Sometimes you need to be patient. At other times, you must treat the customer as a king. I made that man feel powerful by being so humble. He wanted to exercise his power. If I hadn't treated him so well, he would never have bought a carpet. Sometimes you need to teach, to establish your authority with customers who take you for a mere peddler.' He compares the different modes of selling to gears in a car. 'If the gear needs changing, you change it,' he says.

▶ 25

No business represents this marriage between traditional and modern selling as well as Apple. When it was planning its first stores in 2000–2001, it emphasised the importance of putting them in urban locations to attract passersby, and letting visitors use the products, much as Majid lets his customers wander round his shop looking at the merchandise. Even if a potential customer would never have seriously considered switching from a PC to a Mac, the company knew that if they could get them into the store, they had a chance of converting them. That's why the stores were like latter-day cathedrals and why the company adopted a selling method akin to missionary work.

The stores were laid out with the new products up front, so customers who had never owned an Apple product could try them out. Next was a Red Zone, abuzz with staff and energy, where the conversion could take place in the form of a sale, and then a Family Room, where customers would be called by name and helped with service, support and lessons.

At a time when its rivals were trying to sell $2,000 computers in soulless big-box stores using cut-throat sales tactics, Apple went in the opposite direction. Ron Johnson, the former Apple executive charged with coming up with its retail offering, says that if the other companies had moved on from their aggressive shark-like approach to selling PCs, they would probably represent much stronger competition for Apple today. Apple sought 'not sharks, but . . . teachers, photographers and filmmakers'. In other words, converts themselves who sold out of enthusiasm, not just on commission.

Technology creates transparency and gives us more information. It should lead to better prospecting and franker negotiating. But so far it hasn't eliminated the ghost in the machine, which remains the human interaction.

▶ 26

I = Interviewer E = Elena A = Adam

I: I have with me in the studio this morning Elena Vincent and Adam Carlisle, both of whom work in marketing, an industry which fascinates us all but one that also comes in for criticism from time to time. Elena, you started out in the industry when you were quite young, didn't you?

E: Relatively, yes. I was 22 when I got my first job as an administrative assistant with an advertising agency. It wasn't very exciting, but it was certainly a foot in the door. They were working on a campaign for a hotel that had once been a very popular holiday destination. Coincidentally, my grandparents had stayed there a couple of times. I did some research and discovered that a lot of famous people had also been regulars. I mentioned this to an account executive and they decided to theme the whole campaign around the idea of the past and the present. I didn't get to write any of the advertising copy, but I was really chuffed to see my idea made reality.

I: I understand that it was also a bit controversial because of some celebrities who were used in the campaign.

E: I wouldn't have called it controversial, although it did cause a bit of a stir. That was mainly because the celebrities disliked the images we used. I'd managed to find photographs of them at the hotel in the 70s and 80s. We put the old photographs alongside new ones taken in the same places and with the same posture and facial expressions. They'd all agreed to our using the photos, so I thought it was out of order to object after the event. They didn't like the sharp contrast between how they'd looked when they were young and how they look today.

I: But this campaign actually led to your being given a chance to do a marketing course, didn't it?

E: Yes, the agency wanted to move into marketing strategies aimed at services and they gave me a chance to do a course. I really put my heart and soul into it, though at the time I thought some of the techniques they presented on the course were a bit far-fetched. Now that I've seen how they work in practice I realise just how they can help marketers create very successful campaigns for services like hotels and restaurants. Through making use of the senses – visual appeal, sound and even smell – marketers can create a lasting positive impression. Smell is probably the most difficult sense to use successfully but we did a lot of activities where we actually saw how the various strategies could be applied. I still use what I learnt in my work, to great effect I must say.

I: Now that you've mentioned scent marketing, I'm going to bring Adam in here if I may. You started off researching the psychological effects of scents, didn't you?

A: Well no, not quite. My original dissertation topic focused on the way different perfumes are formulated but I got a bit bored with that. I had a girlfriend who was into aromatherapy and that led me into researching the way in which certain smells can change emotional states. It's an area that's attracted a lot of attention from businesses using scents to enhance the appeal of their products and services. I knew my work would always find an audience and that I would see it applied in the marketing industry. That really gave me the incentive to go on doing research.

I: I understand scent marketing has come in for quite a lot of criticism though. Could you both give me your views on why you think that is?

E: No one has an issue with bread smelling like bread or coffee smelling like coffee. It's more complicated when smell is being used to manipulate people. I mean, when a powerful and irresistible scent is used to entice them into a shop only to find nothing identified with that smell actually on sale.

A: Yes, that's where problems arise. There's an advertisement aimed at getting people to drink more milk but milk is one of those smells that most people dislike. The marketing company opted, very cleverly in my opinion, for pumping out the smell of freshly baked cookies. They thought the cookie smell would make people want to eat some cookies and, by association, drink some milk. It worked but people did say it was manipulative.

I: I've heard that there are medical reasons why some people object to scent marketing.

E: The allergy lobby object very strongly. They don't like our environment being manipulated through pumping scented oils into the air – because it is potentially dangerous for this group, especially if the scent is so subtle that they would be potentially unaware of the danger. It's fair enough, really. If they start having breathing difficulties but can't actually smell whatever it is that is being pumped out, they won't realise they need to move away. This is a real problem because scents and aromas are being used in a whole range of contexts to market services: airlines, hotels and even, somewhat worryingly, casinos to encourage people to stay and keep gambling. They're really difficult to avoid.

A: Yes, allergy sufferers do have a problem. The gambling issue is an important one too; our motives are not always sinister though!

I: I'm sure they're not but there we must leave it. Thank you both … coming up now …

▶ 27

A: What I think makes messages like these particularly effective is the fact that they're using anti-advertising slogans to attack the advertising industry.

B: Absolutely! It's a clever way of warning people not to be taken in by the power of advertising. Having said that,

I do have some reservations. Some of these messages are a bit obvious, after all. I mean, we all know the whole point of advertising is to sell us things.

A: I can't argue with that but, as obvious as it may seem, we are still manipulated by the whole marketing industry. What campaigns like this do is make people stop and think. I especially like the use of humour – that's the key tool to changing hearts and minds.

B: Indeed it is. Poking fun at advertising robs it of some of its power. I do see that there is value in receiving an anti-advertising message from time to time but I do sometimes find things like this a bit patronising.

A: Patronising? I'm afraid I just don't see it like that at all. I'd really like to see at least one ad like this outside every shopping mall.

B: I can't think of anything worse! That would be the best way of ensuring that the message would lose its impact and its appeal.

A: Oh well, we'll just have to agree to differ on that one then.

▶ 28

Now I'd like you to talk about something together for about two minutes. Here are some ways of promoting fashion products and a question for you to discuss. First you have some time to look at the task.

Now talk to each other about how effective these ways of promoting fashion products would be.

▶ 29

Stealth advertising, or advertising you wouldn't even know is advertising, is coming to a living room, a college classroom or a blog near you. Here's how it works: imagine that you find your rather stylish friend is now looking more stylish than ever. Day after day she comes to college decked out in fantastic outfits that attract compliments from all and sundry. Then she lets slip that, in fact, what she is wearing is the new summer range from such and such a clothing company, available online or in-store and at the moment there happens to be a sale on, with some very attractive discounts. Would you smell a rat or would you think it was just normal chit-chat about clothes and where to get a bargain? Might it be the case that your friend is actually being paid to 'model' these fashion items and sing their praises so as to sell the brand to her classmates? I don't think anybody I know would do such a thing but if I were to learn that a friend was being paid to promote a product to me, I would be really angry.

As unlikely as this scenario might sound, this particular breed of stealth advertising is actually becoming more and more common. For the companies involved, it represents a huge saving on expensive campaigns but what's in it for people like my stylish friend? It sometimes starts with the person being offered the opportunity to trial a product – let's say a lip gloss. They get a year's supply of said lip gloss free and then, a few days later, someone contacts them to ask how they like it and then says, 'Hey, if you happen to be talking to your friends, can you just mention in passing that you use Lipluxe?' No pressure – after all, it's only if you happen to be talking to them. But you realise that you're being manipulated or your friends catch on and, outraged, contact the people who make Lipluxe to complain. In most cases they'll be fobbed off with one of those chillingly formal letters saying that it's normal practice, ending with the challenge, 'Should you wish to make a complaint, we suggest you contact the Advertising Control Board.' I say it's a challenge because nine out of ten times they know you won't.

But sometimes people do fight back. A friend of mine who is something of a fashionista has a blog where she writes about clothes and posts photos of herself wearing some of them. One day she was flicking through a magazine and she happened to see an ad for a brand of trainers in which the image was a lot of different pairs of feet wearing them … including hers! In tiny print at the bottom of the page were all the sources for the photographs, including her website. She was furious! Had the company asked my friend's permission to use her blog to promote the product, she would never have agreed to it. But a lot of bloggers wouldn't think twice about accepting money, though sometimes they're just given the clothes and encouraged to wear them. The really big bloggers demand high fees for this – sometimes as much as $50,000. I wonder what their friends would think if they knew.

Unit 8

▶ 30

I'm Tim Cole and, as an experienced travel writer, I'm here to tell you not to believe everything you read in guidebooks because following some of the recommendations they give can result in the most bizarre situations. I'll never forget the night I arrived in Sydney, for example. I'd decided to check into a hotel recommended in my guidebook. My flight was late and I turned up at the address at 1 a.m., exhausted and looking forward to a few hours' rest, but instead found myself at a comedy club, which at the time I didn't find at all funny. It turns out the hotel had moved to what was a department store, according to my useless guidebook.

The problem is that too many travellers are too trusting of their guidebooks and don't bother to research even the most basic facts before they set off. For example, many people don't think to check the publication date. Clearly, if this isn't within the last 12 months, you shouldn't buy it. Some guidebooks are only revised every couple of years, so it's no wonder the majority of guidebooks contain various inaccuracies and omissions.

This doesn't tend to apply as much to museums or other places of cultural interest, as this kind of information doesn't vary that much – so guidebooks are generally pretty dependable on these. But what I'm always extremely wary of are recommendations on restaurant prices, which can often come as a nasty shock. This can be a real problem for people

on a budget. It wouldn't be such a disaster if other kinds of information were wrong, about the food or the ambience, for example – but these tend to be more or less OK.

Some people believe maps are now redundant in guidebooks because online versions are available – but I don't agree. Studying a real map is the best way to get to know a place. But some information I think is unnecessary. A special pet hate are those books which insist on including a multitude of photos. We already know what the Eiffel Tower looks like! Why not include more background information instead?

Of course, most guidebooks are also now available in a digital format and many travellers prefer using these because they're obviously not heavy to carry, so you can download as many as you like. But I avoid them because navigation is much harder than flicking through the index at the back of a book. Life's just too short and you can never guarantee you'll have internet access anyway. The only digital travel guide I'd consider using would have to be what you might describe as 'tailor-made' – specially designed for my individual trip. Otherwise, I'm happy to stick with the traditional form of guidebook.

However, on my trip to Hawaii last summer I experimented with a new way of getting good travel advice: an app called 'In-the-know'. This relies on insider advice from locals who have cool and interesting lifestyles – in Hawaii this didn't just include surfers – I actually got some really surprising tips from a sportswear designer. Without his advice I'd never have visited the unique Ukulele Festival or eaten spam sushi. But the thing I'll never forget was a ten-kilometre kayak expedition along the coast for a night-time swim with manta rays in a huge cave. A truly magnificent sight. And my top tip for anyone visiting Hawaii!

▶ 31

Matt:	Mia, you went to Thailand last year, didn't you?
Mia:	Yes, I did. It was amazing! You have to go there, Matt!
Matt:	Well, I'm already planning to go there. In the summer, hopefully. I was wondering if you can recommend a guidebook.
Mia:	Well, the guidebook I used was so out of date I really wouldn't recommend it. In fact, I don't think I'll ever use one again. I'm thinking of just relying on travel apps next time I'm travelling. I think they're a much more reliable way to get advice.
Matt:	I expect that's true.
Mia:	I'll show you my photos if you like. Are you free this evening?

▶ 32

Here are your pictures. They show people on holiday buying souvenirs. I'd like you to compare two of the pictures and say why the people might want to buy these items and how useful each item might be as a reminder of their holiday.

▶ **33**

In both pictures the people are interested in buying local products or crafts but in one picture a man is selling typical baskets and hats from his bicycle, whereas in the other one the people are at an expensive airport shop, which looks as if it's mainly selling food products. Um … I would imagine that most people who travel to a new country that they may never visit again are interested in buying souvenirs that are typical of that area. But I doubt whether most tourists actually check to see if that item is actually locally made. I think some of these things are often mass-produced in countries like China. I'd be surprised if the street seller had actually made these things. It's not certain in either picture whether the people are actually going to make any purchases. I couldn't say if they're buying presents or not. Often these kinds of products are bought as gifts but they could just be shopping for themselves. The people talking to the street seller may just want to give the man some business and the people at the airport may just be trying to pass the time. In all likelihood they'll buy something that'll never be used and will be a waste of money.

▶ **34**

New York City's population in April 2000 stood at just over eight million – the highest it had ever been since records began. However, while the city's population grew substantially in the first half of the 20th century, it dropped from nearly 7.9 million in 1950 to 7.1 million in 1980. This was despite the baby boom and the surge in immigration from Europe, which started in the 1950s and continued through the 1970s. It was during this period that many families left New York City for the suburbs. But this trend was reversed over the next two decades as parts of the city were regenerated and a rise in immigration from Asia boosted the population to a peak of eight million by the year 2000.

It is unlikely that population growth will reach the levels seen in the first part of the 20th century, when the city's population went up by 38 percent between 1900 and 1910, but sharp declines are also unlikely. A period of relative stability in population levels seems likely during the first few decades of the 21st century. Moderate growth is expected, although it will be sufficiently high to push the population up to nine million by 2030.

▶ **35**

1

I hate to admit it but I've got no choice. I have to leave here to find work.

2

Don't worry, Mum. I'm not lonely. I've made loads of friends here already.

3

I wish I hadn't left. I think I would have had a better chance of starting my own business at home.

4

The government hasn't done enough to create jobs – that's why so many people are leaving.

5

Listen, Son, I really think you should stay in Australia. You've got lots more opportunities there.

6

I don't regret emigrating for one minute. It's the best decision I've ever made.

Unit 9

▶ **36**

Babies and small children pass a number of developmental milestones as they grow. Only weeks after a child is born she knows a smile for what it is and may even smile back, though she is not yet able to actually recognise the important people in her life. This comes a little later, when, at four months, the baby can identify her mother and begins to know who's who among all the people she encounters regularly. Mind you, names don't mean much to her at this stage but at ten months she will begin to recognise her own name and react to it appropriately. It's at this age also that she'll start to get a real kick out of the game of *peekaboo*. The adult hides his face behind his hands or some other object and then reveals it. This usually gets a laugh from the baby and is early evidence of a burgeoning sense of humour. She will begin to display helpful behaviour when she is little more than a year old but bear in mind that the child might actually be more of a hindrance than a help. Still, it's the thought that counts, so don't discourage her. It won't be long before she'll also get the hang of dressing herself – usually at around two. Once again, don't crush the child's enthusiasm as this may actually be slowing down her development and hanging on to an extra responsibility an adult can actually share with her.

▶ **37**

In this part of the test I'm going to give each of you three pictures. I'd like you to talk about two of them on your own for about a minute and a half, and also to answer a question briefly about your partner's pictures.

It's your turn first. Here are your pictures. They show people doing things on their own. I'd like you to compare two of the pictures and say why people might be doing these things on their own and what reactions they might get from other people.

▶ **38**

Both these photographs show people doing things alone that we often do with others. Apart from that similarity, they are in some ways rather different from one another. In the first picture there is a young boy by himself watching a film in a cinema. He seems completely engrossed in whatever it is he's watching and perfectly happy to be there without anyone else. What's more, he's got a huge container of popcorn all to himself. In the second picture a man is having a solitary meal in a restaurant and although he too seems quite engrossed in what he's doing, I have the impression that he's reading a magazine because he's feeling a bit self-conscious about being a lone diner. A woman on her own in a restaurant might attract a bit of attention, but a man on his own, on the other hand, probably wouldn't attract very much attention at all. It depends on the kind of restaurant of course. In a fast food restaurant people probably wouldn't even notice whether people dining were unaccompanied or with friends. Even if they did, I don't think they would think anything of it.

▶ 39

E = Examiner C = Candidate

E: Who do you think is happiest doing these things on their own? Why?

C: It strikes me that the woman playing solitaire may actually be quite content even if she's not smiling or laughing. Perhaps she would prefer not to have someone across the table playing against her.

▶ 40

1

It was Saturday, so the multi-storey car park was jam-packed. I had to drive around for ages to find a space. I locked the car, headed for the lift and got out at ground level where the shops are. It was only then I realised I hadn't registered which row I'd parked in or even which floor I was on. I think I've finally got it through my own thick skull that the secret is to make a mental note of where I am. Everyone kept staring at me hanging around in the car park on my own. I could feel myself blushing. When most of the other cars had gone, I finally found mine.

2

I've always had trouble remembering my girlfriend's cousin's name. What pops into my head first is 'Antoinette' and then I think it's 'Brigitte'. I usually avoid calling her anything, which was what I did last time we met. I don't think she noticed but my girlfriend certainly did and she was not impressed. She would barely speak to me for the rest of the afternoon, which made me feel pretty uneasy I have to say. Boy did she ever give me a talking to when we got home. There's actually an old song about a girl called Bernadette and the experts say using a song or poem sometimes does the trick. I'll give it a go.

3

I was actually really looking forward to our wedding anniversary, but I was so busy I put it right out of my mind. By the time I remembered, all the decent shops were closed and I ended up downloading a couple of new albums I thought he'd like on iTunes when I got home. He'd bought me some pearl earrings. I could tell he was thinking our anniversary was so unimportant to me I'd let it slip my mind. He looked miserable and I felt terrible. Apparently, there's some kind of anniversary alert app you can get and they'll send you messages with suggestions for gifts. I'll have to go for that next year instead of relying on my memory.

4

My sister used to put these little sticky notes all over the house with things she was trying to commit to memory. You'd find them on packets of cornflakes and on the bathroom mirror – everywhere you'd least expect them to be. That's what I should have done because even if I put things down on paper, if there are lots of facts and figures and so on, I get them all muddled up. For this subject there were heaps of dates and place names. I knew that if I didn't get them straightened out in my mind, my chances of getting a good mark in the final exam were out of the window, and it turned out that I was right.

5

There I was in a busy station in the middle of France and I needed to get some change for the ticket machine and get to the airport or I was going to miss my flight. I studied French for about seven years but I've let it get really rusty. I was desperately racking my brains for the phrase 'I need change' but all that came into my head were words in Spanish. Apparently, if you conjure up an image of the person who told you something, you sometimes remember it. So just when I was beginning to panic I thought of my old French teacher and suddenly a complete sentence popped into my head. I got my change.

Unit 10

▶ 42

1

I did this magazine quiz called 'How well does your partner know you?' I don't usually bother with this kind of thing because I think they're a waste of time. You had to grade statements and then give the same quiz to your partner to answer about you.

There was a huge discrepancy between my results and my partner's, and the analysis said something like, 'You should have spent more time getting to know each other.' Some of our answers really shocked me because they showed that we're actually quite incompatible. It's made me start to question a lot of things in our relationship. I did the quiz for a laugh but I rather wish I hadn't now.

2

I'd already had an interview and had actually been working for the company for a couple of weeks when they said I had to do a personality test. I was kind of surprised as I thought this was only used for recruitment purposes but I didn't really mind as it was actually quite interesting – but they must have got my results mixed up with someone else's because they said I wasn't good at handling pressure. I've never felt so insulted in my life. Me? Not handle pressure? I complained to my boss and she said not to worry about it. Now she realises just how wide of the mark the results were.

3

I'm not generally a big fan of personality tests but I basically had nothing else to do at work so I thought I'd give it a go.

I honestly didn't expect to learn much ... I mean how could choosing colours say anything about your personality? You had to click on eight colours in order of preference, then wait a few minutes and repeat the same test. When I read the results I could hardly believe it. My attitudes, my worries, my problems with my partner, my work habits – it was all absolutely spot on. It didn't tell me anything I didn't already know about myself though.

4

The psychology department at my university were asking for student volunteers to do a personality test. They made us wait for ages in this really stuffy room with only three seats and there must have been at least 15 of us. Some people were getting really impatient. We were all a bit stunned when they explained that the point of the test had been to study our behaviour in the overcrowded room. I was quite proud of myself when they said I'd scored highly for tolerance and resilience, just because I hadn't lost my temper. I'd always wanted to get to the bottom of how these tests work, which is why I volunteered. I found it fascinating.

5

I've got my own translation business but I wasn't getting enough commissions. I decided to see if one of those life coaches could get to the bottom of whatever was going wrong and we both thought it would be useful for me to do a personality test. I was a bit taken aback when she said my test results showed that I needed to work in collaboration with others. It's weird as I've always seen myself as a bit of a loner and as not taking too kindly to people telling me what to do. But this new way of working might be just what I need to inspire me and will actually make a refreshing change.

 43

N = Nadia A = Adam

N: Personally, I'm all in favour of robots doing as much work as possible. But I suppose the key issue here is to decide which tasks a robot is capable of doing as well as a human. I think they'd be just as good, if not better, at flying a plane. Would you go along with that?

A: I would, up to a point. I mean, most planes already depend on an automated system but pilots are still needed to make decisions in an emergency and I'm not sure I'd trust a robot to do that instead. Also, I think passengers feel reassured when the pilot talks to them.

N: Sure. But don't you think having a robot instead of a human pilot would remove the possibility of human error?

A: Possibly, but I think most people would still rather have a real person in charge. I think tasks with less responsibility are more appropriate for robots.

N: I suppose so. I hadn't thought of that. How would you feel about a robot looking after your grandmother? There are some practical tasks that a robot could do to help look after the elderly. For example, helping them to get washed and dressed.

A: Mmm. Maybe – as long as they'd also have some human interaction. It would be terrible to only have a robot as a companion.

N: Oh yes, absolutely. That would be terrible. I wouldn't mind having my meals cooked by a robot.

A: Simple meals would be OK. I can't see there'd be a problem with robots preparing things like pizzas. In a pizza restaurant, all they'd have to do is to put the right toppings on and put the pizza in the oven for the correct amount of time. But I just wonder how useful robots would be in a high-class restaurant where the cooks need to be able to taste the food!

N: So we're saying that a robot could cook effectively in certain circumstances.

A: Right.

Unit 11

 44

P = Presenter M = Mark D = Diana

P: Welcome to the *Review Show*. Joining me today are Diana Abel and Mark Shaw. The first book we'll be discussing is Robert Provine's *Laughter: a scientific investigation*. Mark, what did you make of it?

M: Well, he talks a lot about the idea that laughter is not primarily a response to humour but a social lubricant – something used to smooth interaction between people – interesting but I don't think Provine is the first psychologist to make this claim. But he is the first to popularise this theory. I think a lot of people will reject the notion that we don't just laugh because we find something funny and that laughter actually has a much more complex role. But what I found really disturbing is that, according to a recent study in the UK, we're laughing much less than we used to.

P: Indeed ... Diana, I know you were particularly struck by the comparisons between male and female laughter in the book.

D: Yes, that's right. While researching the book, Provine found that one of the key qualities women look for in a potential partner is a good sense of humour – something sought after much less commonly by men. That was certainly news to me. It seems women want a man who will make them laugh, while men like women who laugh at their jokes. Men may even feel threatened by a woman who's funny, which goes a long way to explain why until relatively recently there were so few female comedians around.

P: Provine does stress the importance of increasing laughter in our lives and gives some advice on how to achieve this. Were you persuaded by any of his suggestions, Diana?

D: Well, while Provine thinks we should all try to laugh more, he's not advocating attending laughter workshops or anything like that in order to be able to tell an amusing anecdote. His message is really quite simple. If you want to laugh more or better still make other people laugh, rather than trying to learn to play the clown, engage with people who have a humorous outlook and avoid those who are always gloomy – which makes sense to me. One thing I'm in favour of, which Provine neglected to mention, is that people should lighten up and laugh at themselves more.

P: Did either of you find your own attitude to laughter had changed after reading the book?

M: I certainly started noticing when people actually laughed and found it confirmed Provine's theory, that is, people were laughing at things that weren't remotely funny and also in odd places during a conversation.

D: The effect it had on me was to monitor my own impulses to laugh – it made me less spontaneous in a way.

M: … analysing what made you want to laugh instead of reacting naturally – I experienced that too. And it also made me aware of how little I actually laugh. I've found I am making more of an effort to be funny.

P: So did you find the book answered everything you ever wanted to know about laughter?

M: It was pretty comprehensive, especially the parts on how humour and comedy work. He also focuses on how humour can be abusive and cruel – anyone who's experienced this in the playground will be able to relate to that. The section on the mechanics of breathing and laughing I could have done without.

D: I was drawn to the social aspects of laughter. Provine argues that laughter existed long before comedy and I wish he'd gone into more depth about how the need for laughter may have been triggered.

M: That was the most informative section of the book, so that could have been expanded in my view. The descriptions of how laughter may have started with chimpanzees tickling each other are wonderful.

P: But, overall, would you recommend this to someone who hasn't got a professional or academic interest in laughter?

M: Without question, yes. There were some bits where I felt my lack of a background in neuroscience was a disadvantage but you can just skip those bits and move on to some of the lovely anecdotes about the research – some of the accounts of the contagious nature of laughter are really amazing. In some places people couldn't stop laughing for days.

D: Yes, incredible.

P: And do you think the book will help people?

M: Well, if you just want to find out about the benefits of laughter, there are more appropriate self-help guides. This is more wide-ranging than that.

P: I see. So, moving on to another book about comedy …

 45

They did an experiment recently which shows that people are able to tell how a dog is feeling by reading its facial expressions. They showed volunteers photos of a dog expressing different feelings and the funny thing was it wasn't dog owners who were able to identify the different emotions best – people who'd never owned a dog were just as good. The researchers think people may have a natural empathy with dogs. But they're not sure why – it may be because humans and dogs have evolved with each other over thousands of years? I think they should do more research to find out if people can read other animals' emotions as well.

46

In this part of the test I'm going to give each of you three pictures. I'd like you to talk about two of them on your own for about a minute, and also to answer a question briefly about your partner's pictures.

It's your turn first. Here are your pictures. They show people creating an image. I'd like you to compare two of the pictures and say how successful the people are at creating the image and how people might react to them.

47

E = Examiner   C = Candidate

E: Which image do you think is the most powerful?

C: Well, it's quite hard to say because these can all be extremely influential; they can make us decide to buy a product or vote for a politician – but I suppose the most powerful might be the image created by the fashion shoot because it's more subtle, while the others are more direct. These kinds of images can help to sell thousands of products and can change people's attitudes to the way they dress or whatever.

Unit 12

48

Hi, I'm Max Bignall. When I arrived in New York six months ago to study physics at university, I was interested to hear about something called the Secret Science Club. It really is quite something. I knew that the club was started by two science writers, but not that the third founder was a radio producer. He did have a scientific background too, though. The club started as a small informal gathering held in a Brooklyn bar but soon outgrew this venue and is now held at The Bell House, which is a popular Brooklyn venue for weddings and other private events. But most nights during the week what you can see are the types of acts you would expect from a trendy New York bar, namely performances by musicians – usually up and coming bands. And somewhat bizarrely, once a month you'll find a friendly scientist lecturing in down-to-earth language about a topical scientific issue. The lectures often include experiments at the end, which go down well with the crowd, especially if they involve audience participation.

The talks cover all kinds of issues: they've had a climate scientist talking about super-storms, an evolutionary biologist on the elusive animals that live in our cities, an astrophysicist talking about black holes – which was the highlight for me – and last time we had a mathematical sociologist explaining how ideas spread. The lectures themselves are generally very entertaining and accessible – even for non-scientists – but where I sometimes get lost is at the end, when people ask questions which can be quite specialised. And then there's a chance for everyone to listen to music and talk about the lecture. What's really invaluable for science students like me is the opportunity to network with some of the best experts in their field.

Nobody can agree about the precise origins of clubs like the Secret Science Club but they seem to have started in universities at the end of the 1990s. Of course, the idea itself is much older. In the 18th century people used to meet up in coffee houses in Britain and France to discuss the affairs of the day, including scientific discoveries.

I could be wrong, but I think the majority of people who attend the Secret Science Club aren't academics, just people with an interest in science. The appeal for people like this is that the lectures help them to understand the relevance of science in their daily lives. I like the fact that the Secret Science Club is inclusive and wants to share ideas beyond the scientific community. Scientists have a responsibility to help people see how science continues to shape the way we see the world and the future.

▶ 49

E = Examiner G = Gustave M = Maria

E: Good afternoon. My name is Pam Nelson and this is my colleague, Stephanie Mason. And your names are?

G: Gustave Jansen.

M: Maria Fernández Lourido.

E: Can I have your mark sheets, please? Thank you. First of all, we'd like to know something about you. Gustave, where are you from?

G: The Netherlands.

E: What do you do there?

G: I'm a student.

E: Maria, how long have you been studying English?

M: Well, I started learning English in primary school, so I suppose I must have been studying it for about fifteen years now.

E: Gustave, what do you enjoy most about learning English?

G: The fact that I can watch films and TV series and understand quite a lot.

E: What did you like most about the area where you grew up, Gustave?

G: There are a lot of interesting, old buildings. I really like architecture.

E: Maria, do you ever wish you were rich and famous?

M: To be perfectly honest, not anymore, no. I used to when I was younger, of course, but I now think that there are so many responsibilities and problems that come with having money and fame and that sometimes they actually destroy the person's happiness. I would have to say that I don't enjoy my job because of the money. It's more because it gives me a lot of satisfaction.

▶ 50

E = Examiner M = Maria G = Gustave

E: In this part of the test I'm going to give each of you three pictures. I'd like you to talk about two of them on your own for about a minute and also to answer a question briefly about your partner's pictures. Maria, it's your turn first. Here are your pictures. They show people doing research. I'd like you to compare two of the pictures and say why people might choose to do research like this and what problems they might have.

M: Both these photographs show women scientists carrying out research but they are actually quite different from one another. In the first photograph the woman seems to be doing some kind of ... umm ... chemistry experiment – she has a whole lot of ... umm ... small glass ... umm ... containers in front of her on a bench and she is holding a notebook or perhaps a tablet. Perhaps she is making notes of the results of her experiment. The second woman is obviously doing something quite different. Instead of working in a lab she is outside doing some kind of fieldwork. I think she is probably a biologist. I imagine her work involves examining plants in their natural habitat, like the plant she's looking at. While the first woman could have the problem of an unexpected reaction of some kind, in which an explosion or perhaps some kind of poisonous gas is produced, the other woman is outside in the open air or perhaps in a hothouse and probably has to deal with extreme temperatures. They're both wearing lab coats to protect their clothing and possibly to prevent the chemicals and plants they're working with from becoming contaminated.

E: Thank you. Gustave, who do you think is most involved in what they are doing?

G: The woman in the laboratory.

E: Why?

G: She's looking at the slide very closely.

▶ 51

E = Examiner M = Maria G = Gustave

E: Now I'd like you to talk about something together for about two minutes. Here are some ways that good ideas sometimes spread from one person to another and a question for you to discuss. First you have some time to look at the task.

Now, talk to each other about how effective these ways are for spreading good ideas.

M: OK, let's make a start. I actually think good ideas often spread because one person tells another person about them. Do you agree?

G: I think more good ideas are spread through online communication than by means of face-to-face interaction. The point I'm trying to make is that a lot of conversation is quite trivial but if someone has something important to say, they're very likely to put it in a blog or perhaps record a podcast.

M: It could actually just be telepathy as well, now I come to think of it. I mean, someone has an idea somewhere and then by coincidence it turns out someone else in a completely different country has the same idea.

G: If you look at a lot of nineteenth- and early twentieth century inventions, it's quite difficult to say who was the real originator of the idea because it often seems to have been invented by two or more people simultaneously.

M: Hmm … And in the past there were books and magazines, of course, but nowadays Twitter is a really important way of spreading ideas. As I see it, it's far more important than anything else, at least for young people. People are constantly tweeting things they've read or just thought about.

G: It's amazing how quickly an idea or just a rumour of some kind can spread through a medium like that. I do have a few reservations about whether these things could actually be called good ideas, though.

E: Thank you. Now you have about a minute to decide which method would reach the largest number of people.

G: For me it would have to be online resources like blogs or even online newspapers and magazines. Almost everyone has an internet connection and potentially has access to good new ideas because of that.

M: Yes I suppose so, but I still tend to think that Twitter reaches more people.

G: There are loads of people who don't have a Twitter account.

M: That's true, so perhaps we could say that the internet is our first choice because of its almost universal appeal.

▶ 52

E = Examiner G = Gustave M = Maria

E: How important is it for people to learn about the history of science at school?

G: It's very important. People should study history.

E: Maria, what do you think about studying history?

M: History is an important subject and history of science especially. It's fascinating to learn about when discoveries were made and under what circumstances. I mean often scientists had such passion for their work that they were willing to make huge sacrifices in terms of their health and their relationships to other people. Of course many were rather eccentric as well so their stories make fascinating reading. Would you agree?

G: Sometimes scientists solved an important problem completely by chance. I always enjoy learning about that kind of research. They often ended up getting ill as a result of their work. I mean people like Marie Curie.

E: Some people say they don't see the point of scientific research. Why do you think this is?

M: Well, in some cases I think it is because they don't actually know very much about it. There are reports on science research in the better newspapers but not everyone reads them and they may not be aware of the important contribution research can make to things like curing disease or warning us of dangers like global warming.

E: Gustave, do you think people are well informed about the value of scientific research?

G: No, and in my opinion it's up to scientists to inform them.

E: Why scientists?

G: They know more about it.

M: Yes, but they can inform the press about their work and then it can be presented to the public in an entertaining way. The problem is that it's not easy for people to get access to research reports directly. My father is a scientist and he says that unless your university or research institute subscribes to a journal you have to pay to read the articles and it can be very expensive.

G: If it's taken out of scientists' hands there will inevitably be distortion. There's a lot of false news on social media and so on, offering cures for diseases.

M: So maybe it's a question of educating people so that they can tell the difference between real scientific reporting and false news.

E: Gustave, what do you think about other media like television?

G: There are some pretty good science documentaries on TV but I think the universities themselves should have YouTube channels and so on to publicise research.

M: A lot of them do, actually. The university where my father works gives researchers the opportunity to make a kind of mini-documentary about their research for the YouTube channel. My father has made one on his research.

G: That sounds like a good idea I guess. But how do people know the YouTube channel exists?

M: Yes, that can be a problem and the other issue is talking about science in a way that's interesting and relevant for the general public.

E: Thank you. That is the end of the test.

Practice test

Part 1

 53

1

A: How did it go at the Physics competition in the Netherlands?

B: I couldn't stay for the duration unfortunately … due to a family crisis … but the rest of my group did and the guys did incredibly well. We had lots of resources at our disposal, and that paid off. Anyway, despite being up against some of the best physicists in the world, we came second in the problem-solving category, which was no mean feat considering the opposition! We also won the Best Presentation award for our presentation on string theory. Well, at the risk of sounding smug, I think that was pretty much a given all along.

A: What were the other competitors like? Were they from a similar background?

B: Well, there seemed to be a good balance of males and females this year. Mind you, that's hardly unexpected … that gender gap in physics has been closing for a while now and that's refreshing. It's usually PhD students who enter … I suppose they've got the necessary expertise, so we were unique in that we're not PhD students! And obviously many of them were competition veterans … they've been doing this for years.

2

A: I think that since people have started watching several episodes of programmes back-to-back, they're becoming more demanding. Hence the decision, I suppose, by many TV conglomerates to dump entire series of certain shows online at a time, rather than drip-feed us episode by episode. I suppose it's all about instant gratification for the viewer. And there's a growing distaste for commercials too, which is bad news for the advertising industry. Research shows that one of the things people most enjoy about streaming shows is that they can either mute or fast-forward through the ads, as opposed to waiting them out when watching a live show.

B: That makes sense. It does seem that we're in the golden age of TV. For me, soap operas have never been better. They really do seem to touch on the rhythms of contemporary life. I would say though, that scriptwriters should remember that effective story-telling has to follow certain principles … you know … add some surprise into the mix without being phoney about it. There's a love of the bizarre twist nowadays that often isn't even really based on the characters themselves – there's no clear connection. That's a low-grade form of story-telling, I think. Classic story-telling's about people facing some sort of dilemma and dealing with it.

3

A: How did you rise to the marathon challenge?

B: Well, the night before the marathon I thought I was starting to come down with something dreadful but thankfully it turned out to be nothing more than a few stomach cramps. I fully expected to have a bit of a wobble before it, but I managed to stay composed. Anyway, I thought back to the half-marathon I ran last year and I remembered that feeling of being sure I'd underperform when the day came. And this particular marathon really stirred up a lot of self-doubt too. I think it was a mixture of concern about endurance as well as a fear of the route itself, which is notoriously tough.

A: I know what you mean. When I ran my first marathon, I found it hard going at times for several reasons. Even though I'd followed all the rules about what to eat and drink beforehand, I just couldn't shake off the craving for cold drinks. I was well prepared though, and managed to get the pace just right, so I didn't burn out after the first hour … something that many novice marathon runners do. Then they're so disheartened at not making the finish line.

Part 2

 54

Good afternoon everyone. I'm Leo Anderson and I'm here to talk to you about my work with rhinos in South Africa. I was with an organisation called the African Conservation Group, the ACG.

Several other volunteers arrived in Johannesburg at the same time I did, and we were put into teams such as the maintenance team that's responsible for the upkeep of the centre or the game ranger team. They'd decided I'd be best in the wildlife capture team, which mainly focuses on tagging animals so that their movements can be monitored, but has other duties too.

The first job I had was with the infant rhinos, so I wasn't exactly thrown in at the deep end! I was asked to assist with bottle-feeding these cute animals. We didn't have to prepare the formula – that was done for us – and then we were usually asked to feed them.

Another of my daily duties was clearing the enclosures. Well, that was really hard work to begin with, but I got used to it. I remember there was a huge panic one day as one of the animals almost escaped. That meant that the fences around the site had to be checked and reinforced.

To give volunteers an idea of how physically demanding working on a rhino conservation project is, the ACG established a rating system which is clearly displayed on their website. It's goes from one to five, and the more rhinos you see, the more challenging the experience is. One rhino, for instance, means suitable for all levels of fitness and physical ability but five rhinos means you need to be in excellent health as volunteers will often be on their feet from dawn to dusk.

The centre also does a lot of research on rhino behaviour … things like observing the interaction between adolescent rhinos, though that's not something that I was involved in … and monitoring the sleeping patterns of both males and females. Logging information on the central database about that was something I was regularly required to do. Accommodation-wise, the centre has some beautiful bungalows where many of the permanent staff live, and where we often got together in the evenings. They're astonishingly luxurious. The rest of us had wooden huts, which we had to share. And though I expected them to be pretty basic, they were actually far from it.

Overall, my experience at the ACG was superb. It was fantastic to work with a group that has such a strong commitment to the rhinos, and in particular to the rehabilitation of orphaned rhinos. And the remarkable chemistry between all of us who'd gone there to help was especially memorable.

So how and why did I get involved? Well, back when I was applying for a place at university I knew there'd be a lot of competition for certain courses, like wildlife management and zoology. And as veterinary medicine, the degree I'd hoped to do, is particularly competitive, I was sure that my experience on a conservation programme would help make my application stand out.

Now if you have any questions, please feel free to come up and have a chat …

Part 3

 55

I = Interviewer O = Oliver M = Michelle

I: On *Business Matters* today I'm talking to two young fashion designers, Michelle Barnes and Oliver Grimshaw, who run a very successful start-up company in sustainable fashion called *Ethion*. Michelle, generally speaking, what do you think of the fashion industry today?

M: It needs to change, doesn't it? I mean the industry needs to evolve. To put it simply, environmentally and socially, the way fashion's produced isn't working. It's damaging. But I think we've come some way in recognising this so that there's been a definite shift throughout both the fashion and textile industries towards more sustainable practices that consider the impact on our planet, for instance. The word 'transparency' has become a buzz word for many companies that are really beginning to include sustainable solutions and want the public to know about it. The shift's towards change, but change takes time and comes with its own challenges. You know, we're still dealing with resistance and misinformation along the way on the part of some companies, and consumer scepticism.

I: I see. Oliver, your company's considered to be a pioneer when it comes to sustainable design … by which we mean fashion that can be supported indefinitely in terms of human impact on the environment and social responsibility. Do you feel that progress has been made when it comes to the way fashion collections are produced?

O: Well, we always wanted to just use pre-existing materials, originally for what it meant to us artistically rather than environmentally, but the more we became involved in the industry, the more we felt the urge to break all the rules. We've only ever used waste from designer products that didn't actually get to market, and we've always produced locally with a social conscience, by making a conscious effort to rehabilitate the longterm unemployed through a cooperative.

I: I see. Michelle, do you feel customers are becoming more aware of the negative impacts of the fashion industry?

M: Without a shadow of a doubt! Too many stories have been told … too much awareness of polluted rivers because of chemicals being dumped, for example, and widespread malpractice in terms of breaking the law have appeared for consumers not to have become aware of this issue. And consumers that were aware of this all along are now more outspoken in demanding change. Despite the relatively slow response from the industry itself, consumers are beginning to ask relevant and increasingly more meaningful questions on how the industry operates. And it's that which has had a significant impact.

I: Many believe that it's up to the next generation of designers to make a radical difference. Do students have good role models at the moment? Oliver?

O: If there were too many role models, students would react against them … as they're reacting against the so-called 'fast fashion' companies, and the social and environmental exploitation which means workers are not treated well. It's precisely because there are so few role models that there's this sense that we need to do something about it pretty quickly. Some of my most exhilarating moments are spent among students and very young designers. The role of the designer's changing profoundly in terms of ethics, and I strongly sense that the next generation will relish the chance to collaborate on finding sustainable solutions.

I: Michelle, you founded Ethion … a platform for designers with ethical and sustainable standards, which is a very noble concept. What direction do you think your company should move in?

M: Well, it's taken time for us to get established and I wouldn't say we're there yet, but step-by-step we're heading where we want to be. Top of our agenda is upcycling. In a world still churning out trendy, throwaway fashion pieces at breakneck speed, the idea of recycled, refashioned clothing can be an anomaly.

But it's the way to go as far as we're concerned. We've got a good structure in place now and have come up with some solid plans for growth.

I: Sounds good. And finally, what do you both think about the state of the fashion industry here in the UK at the moment? Michelle?

M: Well, for years now, we've seen more and more of our local manufacturers being abandoned for production facilities much further afield, simply because it's cheaper. It's a shame really because all that expertise we had has been greatly diminished. Perhaps the government needs to provide more of an incentive for entrepreneurs to start new fashion companies in an attempt to get back to where we were …

O: … and when you think about the number of buildings dedicated to fashion that there used to be throughout this country too … you know linen factories, woollen mills and so on. It's a disgrace that we've practically killed our home industry. We've ended up gradually industrialising the globe without keeping our own artisanal skills alive.

I: Indeed … well, Michelle and Oliver, thank you for talking to us today …

Part 4

 56

1

Interviews are not really my thing … I get so worked up. Anyway, I have to say the panel at the last interview I had was superb. They asked me all the usual stuff about where I saw myself in a few years' time, but I was well prepared for that! But I wish there'd been a bit more depth to my answers when they asked for examples of my innovation. I got the job because I reckon I ticked a lot of their boxes, especially in terms of international communication … I suppose it has come in handy that I'd lived in rural places in different countries where English wasn't widely spoken, and mixed with the locals.

2

My last interview was no picnic, I can tell you! It's almost like the panel wanted me to fail! The way they worded one question about the role meant that I got the wrong end of the stick and went on about *their* role as employers instead of mine! Still … it was my own fault I suppose. But I kept my cool and answered the other questions as best I could. I did a good job hiding my nerves and I did my absolute utmost to show that I'd a long way to go in terms of professional development, honing my creative skills etc. … I mean nobody likes a wise guy. Unbelievably, I got the job!

3

I love interviews! I thrive in demanding situations where there's that time pressure. My last interview was with a large energy company. In hindsight, I probably should've

spent a bit more time stressing my plans for career progression. At least I'd done a fair bit of background reading on the organisation, so that obviously went down well because I've now joined the company. Another thing that I feel the interview panel liked hearing about was my experience of training the customer services team … no mean feat I can tell you after what they'd been through with the last manager, but the team members have turned things round and can now operate entirely self-sufficiently.

4

Looking back at my last interview, I think it's a shame I wasn't a bit more on the ball when it came to highlighting the one thing that should have made me stand out head and shoulders above the other candidates … and that's my language skills. It completely slipped my mind! I suppose it's just as well then that I was able to speak knowledgeably about company performance. Anyway, to cut a long story short, I was offered the job and have just started. I think it's important to demonstrate to the interview panel that you can think outside the box. And I think that's possibly where I shone at my last interview.

5

Well, I know looking the part's important for a job in a law firm because lawyers, as you know, tend to be pretty conventional dressers. My black suit did nicely I think. On reflection though, I could've done a better job in turning the tables on them by getting them to talk more. Anyway, that said, my one chance to come into my own was when they asked me about working in stressful situations. My background in the Tokyo stock market, and also that year that I spent in New York, meant I had more than enough examples to give them. They must've been happy with what they heard because they offered me the role!

Speaking Part 1

 57

First of all, we'd like to know something about you.

Where are you from?

What do you do here/there?

How long have you been studying English?

What do you enjoy most about learning English?

If you could live in any city in the world, which one would you live in? (Why?)

Who do you think is the most influential person in your country? (Why?)

What was the most interesting TV programme you've watched recently about?

If you had more free time, what would you like to learn to do? (Why?)

Who do you enjoy spending your free time with? (Why?)

Speaking Part 2

 58

In this part of the test, I'm going to give each of you three pictures. I'd like you to talk about two of them on your own for about a minute, and also to answer a question about your partner's pictures.

Candidate A, it's your turn first. Here are your pictures. They show people relaxing outdoors. I'd like you to compare two of the pictures, and say why the people might have chosen to relax in this way, and how they might be feeling. All right?

Thank you. Candidate B, in which situation do the people seem most relaxed?

Thank you. Now, Candidate B, here are your pictures. They show young people doing sports. I'd like you to compare two of the pictures, and say which sport would be most exciting and why, and how young people could benefit from doing this sport? All right?

Thank you. Candidate A, do you think it's important for young people to take part in sport while they're studying?

Speaking Part 3

 59

Now I'd like you to talk about something together for about two minutes. Here are some things people often have to consider when applying for a job and a question for you to discuss. First you have some time to look at the task.

Now, talk to each other about how important these things are when choosing a job. All right? Could you start now, please?

Thank you. Now you have about a minute to decide which of these things older people might feel is more important when choosing a job.

Speaking Part 4

 60

Is it best for people to find a job close to their home or in another town/city? Why?

Why do you think some people prefer to live and work in another country?

Some people say it's better to work from home than work in an office? Do you agree?

What are the advantages of working in teams?

Some people say it's not a good idea to stay in the same job for life. What's your opinion?

Thank you. That is the end of the test.

Contents

Teaching notes

1A This is me

Aim
to review perfect and continuous tenses

Exam link
Speaking, Part 1 (interview)

Activity type
Providing personal information and guessing

Classroom dynamics
Pairs or groups of three

Time taken
25 minutes

When to use
after Grammar focus, Activity 7 on page 8

Preparation
Make one copy of the activity for each pair or group of three students.

Procedure

1 Write these two topics on the board and choose one to talk about. Talk about one of the topics for up to a minute without using the key phrase in bold.

- *Talk about an important person from your town who **you have met in person**.*
- *Talk about a person **you have been meeting a lot** recently.*

2 Ask students to guess which of the two you were discussing and bring their attention to the fact you didn't use the key phrase in bold (but most probably, a paraphrase of it).

3 Put students into pairs or groups of three and give them a copy of the worksheet. Taking turns, students should choose one of the 'talk about' boxes in secret and then one of the letters (A–C). They should discuss it for up to a minute while their group members listen. They should not use the exact phrase in bold when doing this.

Once finished, the other students should guess which 'talk about' box and letter was being answered and then ask one follow-up question about the topic.

4 This continues until all the boxes have been discussed or the 25 minutes are up. A box should not be chosen more than once during the activity.

5 At the end of the activity, ask students to think about how well their group members discussed the items in terms of content and language used (e.g. Did they expand their answers? How well were the answers organised? Were they easy to follow? Was the grammar used correctly?).

1B Matching halves

Aim
to review and practise using compound words in context

Exam link
Reading and Use of English, Parts 1 and 3

Activity type
putting dominoes together and creating sentences

Classroom dynamics
small groups

Time taken
20 minutes

When to use
after Vocabulary, Activity 6 on page 12

Preparation
Make one copy of the worksheet per group, cut up as indicated.

Procedure

1 Put students into small groups and give each group a set of domino cards face down. Ask them to deal out the cards equally. If there are any leftover cards, these should be placed face down in a pile.

2 Tell students that these are domino cards and they need to match halves. Give an example by writing *WIND* on the board and asking students to recall what word matches with wind to create a compound adjective (*SWEPT*). Use the definition 'a place which is windy because of a lack of trees or buildings to protect it' to help.

3 The activity is as follows. Whichever student has the card with the lowest letter in the alphabet (A, for example) starts and places their card on the table. Moving clockwise around the group, the students then choose from their domino cards to match halves. They should ignore the letters at the top of the cards – these are to check the answers later.

The next student has a choice of completing the compound word to the right or left of the domino. Once placed down, the student should invent a sentence or give an example using the compound word. For example, *Cadiz is a really windswept city*. If a student believes they have no card which fits, they should pick up an extra card from the pile or, if there are no remaining dominoes, simply miss a go.

4 The winner is the student who gets rid of all his/her dominoes first. However, the activity should continue until all the dominoes are on the table and the circle is complete.

5 Ask students to identify the three compound nouns in the activity.

Answers

A long-standing, B run-down, C cut-price, D middle-aged,
E self-esteem, F far-fetched, G life-saving, H part-time,
I built-up, J high-rise, K world-renowned, L purpose-built,
M landmark, N interest-free

Nouns:

landmark, self-esteem, high-rise (can also be an adjective)

1C What's the link?

Aim
to practise and review using conjunctions in context

Exam link
Reading and Use of English, Parts 1 and 2

Activity type
understanding the meaning of conjunctions in context in order to complete sentences

Classroom dynamics
pairwork and small groups/whole class

Time taken
30 minutes

When to use
after Grammar focus, Activity 5, page 13

Preparation
Make one copy of the worksheet per pair.

Procedure
1 Tell the class they are going to have a debate, but first, they must prepare their arguments. The debate will be about the best ways to improve the city they live in.
2 Put students into pairs and give them a copy of the worksheet. Ask students to complete the sentences with the debate topic in mind for about 10–15 minutes.
3 Once complete, put students into groups to conduct the debate. Alternatively, you could do this as a whole-class debate. Tell students to imagine that they are members of the local council and go through the points on the worksheet one-by-one, allowing students to give their opinions and respond to other people in the class.
4 Monitor throughout the process, aiding with sentence completion when necessary. During the speaking element, make notes in order to give content and language feedback at the end of the activity.

2A Tell the truth

Aim
to review the use of narrative tenses

Activity type
telling stories and identifying true and false facts

Classroom dynamics
small groups of three or four

Time taken
30 minutes

When to use
after the Review of narrative tenses, Activity 12 on page 17

Preparation
Make one copy of the worksheet for each student.

Procedure
1 Tell students to think about a past experience when something particularly good/bad happened.
2 Hand out a copy of the worksheet to each student, and ask them to make some notes about their story using the prompts provided.
3 Explain to students that they should now note down in their plan three false pieces of information.
4 Divide the class into small groups of three or four students. One student starts by being the storyteller. They begin telling their story, using their notes.

   While listening, at appropriate moments, the other students should try to think of questions in order to identify the three false pieces of information. They can make notes while listening.

   Once finished, the other students should take a couple of minutes to discuss which parts of the story they thought were untrue, and then ask the storyteller their questions. The storyteller should respond truthfully. Students then guess which elements were true and which were false.
5 This process is repeated for the other members of the group.
6 Monitor closely and give feedback on students' use of narrative tenses at the end of the activity.

2B Ten perfect pairs

Aim
to identify 'follow-on' sentences using reference words and context

Exam link
Reading and Use of English, Part 7

Activity type

matching pairs of sentences

Classroom dynamics

groups of four or five

Time taken

30 minutes

When to use

after Reading focus, Activity 7 on page 20

Preparation

Make one copy of the worksheet for each group of four or five students and cut it into cards. Keep the numbered and lettered cards in two separate sets.

Procedure

1 Divide the class into groups of four or five and give each group a set of numbered cards (1–10).

2 Ask students to work in their groups and predict the sentence that follows each of the numbered sentences. Allow about ten minutes for this.

3 Hand out the lettered sentences (A–J). Ask students to match each lettered sentence with one of the numbered sentences. Allow about 10 minutes for this, then tell students to stop and review their answers. The winning group is the group with the most correct matches.

4 Ask students how they knew which lettered sentences followed on from which numbered sentences. They should have done this using a combination of reference pronouns (e.g., *this*, *these*) and the context of the sentences. Ask students if any of their predicted sentences were similar to the lettered sentences.

Answers

1 H   2 E   3 A   4 J   5 C   6 D   7 I   8 F   9 G   10 B

2C   Who fits which role?

Aim

to review collocations related to communication

Exam link

Speaking, Part 1 and Reading and Use of English, Part 1

Activity type

discussion and sentence completion

Classroom dynamics

individual, whole class and small groups

Time taken

25 minutes

When to use

After Vocabulary focus, Activity 8, page 22

Preparation

Make one copy of the worksheet per student.

Procedure

1 Tell students to imagine that they work on the board of a new company which likes to pioneer new developments in technology. They need to complete a survey in order to decide who would be the best person for each role in the company.

2 Give a copy of the worksheet to each student and ask them to complete the missing words in questions 1–8. Point out that these are all collocations related to communication.

3 Tell students that they now need to mingle and talk to all members of the class. Students stand up with their worksheets and a pen, and survey the other members of the class. They should write the names of the person they interview in the table and ask follow-up questions. Monitor and take notes to give some feedback at the end of the activity.

4 Once completed, put students into small groups of three or four and ask them to report their findings to each other. They should give their opinions as to who in the class should be given each role, and give reasons. Each group should try and agree.

5 Each group then gives a short presentation of their 'new employees' to the whole class.

6 Give some language and content feedback at the end of the activity.

Answers

1 have
2 making/giving/delivering
3 having/holding
4 keeping
5 making
6 conversation
7 give/make
8 lead/have/hold

3A   The *it* race

Aim

To review and practise the use of introductory *it*

Exam link

Reading and Use of English, Part 4

Activity type

reading texts to identify sentences that could use introductory *it*

Classroom dynamics

pairwork, small groups

Time taken
25 minutes

When to use
after Grammar focus, Activity 5, page 30

Preparation
Make one copy of the worksheet per pair.

Procedure

1 Ask students what they consider to be the main stages of life and what the main difficulties or advantages of each stage are.

2 Put students into pairs and tell them they will have a few minutes to quickly read the four texts and check if the stages and difficulties/advantages mentioned match their own ideas.

Give a worksheet to each pair and give students up to three minutes to read it. Give them time to discuss ideas after reading before getting whole-class feedback.

3 Write this example on the board and ask students how the sentence could be rephrased using introductory *it*: *Finding time to work out when you have a full-time job is difficult.* (It is difficult to find time to work out when you have a full-time job.)

4 Now tell the students to race to find as many example sentences as possible that can be transformed using introductory *it* in the four texts. Give pairs at least 10 minutes to do this and tell them there are a possible 15 in total.

5 Go through the answers after the activity – the pairs get 10 points for each correctly transformed sentence. The winning team is the one with the most points. Explain that you wouldn't necessarily use all these examples of introductory *it* in one text.

6 Now put students into small groups of four and ask them to discuss if they agree with the comments made in the texts or not. Within their groups, they should debate what they believe to be the easiest/most difficult stage of life and why.

Suggested answers

1 It is (definitely) young children who have the easiest lives.

I find it frustrating to explain this to children while they are young.

It is a dream come true to have someone cook all your meals for you …

2 I hated it when I was expected to know what I wanted to do when I grew up.

It is ridiculous to ask a 16-year-old to choose subjects to study which affect their future choices.

It was my parents (not me) who picked which exams I was going to take.

It is thought that teenagers aren't bothered by these things.

3 It is the responsibility of being an adult that frightens me the most.

It is always said that you are more comfortable in your own skin as an adult, but what about the stress that comes with growing older?

It's exhausting to work all day to provide for yourself and other people.

It is even frightening for me to have a pet dog because of the responsibility it brings.

4 It is amusing to think about the fact we start and finish our lives in a very similar way.

It is good that elderly people spend their days just relaxing.

3B A good answer

Aim
to practise collaborative speaking

Exam link
Speaking, Part 3

Activity type
answering Speaking questions while being assessed by other students

Classroom dynamics
groups of four, divided into pairs

Time taken
20 minutes

When to use
after Speaking focus, Activity 5, page 31

Preparation
Make one copy of the worksheet for each group of four students and cut it into cards.

Procedure

1 Divide the class into groups of four and ask each group to divide into pairs (Team A and Team B). Give each team a *Team A* or *Team B* set of cards.

2 Explain that, in their teams, students are going to do a collaborative speaking activity and their responses are going to be analysed by the other team in their group.

3 Team A begins by asking Team B their Question 1. The students in Team B should take a few seconds to read the question and then answer it. They should make sure they:

- discuss all five points in the question and the summary question at the end.
- interact with each other.
- expand on what their partner says.
- speak for up to three minutes, without too much repetition or hesitation.

4 The students in Team A time the Team B students and use the checklist on their score sheet to tick the things the Team B students do. When the Team B students finish speaking, Team A should give them feedback based on how they did. They should then award points based on their answer.

5 Team B then gives their Question 1 to Team A and follows the same procedure.

6 The process is repeated with the Question 2 cards. The winning team is the one with the most points.

3C Word exchange

Aim
to identify incorrect words in sentences

Exam link
Reading and Use of English, Part 1

Activity type
identifying incorrect words in sentences and exchanging the wrong words with other students

Classroom dynamics
groups of four, divided into pairs

Time taken
20–25 minutes

When to use
after Use of English Focus, Activity 6, page 32

Preparation
Make one copy of the worksheet for each pair of students.

Procedure
1 Explain that this task focuses mainly on collocations. Make sure students know what these are and give an example (we *run a bath*, we don't *pour a bath*).

2 Divide the class into pairs and give each pair a copy of the worksheet. Ask them to fold it and only look at Part 1. Explain that in each sentence there is an example of a collocation which is either wrong, or a weak collocation (as in, there is a better word which could be used).

3 Give students around 10 minutes to look at the sentences and try to identify these words. They should underline them. Put two pairs together to create a group of four and ask them to compare their answers.

4 Now back in their original pairs, ask the students to unfold the bottom half of the worksheet. Explain that all the underlined words in the examples in Part 2 can be 'exchanged' for one of the words in their example sentences in Part 1. These should (if they have predicted correctly) be the words they have previously underlined. Give an example first: *identified* in 1 can be exchanged for *known* in F. The letter of the matching sentence should be written in the column provided.

5 Give students another 10 minutes to complete this before asking them to compare answers with another pair.

6 Encourage students to make a note of any new collocations to create their own personal collocation dictionary.

Answers
1 F: identified, known
2 D: demanded, begged
3 I: concluded, settled
4 B: figure, amount
5 J: anticipation, hope
6 E: completed, achieved
7 A: partners, colleagues
8 C: pushed, drove
9 H: produce, lead
10 G: proportion, number

4A Same word, different sentences

Aim
to review verbs and collocations

Exam link
Reading and Use of English, Part 1

Activity type
crossword and exam practice task

Classroom dynamics
pairs

Time taken
15–25 minutes

When to use
after Vocabulary focus, Activity 7, page 40

Preparation
Make one copy of the worksheet for each pair of students and cut it into three sections.

Procedure
1 Divide the class into A/B pairs and give each student their A or B part of the worksheet. Do not give out the crossword yet. Put students into AA and BB pairs. Explain that they have a set of gapped sentences. They must look at their sentences and think of all the verbs that could go in the gaps. Allow around 5–10 minutes for this.

2 Put students into A/B pairs and give them a copy of the crossword. Students now work together to look at their sentences and complete the crossword. Each verb in the

crossword must fit the sentence with that number on both sheets. For example, answer 1 in the crossword (*realised/achieved*) fits in the gap in sentence 1 on sheet A and sentence 1 on sheet B.

3 Let students continue until one group has completed their crossword or set a time limit of about 10 minutes, then check their answers. The winning pair is either the first pair to finish or the pair with the most correct answers when the time is up.

Answers

1 realised/achieved 2 exceeded 3 grabbed 4 gaining
5 follow 6 grasp 7 encountered 8 doubted 9 trust
10 seized

4B Get the message?

Aim
to practise reading for gist or the author's implied message

Exam link
Reading and Use of English, Part 5

Activity type
identifying the gist or main message

Classroom dynamics
groups of three or four, pairwork

Time taken
35 minutes

When to use
after Reading focus, Activity 4, page 42

Preparation
Make one copy of the worksheet for each group of three/four students and cut into cards.

Procedure

1 Divide your class into groups of three or four and give each group a set of cards.

2 Explain that each card contains a short paragraph about a product that has failed. The paragraph is followed by a sentence that either conveys the message being implied by the writer of the paragraph or gives the gist of that paragraph. Three of the sentences are an accurate reflection of the message implied in the paragraph but three of them are not.

3 Working in their groups, students read the paragraphs and decide which sentences are correct and which are not. They should then decide what the message *should* be for the paragraphs where the sentence is incorrect.

4 Let students do the activity for about 15 minutes, then review their answers. Award the groups one point for each message identified as being correct or incorrect and up to three points

for the message they think *should* be there (see suggested messages below).

5 Next, put students into pairs. Write the following question on the board for them to discuss: *Which of the products would you like to have seen on the market and why?*

Answers

1 Yes

2 Yes

3 No. (Suggested message: People associate some brand names with particular products.)

4 No. (Suggested message: A product can fail for no particular reason.)

5 Yes

6 No. (Suggested message: Trying to monopolise the market is not always a good thing.)

4C Modal Me

Aim
to review and practise the use of modal verbs

Exam link
Speaking, Part 1

Activity type
writing and discussing sentences

Classroom dynamics
pairwork

Time taken
25 minutes

When to use
after Grammar focus, Activity 5, page 44

Preparation
Make one copy of the worksheet per student.

Procedure

1 Write this example on the board and elicit what modal verb might be missing: *I _____ have studied languages at university.* (e.g. *should*)

2 Give each student a copy of the worksheet. Ask them to choose six topics to write about, and then write six sentences – one in each of the circles. They should write their sentences in any order they want. They should use one of the modal verbs from the box in their sentences. Point out that they do not have to use all the modal verbs. Explain that they should not show the other members of the class their sentences at this stage.

3   Monitor closely and assist students where necessary. Make notes of any common mistakes and give students some ideas if they are having problems.

4   Once finished, put students into pairs and ask them to exchange worksheets. They should take turns to guess what each sentence refers to and then discuss it for a minute (by asking and answering questions about the situation).

5   Let students talk for at least 10 minutes and then give them some feedback.

5A   You wish!

Aim
to review hypothetical structures

Activity type
completing sentences and guessing based on short conversations

Classroom dynamics
pairwork

Time taken
25–30 minutes

When to use
after Grammar focus, Activity 5, page 54

Preparation
Make one copy of the activity for each student in the class.

Procedure

1   Write this prompt on the board: *My boss would rather I …* Tell students that you are going to describe an invented situation related to this prompt and they must try to complete the sentence. Imagine the full sentence is: *My boss would rather I worked later in the evening.* Without saying the full sentence, give more information about this situation. For example, *He always gets annoyed when I leave at five, and gives me jobs to do just as I'm about to leave the office. He stays until after seven and expects his employees to do the same. I stayed until nine once and he was very happy with me.* Let students guess before giving them the correct answer.

2   Give a copy of the worksheet to each student and ask them to complete the sentences in Part A. Explain that the answers do not have to be true and can be invented. Give students at least 10 minutes to do this. Monitor closely and assist with any language.

3   Put students into A/B pairs. Student A begins by describing his/her situation without mentioning the actual completed sentence 1. Student B listens and tries to complete the sentence for their partner in Section B of the worksheet. This process is then repeated, with students taking turns to describe and guess the sentences.

4   When all the sentences have been discussed, students should compare their worksheets. The winning student is the one with the most sentences which are the same as or similar to their partner's original.

5B   Hit and *mis-*

Aim
to review the prefix *mis-* and false opposites

Exam link
Reading and Use of English, Parts 1 and 3

Activity type
completing sentences in a *Battleships*-style game

Classroom dynamics
groups of four, divided into pairs

Time taken
15–20 minutes

When to use
after Vocabulary focus, Activity 4, page 55

Preparation
Make one copy of the worksheet for each group of four students and cut it into two sections.

Procedure

1   Divide your class into groups of four and ask each group to divide into pairs (Team A and Team B). Give each team a *Team A* or *Team B* section of the activity. They should not show these to each other.

2   Explain that each team has four sentences and each sentence has two words missing. Their opposing team has the words they need to complete their sentences and they need to obtain these words from them.

3   Team A begins by giving Team B a letter+number reference from their left-hand grid (e.g. *C7*). They tick off this space on their left-hand grid so they don't repeat it. Team B looks at that space in their right-hand grid and tells Team A if there is a word there and what that word is.

4   If there is a word in that space, Team A decides which sentence that word goes into and writes it in the gap in the sentence. Play then passes to Team B, who repeat steps 3–4.

5   Steps 3–4 are repeated until one team in each group has completed all their sentences.

6   At the end of the game, you should go through the answers as a class and clarify any that students got wrong.

Answers

Team A

1 misleading, nonchalant 2 unassuming, inadvertently
3 mistrustful, misspellings 4 misconception, insipid

Team B

1 nondescript, disgruntled 2 misunderstanding, misinterpreted
3 misconception, misguided 4 misgivings, unassuming

5C Speedy pairs

Aim
to review the use of ellipsis and substitution and adverbs of opinion in reviews

Exam link
Writing, Part 2

Activity type
reading and modifying a review

Classroom dynamics
groups of four, divided into pairs.

Time taken
20-25 minutes

When to use
after Writing focus, Activity 8, page 56

Preparation
Make one copy of the worksheet for each pair.

Procedure
1   Give a copy of the worksheet to each pair of students and ask them to read it quickly in two minutes to answer the questions at the top of the activity, ignoring the gaps and underlined sections.

2   Put students into pairs and tell them that they are going to have a race to 'improve' this film review by firstly adding opinion adverbs. Give students five minutes to complete the gaps with one of the adverbs in the box before going through the answers as a class.

3   Now tell students that they are further going to improve the review by finding examples of ellipsis. Students should look at the underlined words in the text and decide which parts could be elided or not.

4   Give students 10 minutes to do this in their pairs.

5   Now bring the students' attention to the missing paragraph and ask them to complete the review by inventing more information about the film. Monitor closely in order to give both content and language feedback after the activity.

6   Ask students to read each other's paragraphs to see if they have written similar information.

Answers
The review is mainly negative.

Liked: cast, jokes.

Disliked: Plot and its predictability, cinema experience.

It'd been months since I'd been to the cinema because of work, so I was excited to get out on a Friday night and I was excited to watch Tom Grady's new film, *The Honour*. 1 **Curiously/ Oddly enough**, I had seen the trailer the week before my sister

had called to invite me, and I thought that it looked excellent. 2 **Ironically**, my one night out in a long time was spent watching something completely second-rate.

Due to its star-studded cast, *The Honour*, 3 **understandably** drew in the crowds, but we had booked in advance, so we had no problems getting good seats. 4 **Unfortunately**, a Tom Grady fan club had also decided to pick this specific Friday night to visit the cinema, so we had to endure various whooping moments and clapping moments throughout the showing.

The storyline wasn't so bad and it was entertaining and it was funny at least, if not a little predictable 5 **Curiously/Oddly enough**, the trailer had given away most of the plot, so both my sister and I already felt as though we knew what was going to happen next.

Overall, we had a good night and we enjoyed being together, but I wouldn't necessarily recommend spending money on it or recommend watching *The Honour* on the big screen. 6 **Hopefully**, my next cinema visit will be a bit more successful and a bit more worthwhile.

6A Three in a row

Aim
to review modified word forms (including prefixes and suffixes)

Exam link
Reading and Use of English, Part 3

Activity type
completing gapped sentences with correct word forms while playing a board game and answering questions

Classroom dynamics
groups of four, divided into pairs

Time taken
25 minutes

When to use
after Use of English and Listening focus, Activity 7, page 59

Preparation
Make one copy of Part A for each group (cut into squares as indicated) and a copy of the board (Section B) per group.

Procedure
1   Divide the class into groups of four and then into two teams of pairs (A and B). Hand out a board (Section B) and a set of the Part A cards to each group and ask them to place the cards and the board face up on the desk in front of them. Explain that they are going to use these Part A cards in a board game by completing the gaps with a modified version of one of the words at the top of the board.

2   Without discussing with or giving away any answers to the other pair, give the pairs five minutes to look at the Part A cards and try to think which words might go in each gap. At this point, they should not write anything down.

3   Now the students are ready to begin. The aim of the activity is for the pairs to create (or block!) a four-in-a-row line horizontally, vertically, or diagonally by placing the question cards with the same base word on the board.

   Pair A begins by choosing a card and completing the gap with the correct form of one of the base words at the top of the board (Part B). If all students agree this is correct, then Pair A can 'claim' a square by placing it on the board in the desired position.

   This process is then repeated with Pair B. They must think tactically by either starting their own four-in-a-row line, or by choosing a card to block the other pair.

   This continues until all the squares on the board are taken, or one of the pairs has managed to create a line of four. If none of the pairs manage to make a line, the pair with the most squares taken is the winner.

4   Monitor closely throughout the activity and make any notes of errors, including spelling. Go through the answers to all the cards at the end of the activity.

Suggested answers

analyse: 23 analysed, 25 analysis, 27 analysts

astonish: 8 astonishes, 21 astonishing, 26 astonishment

able: 6 disable, 19 inability, 24 unable

consider: 4 consideration, 17 considering, 22 inconsiderate

discover: 16 discoveries, 18 undiscovered, 20 discovering

excite: 13 exciting, 28 excitement, 30 excitable

hunt: 10 hunters, 12 hunted, 14 hunting

perfect: 2 perfectly, 15 perfection, 29 imperfection

power: 1 powerful 3 powerless 5 powerfully

remain: 7 remains, 9 remained, 11 remainder

6B   Opinionated!

Aim
to review comparative structures using modifying adverbs/adverbials

Exam link
Speaking, Part 4

Activity type
creating comparative sentences and then discussing them

Classroom dynamics
individual and small groups of 3–6

Time taken
25 minutes

When to use
after Grammar focus, Activity 8, page 60

Preparation
Make one copy of the worksheet (Part A and B) per group, cut up as indicated.

Procedure

1   Write this example on the board and elicit a sentence using a comparative structure. *Italian or Mexican food in my country. (popular).* Encourage the use of an adverb/adverbial phrase in the sentence, e.g. *Italian food is far more popular than Mexican food.* Ask students why they believe this and give your opinion on their statement.

2   Tell students they are going to have a discussion with other members of their group, but they will all have specific roles. Put students into small groups of 3–6 and give each student a card from part A of the worksheet. Students should take a minute to read about their character.

3   Now hand out a copy of Part B of the worksheet to each student and give them 5–10 minutes to create sentences for the six examples on the worksheet. Tell students they must use one of the adverbs/adverbials from the word cloud and that the sentences should be completed with their character from Part A in mind. Monitor closely, and help students if necessary.

4   Put students into small groups of 3–4. Taking turns, students read out one of their sentences. The other students should ask questions about their opinions and give their ideas too. Monitor and take notes in order to give feedback at the end of the activity. If students are in groups of three, this can be repeated with a different card from Part A.

6C   Absolutely right

Aim
to review modifying adverbs

Exam link
Reading and Use of English, Part 1

Activity type
completing sentences to reveal a missing word

Classroom dynamics
groups of 3–4 and pairwork

Time taken
35 minutes

When to use
after Grammar focus, Activity 8, page 65

Preparation
Make one copy of the worksheet for each group of three or four students.

Procedure

1 Divide your class into groups, and give each group a copy of the worksheet.

2 Explain that each sentence can be completed with a modifying adverb and adjective from the box, and these words should be written into the grids underneath each sentence (one letter per space). Point out that one of the adverbs will be used twice and one will be used three times. In some cases, more than one answer may be possible but only one combination of words will fit into each grid. When completed, the letters in the shaded spaces will spell out another modifying adverb.

3 Invite one student from each group to the front of the class and show them the answer to the first sentence (*absolutely enormous*). They should read this to themselves, then return to their desk.

4 They then convey the meaning of the adverb and adjective to their group but *without* using the words. The other members of their group must guess the correct adverb and adjective. When they have guessed the answer, they can write it in their grid, and another student from their group comes to you for the next answer.

5 The activity continues until one group has completed all the sentences. Check answers and ask students to use the letters in the shaded boxes to form the mystery word.

6 Now put the students into pairs and ask them to choose six example adverb-adjective collocations from the above activity. Tell them to invent some sentences using these collocations, but to gap them out. Monitor closely here in order to give some on-the-spot feedback.

7 Ask students to swap their sentences with another pair, who should attempt to fill the gaps with an adverb/adjective without looking back at their worksheets.

Answers

1 **absolutely** enormous
2 **quite** unremarkable
3 **fairly** predictable
4 **practically** impossible
5 **somewhat** surprised
6 **bitterly** disappointed
7 **absolutely** furious
8 **quite** exceptional
9 **deeply** emotional
10 **highly** plausible
11 **absolutely** perfect
12 **seriously** worried

mystery word: surprisingly

7A Collocation Bingo!

Aim
to review collocations related to sales and marketing

Exam link
Reading and Use of English, Part 1

Activity type
completing sentences

Classroom dynamics
groups of four and pairwork

Time taken
20 minutes

When to use
after Grammar and Vocabulary focus, Activity 14, page 71

Preparation
Make one copy of the worksheet for each group of four students, cut up as indicated.

Procedure

1 Tell students they are going to play a game in groups of four. Put students into groups of four and give each student in the group Part B of the worksheet. Allow students a few minutes to consider what the missing words could be. They should not discuss this with the other group members, nor should they write anything down yet.

2 Now hand out a set of cards from Part A to each group. They should place them face down on the table. Students take turns to pick up a card and read the word aloud. All of the students in the group then check their worksheet to see if one of the words fits in a gap. If they think so, they should take turns to read the sentences to their group. If all agree the word fits, the students should write them in the gaps.

3 This process is repeated until one of the students completes the full card and shouts 'Bingo!'. Monitor closely and help if necessary.

Answers

1 customers 2 mail 3 Loyal 4 marketing/retail
5 campaign 6 rapport 7 marketing/retail/sales
8 campaign/product 9 Retail 10 marketing/campaign
11 customers 12 mail 13 sales 14 mail 15 retail
16 loyal

PHOTOCOPIABLE ACTIVITIES

7B Make your pitch

Aim
to practise using language of agreement and disagreement in a collaborative/decision-making task

Exam link
Speaking, Part 3

Activity type
choosing a motto for a new product and promoting that product to the class

Classroom dynamics
groups

Time taken
25–30 minutes

When to use
after Speaking Focus, Activity 7, page 76

Preparation
Make one copy of the worksheet and cut it into cards.

Procedure
1 Divide your class into six groups and give each group a card. Explain that they work for an advertising company and have been asked to come up with an advertising campaign for a new product or service. So far, their company has come up with four possible mottos for this product, which they will see on their card.

2 In their teams, they should discuss the advantages and disadvantages of each motto on their card, using language of agreement and disagreement where relevant. If they are not happy with any of the mottos, they can make up their own. Allow about 10 minutes for this, monitoring the groups to make sure that everybody is participating and that no students are dominating the discussion.

3 When the time is up, tell them that they are going to promote their product/service to the rest of the class. In their groups, they should decide what they are going to say and how they are going to say it. The presentation should follow this structure.
   * What is the product?
   * What type of message do you want to convey with your product?
   * Who is your target market?
   * What types of advertising will be used to promote the product?
   * Why is this the best type of advertising for the product?
   * What is the motto and why have you chosen it?

4 In their groups, students should decide who is going to say what during the presentation.

5 Taking turns, the groups should present their product. When all the groups have finished, groups should award points to each presentation, based on how persuasive they thought the advertising pitch was (5 = very persuasive, 1 = not at all persuasive). Ask groups to explain why they awarded the points they did. The winning group is the group with the most points.

7C Just supposing …

Aim
to practise different forms of conditionals

Exam link
Speaking, Part 4

Activity type
making decisions based on moral dilemmas

Classroom dynamics
groups of 3–4

Time taken
30–40 minutes

When to use
after Grammar focus, Activity 5, page 77

Preparation
Make one copy of the worksheet for each group of three or four students, cut into cards and shuffle.

Procedure
1 Tell your class that you are going to give them a dilemma to think about. The dilemma is this: *It is dark, and you are driving home from work along a lonely stretch of road. You see a desperate-looking young couple hitch-hiking by the side of the road. Do you stop to pick them up?* Ask students if they would stop and to qualify their answers using a conditional sentence. For example: *It depends – if there was someone else in the car with me, I probably would but if I was on my own, I wouldn't.*

2 Give each group a set of cards, which they should place face down on the desk. All the students in the group should pick a card and take a few minutes to prepare their answer to the dilemma. They then take turns to read out the dilemma on the card, saying what they would do and qualifying their answer with a conditional sentence. The other students should join in the discussion, giving their ideas too.

3 Monitor closely at this stage of the lesson, jotting down errors made with the conditional structures, or making note of other advanced conditional structures that could have been used instead. Let this continue for about 20 minutes, then ask students to stop.

4 Now put students into pairs from different groups, and ask them briefly to report back which dilemmas they discussed and the best answers they heard from other group members.

5 Give the class some language and content feedback.

8A Four texts

Aim
to practise reading for detail

Exam link
Reading and Use of English, Parts 6 and 7

Activity type
arranging sentences to form complete texts, then answering questions about the texts

Classroom dynamics
groups of four

Time taken
20 minutes

When to use
after Reading focus, Activity 7, page 84

Preparation
Make one copy of the worksheet for each group of four students. Cut it into cards.

Procedure

1 Divide your class into groups of four and ask each group to divide into pairs. Give one pair the cards for Andy Watson and Alice Griffin, and the other pair the cards for Olivia Jenkins and Peter Carter. Give each group a Questions card, but ask them to put this face down on the table until later.

2 Explain that each card contains a short text in which someone gives their opinion on moving or living abroad. The text has been broken up into five sections (A–E) and these sections are in the wrong order. Working in their pairs, they should put these sections in order. They should then decide if the three statements (1–3) which follow each text are true or false, or if the information is not given.

3 When they have done this, the pairs should swap their texts to read through and check if they agree with the order.

4 Once students have all agreed that their text sections are in the correct order, they then look at the Questions card and answer the questions. At this stage, they can look at all the text cards together. The first group to correctly answer all of their questions is the winner.

Answers
Andy Watson: C, A, E, D, B (1 true, 2 not given, 3 false)
Alice Griffin: B, E, C, D, A (1 true, 2 not given, 3 true)
Olivia Jenkins: C, E, B, D, A (1 not given, 2 true, 3 not given)
Peter Carter: E, A, D, B, C (1 true, 2 not given, 3 false)
Questions
1 Alice Griffin 2 Andy Watson 3 Peter Carter 4 Olivia Jenkins

8B Interviews with the famous

Aim
to review reported speech, reporting verbs and structures

Exam link
Speaking, Part 3; Writing, Part 2

Activity type
interviewing and reporting, article writing

Classroom dynamics
pairwork and small groups

Time taken
40 minutes

When to use
after Grammar focus, Activity 4, page 87

Preparation
Make a copy of Part A cut up as indicated (one card per pair). Make one copy of Part B per student.

Procedure

1 Tell students that they are going to role-play being researchers from a university who want to create and conduct interviews with different famous people in order to find out the answer to the following questions: *What are the secrets of the rich and famous?*
What are the best ways to become and stay successful?

2 Put students into pairs and give each pair a different role from Part A of the worksheet. Now hand out a copy of Part B of the worksheet to each student, and give them a few minutes to read through it. They should think of at least 3–4 more questions for the interview which will help them answer their research questions.

3 Students take turns to interview each other. Give them around 5–10 minutes to do this, in the roles of their famous person. Students should take some brief notes in order to remember what was said during the interview. During the interview, the interviewer should always consider the research questions, as they will need to answer these later.

4 Put students into new pairs. Give them 5–10 minutes to tell each other about the famous person they interviewed and what they said. They should collate ideas here and discuss which are best, using their interview notes to support their ideas. This discussion should finish with the students answering the research questions.

5 Tell students they are going to write a short report on the research questions, using their research from the interviews. Give students some time to plan what they want to include and then write the text together. Monitor closely and take notes in order to give some feedback at the end of the activity.

6 Ask students to read each other's reports and make comments on the research.

8C City of the year

Aim
to practise using an appropriate style in proposal writing

Exam link
Writing, Part 2 (proposals)

Activity type
planning and creating a proposal; making a presentation

Classroom dynamics
small groups

Time taken
60 minutes

When to use
after Writing focus, Activity 6, page 88

Preparation
Make one copy of the worksheet per student.

Procedure
1 Tell students that they all work for different local councils hoping to win *City of the Year*. The winning city gets extra investment to make improvements to their city/town.

    Put students into small groups and ask them to choose a city/town. It can be real or invented, but each group must have somewhere different.

2 Tell students to imagine they are going to have an important meeting in which they will discuss what to include in their proposal to the board of *City of the Year*. Give a copy of the worksheet to each student and tell them they have around 15–20 minutes to make notes in the boxes provided. Encourage one member of the group to run the meeting.

3 When the meeting has finished, tell them they will now write a proposal. This should be written by the whole group, with all students involved in the writing process. Encourage students to divide the proposal up into four paragraphs, which different group members could be responsible for:
    * Introduction (information about the city)
    * Possible benefits
    * Proposal as to how the extra money could be spent
    * Recommendation to the board.

    Give students another 20 minutes to write their proposals. Monitor closely and help if necessary.

4 Tell students they will now choose who should win *City of the Year* by reading all of the proposals (they cannot choose their own city!). Ask all the groups to pass their proposals to the group sitting to their right. Give them five minutes to read and discuss the proposal. When the five minutes are up, call *change* and each group should pass the proposal to the next group.

5 When all proposals have been read, give a few minutes for students to make their decision as to who had the most convincing one. Have a class vote to decide who wins the *City of the Year*.

9A As quickly as you can

Aim
to review expressions with *mind* and *brain*

Exam link
Reading and Use of English, Parts 1 and 4

Activity type
matching and completion game

Classroom dynamics
pairs and groups of four

Time taken
20 minutes

When to use
after Use of English and Vocabulary focus, Activity 8, page 91

Preparation
Make one copy of the worksheet for each group of four, cut up into two.

Procedure
1 Put the students into groups of four and then divide them into two teams (A and B).

2 Give each pair a *Team A* or *Team B* card. Explain that each team has eight prompt sentences (1–8) and eight responses to the other team's prompts (A–H). Each response is missing an expression with *mind or brain*, which can be found in the word box. The aim is for teams to match their responses with the other team's prompt sentences using one of the expressions with *mind or brain*.

3 Students in Team A take it in turns to read out one of their prompt sentences. Team B must listen and work together to identify the correct response and correct expression with *mind or brain*. They write their answers down on the sheet, e.g.*1 C never mind*.

4 When they have finished, the roles are reversed, with Team B giving the prompt sentences and Team A choosing the responses and the correct expressions with *mind* or *brain*.

5 Review all the answers and award points. Teams get one point for each correct response and one point for each correct expression with *mind or brain*. The winning team is the team with the most points.

6 (Optional:) Ask students to write their own gapped sentences, which they then swap with another member of the group and try to complete.

Answer

Team A

1 C mind your language
2 E mind-boggling
3 D bear that in mind
4 A wouldn't mind
5 H brain damage
6 G brainstorm
7 F childminder
8 B brain scan

Team B

1 C never mind
2 B Mind you
3 E if you don't mind my asking
4 H mind reader
5 A brain teaser
6 G brain drain
7 F brainwave
8 D brainwashed

9B I was going to, but …

Aim
to practise using the future in the past

Exam link
Speaking, Part 1

Activity type
talking and asking questions about the past

Classroom dynamics
pairwork

Time taken
30 minutes

When to use
after Grammar focus, Activity 6, page 92

Preparation
Make one copy of the worksheet per pair, cut in two.

Procedure

1 Put students into A/B pairs and give them their part of the worksheet. Tell them to read the statements (1–8) at the top. Individually, students should choose six of the statements to answer, then write one or two words to answer these in one of the circles. They should not write full sentences at this point.

2 Explain to the students that they are now going to show each other the information in the circles and ask extra questions about them, e.g. *Who is Martin?* in order to work out or guess what the information in the boxes is referring to.

3 Allow students around 20 minutes for the activity. Monitor and make notes on how students talk about the future in the past, in order to give some language and content feedback after the activity.

9C Invented words

Aim
to practise working out the meaning of vocabulary from context

Exam link
Reading and Use of English, Parts 5–8

Activity type
reading sentences and guessing the meaning of invented words

Classroom dynamics
small groups

Time taken
20 minutes

When to use
after Reading focus, Activity 6, page 94

Preparation
Make one copy of the worksheet per group, cut up as indicated.

Procedure

1 Write this sentence on the board and underline the invented word: *My friends didn't come to my party, and I felt really glopped.* Ask students if they know the word and if so, what it means (they shouldn't know what it means because it's completely invented!). Ask students to take a few minutes with the person sitting next to them to try to work out what the underlined word might mean. Elicit from the students that *glopped* is likely to be an adjective with a negative connotation, and could mean *sad/upset/disappointed*.

   Explain that you have invented the word and it doesn't exist, but that it was still possible, using the clues in the sentence, to work out the meaning.

2 Put students into small groups and explain they are going to compete against the other groups in the class to work out the possible meaning of some other invented words. The winning team is the one that guesses the most. Hand out a set of cards to each group and place them face down on the table. When you say *go*, they should take a card and try to guess the meaning of the invented words from context.

3 At the end of the activity, check the answers and go through some of the processes as to how the students worked out the meaning.

PHOTOCOPIABLE ACTIVITIES

Suggested answers

1 odd/strange/weird/surreal
2 crossword/puzzle
3 technology
4 breakthrough
5 self-conscious
6 picking/choosing
7 innocent
8 anecdote

Answers

1 Whichever/Whatever
2 Whenever
3 However
4 Whoever
5 Wherever

10A Perfect advice

Aim

to review *whatever*, *whoever*, *however*, etc.

Exam link

Reading and Use of English, Parts 1 and 2

Activity type

completing sentences with pronouns and writing advice

Classroom dynamics

pairs and groups

Time taken

30 minutes

When to use

after Vocabulary and Grammar focus, Activity 10, page 103

Preparation

Make one copy of the worksheet for each pair.

Procedure

1 Divide the class into pairs and give each pair a copy of the worksheet. Give students five minutes to complete the sentences in Part 1 with one of the pronouns in the box. Check answers as a class.

2 Now ask students to consider in their pairs what they would like advice on. Provide/elicit some ideas, for example, *making new friends*, *lowering stress levels at school/work*, etc. Give students a few minutes to think of something together, and to write the topic on Part 2 of their worksheet.

3 Explain to students that it is their turn to write some advice for each other. Ask the students to swap their paper on which the advice topic is written with another pair in the class. Now give students at least 10 minutes to create advice for the other students. Monitor closely at this point and give help if necessary.

4 Once completed, students should give their advice back to the original pair. They should discuss the advice, ask questions, and say whether they agree or not.

10B Compatibility

Aim

to practise reading for general meaning, the main idea, and attitudes

Exam link

Reading and Use of English, Part 5

Activity type

reading to find pairs of people who have something in common

Classroom dynamics

pairs or small groups of three

Time taken

20–25 minutes

When to use

after Reading focus, Activity 5, page 104

Preparation

Make one copy of the worksheet for each pair or group of three students, cut into cards.

Procedure

1 Divide your class into pairs or small groups of three and give each group a set of cards.

2 Explain that the cards contain short monologues by ten people, each one on the theme of work. Each person has something in common with another person in the set. The aim of the activity is to match these people with a compatible partner.

3 Allow your groups about ten minutes to read through their cards, discuss and identify the people who have something in common.

4 When the time is up, read out the following questions, pausing between each one. On a separate sheet of paper, students write down the names of the people.

   1 *Can you name two people who place great demands on themselves?*

   2 *Can you name two people who always come up with great ideas?*

   3 *Can you name two people who work well under pressure?*

   4 *Can you name two people who work well in collaboration with others?*

   5 *Can you name two people who are an inspiration to others?*

5 Review students' answers and award one point for each correctly matched pair. The winning group is the group with the most points. Encourage students to identify the clues in the text which led them to their answers.

Answers
1 Ron + Jane
2 Amelia + Ollie
3 John + Teresa
4 Roberta + Mark
5 Jo + Alan

10C Participle clause match

Aim
to review participle clauses and past forms

Exam link
Reading and Use of English, Part 4

Activity type
completing participle clauses in full sentences

Classroom dynamics
pairwork

Time taken
20 minutes

When to use
after Grammar focus, Activity 6, page 108

Preparation
Make one copy of the worksheet for each pair. Cut up Part A into cards. Cut up Part B into Student A and B sections.

Procedure
1 Divide the class into pairs (Student A and B) and hand out a set of Part A cards, which students should place face down on the table in front of them. Explain that these cards form part of some sentences and that the aim is to complete sentences as quickly as possible.

2 Give Student A and B their corresponding part of the worksheet. Students take turns to turn over a Part A card and read it aloud. Both students then look through the sentences on their worksheet in order to find an example in which it can be used. The student who finds the sentence the most quickly wins a point. Students should read the sentence to their partner, but not write anything on the worksheet yet. If there is a disagreement as to whether the sentence is correct/incorrect, you should be consulted.

3 This is repeated until all of the cards have been turned over and the sentences are complete. The student with the most points at the end of the activity is the winner.

4 Ask students to place the Part A cards face down again and, together, try to remember the participles missing from the sentences. These should be written in the gaps provided.

Go through the answers as a class at the end of the task.

Answers
A1/B3 Having offered
A2/B8 Needing
A3/B1 Not expecting
A4/B7 Not having seen
A5/B5 Being
A6/B2 Wanting
A7/B6 Walking
A8/B4 Being convinced/Convinced

11A The right word, the right form

Aim
to review words to describe emotions

Exam link
Reading and Use of English, Part 3

Activity type
dominoes-style sentence matching and completion activity

Classroom dynamics
groups of three

Time taken
15–20 minutes

When to use
after Vocabulary and Use of English focus, Activity 3, page 112

Preparation
Make one copy of the worksheet for each group of three students. Cut it into cards along the dotted lines (do *not* cut along the solid lines) and keep in three separate sets (Student A, Student B and Student C).

Procedure
1 Divide your class into groups of three and give each student in the group a *Student A*, *Student B* or *Student C* set of cards. They should not show their cards to one another.

2 Explain that their cards contain short situations or conversations, broken into two sections. The aim of the activity is to match the sections together (the left-hand sections of each card follow on from the right-hand section of a different card). At the same time, students must also complete the sentences with the words to describe emotions. The same word must be used in both sections of a situation but in a different form (e.g. a noun + an adjective).

3 Student A has the *Start* card. He/She reads out the sentence on the right-hand side of that card (*When his chair collapsed under him, he went bright red with …*). As a group, the three students discuss which word might be missing. Student A writes this word in the gap and puts the card down.

The other two students decide who has the follow-on sentence for Student A's sentence (in this case, it is student B's number 14). Student B reads this out, then together they decide if it is the correct follow-on sentence and agree on the word form. Student B places his/her card alongside the first card.

4 Play continues with the next square to the one students have just filled in, which in this case is 11. Students repeat the steps with the other cards. The winning group is the group that correctly match all of their cards and complete all of the sentences first.

Answers

1 + 14 embarrassment/embarrassed

11 + 16 frustrating/frustration

7 + 20 astonishment/astonishing

6 + 10 contentment/content

5 + 15 exhilaration/exhilarating

2 + 4 bitter/bitterness

19 + 21 delight/delighted

17 + 22 hysteria/hysterical

3 + 12 indifferent/indifference

8 + 13 amusing/amusement

18 + 9 confusion/confused

11B A myth or not?

Aim

to review passive forms

Exam link

Speaking, Part 4

Activity type

completing sentences using passive forms

Classroom dynamics

pairs and groups of four

Time taken

25 minutes

When to use

after Grammar focus, Activity 6, page 115

Preparation

Make one copy of the worksheet for each pair, cutting it where indicated.

Procedure

1 Divide the class into pairs, A and B, and give each pair the corresponding part of the worksheet. Tell students they are going to read some statements with gaps which they will later discuss in groups.

Firstly, ask students to complete the gaps using a passive form. Give them around 5–10 minutes to do this. Go through the answers with the class and make sure they are correct.

2 Give students a few minutes in their pairs to now consider the sentences and if they agree with them or not.

3 Put two pairs together to create groups of 4. Pair A starts by reading out sentence 1 from their worksheet. As a group, the students discuss if they agree with the statement or not and what they know about it. They should give their own opinion and listen carefully to what the other members of the groups say in order to respond appropriately.

4 This process is then repeated with sentence 1 from Pair B's worksheet. Taking turns, the groups should read their sentences aloud and discuss them.

Monitor carefully, but do not intervene. Make a note of any errors (especially with the passive forms) in order to give feedback after the class.

Answers

Student A

1 is said, can be influenced

2 have been referred to

3 is sought/is being sought

4 are taken, are considered, have been painted

Student B

A are regularly told, should be given

B are thought

C were targeted, aren't shown/aren't being shown

D is believed

11C Can you continue?

Aim

to review linking adverbials

Exam link

Speaking, Parts 2–4 and Reading and Use of English, Part 2

Activity type

card game requiring students to continue sentences using linking adverbials

Classroom dynamics

groups of four divided into pairs

Time taken

20–25 minutes

When to use

after Grammar focus, Activity 6, page 119

Preparation

Make one copy of the worksheet for each group of four students, cut into two sets of cards.

Procedure

1 Divide your class into groups of four and give each group two sets of cards: the shaded (adverbial) cards and the white (sentence) cards. They should spread these out face-down on their desk. Ask the groups to split into pairs.

2 Explain that the aim of the activity is to be the first pair to collect ten of the sentence (white) cards.

3 One pair turns over one of the sentence cards, and reads the sentence on it. They then turn over one of the adverbial cards and decide if they can use the linking adverbial on it to add another sentence that is relevant to the one on their sentence card. For example: *I usually dress very casually at the weekend. + On the other hand, I like to dress smartly when I'm at work.* In some cases, it may not be possible to add another relevant sentence with the adverbial they pick.

4 The other pair decide if the follow-on sentence works in that context. If they decide it does, the first pair keep their sentence card and return the adverbial card to the desk (face down). Both pairs should try to remember what is on that card, as it may be used again. You might want to make a rule that adverbials can only be used a certain number of times so that they are not overused. If the first student pair are unable to give a follow-on sentence, *both* cards are returned to the desk. Note that in any dispute as to the relevance and grammatical accuracy of the follow-on sentence, students should consult you.

5 Steps 3 and 4 are repeated, with the second pair of students picking a sentence card and an adverbial card and seeing if they can add a follow-on sentence.

6 The activity continues until one pair has ten sentence cards and so becomes the winner.

12A   That's what you need

Aim

to practise listening for specific information

Exam link

Listening, Part 2

Activity type

listening to monologues and completing sentences with the correct word to reveal a 'mystery' word

Classroom dynamics

Groups and whole class

Time taken

20 minutes

When to use

after Listening focus, Activity 5, page 122

Preparation

Make one copy of the first page of the worksheet and cut it into cards. Make seven copies of the second page of the activity.

Procedure

1 Divide your class into seven groups and give each group a copy of the second page of the activity. Give the group five minutes to look at the gaps and guess what the missing words could be.

2 Now give one student in each group one of the cards. They should not show this card to the others in their group.

3 Explain to the class that they are going to hear seven short monologues read by a student from each group. They should listen carefully and complete each sentence with one word, which they will hear in the monologue. They should then look at the words they have written and take the letters indicated by the numbers after each sentence. They should use these letters to complete the final sentence with the mystery word.

4 The student with card number 1 comes to the front of the class and reads out their monologue twice. They then rejoin their group. The groups decide what the answer is for sentence 1 (note that the student who read out the monologue cannot help their team).

5 Step 3 is repeated for monologues 2–7.

6 Review the answers. Groups get one point for each correct answer and three points for revealing the mystery word in the final sentence.

Answers

1 discouraged
2 disappointment
3 concern
4 inspiration
5 respect
6 opposition
7 confusing
mystery word: dedication

12B   Crossword links

Aim

to review multi-part verbs

Exam link

Reading and Use of English, Parts 1, 2, and 4

Activity type

creating sentences with gaps as clues for a crossword

Classroom dynamics
individual, pairwork, small groups

Time taken
30 minutes

When to use
after Listening and Vocabulary focus, Activity 11, page 123

Preparation
Make one copy of the worksheet per pair (divided into Student A and B). Do <u>not</u> cut on the dotted line beneath the crossword in preparation.

Procedure
1 Put students into A/B pairs. Give the corresponding part of the worksheet to each student. Ask students not to look at each other's papers.

2 Ask students to try to recall the meaning of the part verbs on their crossword. They shouldn't write anything at this point. Write this example on the board and ask students to look at it: *When a machine (e.g. a car or computer) stops working.* Give students a minute in their groups to guess what the multi-part verb is. Elicit the answer (*break down*).

3 Students should now create their own clues for the words in their crossword, writing them at the bottom of the worksheet. Monitor closely here to ensure the clues are well written and are clear.

4 Once completed, ask students to cut or tear along the dotted line and give their partner the clues they have just written. Students should then try to complete their crossword by using the clues. The winner is the student that completed the crossword first in each pair.

12C Inversion chat

Aim
using emphasis with inversion

Exam link
Speaking, Part 1

Activity type
answering and discussing questions using inversion for emphasis

Classroom dynamics
pairwork

Time taken
20 minutes

When to use
after Grammar focus, Activity 6, page 126

Preparation
Make one copy of the worksheet per pair. Cut into A and B sections and cut Part B into cards.

Procedure
1 Divide the class into A/B pairs and give each student the grid from Part A which they should place face up on the desk in front of them.

Ask students to go through the adverbs/adverbials on the sheet in order to recall their meaning. Then hand out a set of cards (from Part B) to each pair, which they should place face down in front of them.

2 Student A takes a card and asks Student B the questions. Student B answers and, while doing so, should try to use one or more of the adverbials from Part A. If Student B successfully does this, they can put a tick next to the adverbial.

3 This continues until all the questions have been asked and answered. Explain to students that the adverbials can be used more than once, so some boxes may have more than one tick. Monitor closely and make notes in order to give feedback at the end of the activity. The winning student is the one with the most ticks at the end of the activity.

1 Talk about one of the following:
- **A** something **you have changed** in your house recently.
- **B** something **you are changing** in your house at the moment.
- **C** something **you will have changed** in your house in the next year.

2 Talk about one of the following:
- **A** a place **you have visited** many times in your city or town.
- **B** a place **you are visiting** in your city in the near future.
- **C** a place **you have been visiting** in your city since you were a child.

3 Talk about one of the following:
- **A** Something that **will have changed** in your home town or city by the time you have retired.
- **B** Something that **is changing** in your town/city.
- **C** Something that **has changed** in your town/city in the last 10 years.

4 Talk about one of the following:
- **A** a tradition the people in your country **will still be upholding** long into the future.
- **B** a tradition the people in your country **have started upholding** in recent years.
- **C** a tradition the people in your country **have stopped upholding** recently.

5 Talk about one of the following:
- **A** something **you have been planning** to do for a while.
- **B** something **you planned** to do in the past, but never did.
- **C** something you **have always planned** to do that you will have done by this time next year.

6 Talk about one of the following:
- **A** something **you've been spending** a lot of time on.
- **B** something **you are spending** a lot of time on at the moment.
- **C** something **you will be spending** a lot of time on in the future.

7 Talk about one of the following:
- **A** something in your life **you have wanted** to give up recently.
- **B** something in your life **you are giving up.**
- **C** something in your life **you will have stopped doing** in 20 years' time.

8 Talk about one of the following:
- **A** a group or society **you are part of** in your city or town.
- **B** a group or society **you have been a part of** since you were young.
- **C** a group or society **you will be part of** in the near future.

9 Talk about one of the following:
- **A** something **you have done** for your community that you are proud of.
- **B** something **you are doing** for your community that you are proud of.
- **C** something **you will have done** for your community that will make you proud in the future.

A FREE	LONG	**B** STANDING	RUN
C DOWN	CUT	**D** PRICE	MIDDLE
E AGED	SELF	**F** ESTEEM	FAR
G FETCHED	LIFE	**H** SAVING	PART
I TIME	BUILT	**J** UP	HIGH
K RISE	WORLD	**L** RENOWNED	PURPOSE
M BUILT	LAND	**N** MARK	INTEREST

1 **As** the number of inhabitants increases, the need for …

2 **As long as** we have enough money, we should invest more in …

3 **Provided** there is sufficient time, we could …

4 Closing down smaller schools and increasing class sizes is not beneficial. **Nor is** …

5 **Whereas** it's a good idea to encourage people to use public transport rather than their own cars to cut pollution, firstly we must …

6 **Since** this is a relatively small city, we need to consider …

How did you feel?

When?

Any other information

A past experience when something good/bad happened.

Where?

Who were you with?

What happened?

Why was it good/bad?

1
The article says that the screen on Tekfone's new mobile isn't very sensitive and compared with some other models it can be a bit slow downloading large files.

2
The person reviewing the forthcoming CherryPhone in *Technology Today* began with an in-depth analysis of some of its good and bad points.

3
The presenter opened the programme by explaining that he was going to show the viewers how mobile phone tariffs work and why they vary so much from network to network.

4
The shop assistant was very helpful, even transferring the SIM card over to my new phone.

5
The presenter gave examples of people who had received huge phone bills in spite of signing up to package deals offered by their network.

6
Many callers to the radio show complained that texting, and in particular textspeak, is killing the written language.

7
My friend Chris, who's a bit of a techie and knows about these things, gave me a few tips for maximising the battery life on my new phone.

8
The conference on the future of information technology was split into five main sections.

9
When my new phone stopped working, the man in the shop told me that I would need to restore the factory settings, which would mean losing all the apps I had downloaded.

10
When social networking websites first appeared in the 1990s, very few people thought they would catch on.

A
Somewhat surprisingly, what followed instead was a vicious exposé on the way some phone companies rip people off with hidden charges.

B
However, such is the impact they have had since then, it is almost impossible to imagine living without them.

C
The reason for this, he said, is that it's easy to accidentally end up using another network which does not honour the agreement you have signed up to.

D
This might well be true but none of them had any proof to back it up, and I think it's wrong to make claims without having all the evidence.

E
She went on to compare it with some similar models currently available, using a team of expert volunteers to test it.

F
The most interesting one was a discussion on the way in which more advanced smartphones will have a major impact on the way we do business.

G
This was not what I wanted to hear, of course, especially as I had been hoping for a solution that wouldn't inconvenience me so much.

H
Despite these shortcomings, I still think it's the one I'll go for, since it seems to be the most user-friendly one available.

I
'Shut down apps when you're not using them,' she said. 'And the same goes for 3G and 4G when you don't need them. And don't charge it to full each time.'

J
Then he demonstrated how, with just one key, I could block unwanted emails and texts with something called *SpamShield*.

Survey

Who fits which role?
✔ CEO of the company.
✔ Head of sales.
✔ Head of marketing and advertising.

✔ Responsible for fundraising.
✔ Head of tech.

Who ...	Name	Extra information
1 loves to .... a gossip?		
2 doesn't mind .... speeches in front of lots of people?		
3 enjoys .... debates about controversial topics?		
4 is good at .... conversations going and hates awkward silences?		
5 is not a fan of .... small talk?		
6 regularly has to make polite .... as part of his/her job?		
7 has to .... presentations at work or university/school?		
8 likes to .... discussions?		

1

So, which stage of our lives is the easiest and most stress-free? Young children definitely have the easiest lives, don't you think? However, explaining this to children while they are young is something I find frustrating. They just don't understand how good they have it! Having someone cook all your meals for you, take you where you want to go, and letting you spend all day with your friends is a dream come true.

2

At school, I really hated it when I was expected to know what I wanted to do when I grew up. Asking a 16-year-old to choose subjects which affect their future choices is ridiculous. My parents picked which exams I was going to take, not me. I was too immature, but I remember being really stressed about it. People think that teenagers aren't bothered by these things. But believe me, they are.

3

The responsibility of being an adult frightens me the most. People always say you are more comfortable in your own skin as an adult, but what about the stress that comes with growing older? And having a family? Wow! Working all day to provide for yourself and other people is exhausting, both physically and mentally. Even having a pet dog frightens me because of the responsibility it brings.

4

Thinking about the fact we start and finish our lives in a very similar way is amusing. Like children, old people don't really have to worry about much. Elderly men and women spend their days just relaxing, and that's good. If you're careful with your money when you're working, this last stage in our lives could truly be the best.

Team A: Question 1 for Team B

How might these things have a negative impact on a young person? (2 minutes)

- school/college exams
- overly ambitious parents
- peer pressure to do things they might not usually do
- too much freedom to do what they want
- the environment in which they live

Which of these things would have the biggest negative impact on a young person? (1 minute)

Team B: Question 1 for Team A

How might these factors have a positive influence on a young person's sense of well-being? (2 minutes)

- having plenty of hobbies or interests
- having a large circle of friends
- getting out and about as much as possible
- spending time with their family
- balancing work/study time and leisure time

Which of these factors would have the biggest positive influence on a young person's sense of well-being? (1 minute)

Team A: Question 2 for Team B

How might these life skills help a young adult get on in life? (2 minutes)

- being able to drive
- being able to speak two or more languages
- computer literacy
- good manners
- being able to socialise easily

Which of these skills would be the most beneficial? (1 minute)

Team B: Question 2 for Team A

Which of these qualities should a young person possess if they are to succeed at work? (2 minutes)

- ambition
- the ability to learn from their mistakes
- self-discipline
- being a team player
- enjoying the work they do

Which of these qualities would be the most useful? (1 minute)

Team A: Score sheet for Team B

Did they …

- discuss all five points in the question?
- interact with each other?
- expand on what their partner said?
- speak for three minutes without too much repetition or hesitation?
- provide a satisfactory answer to the question at the end?

Total:
Question 1: ....

Question 2: ....

Team B: Score sheet for Team A

Did they …

- discuss all five points in the question?
- interact with each other?
- expand on what their partner said?
- speak for three minutes without too much repetition or hesitation?
- provide a satisfactory answer to the question at the end?

Total:
Question 1: ....

Question 2: ....

Part 1

		Match
1	Little is identified about the author's early life, apart from the fact that he spent his childhood in Tanzania.	
2	I demanded my tutor for more time to complete my assignment but he was adamant that I handed it in on the due date.	
3	This dispute has been going on for weeks now and I personally feel it's time we concluded it once and for all.	
4	Most people feel that the council has spent a considerable figure of money on promoting tourism in the city without any positive benefits.	
5	The local economy has suffered a great deal since the closure of several major companies in the town and there's very little anticipation of it recovering in the near future.	
6	Going to my cousin's wedding in Essex last week meant that I finally completed my ambition of visiting every county in the country!	
7	Generally speaking, I get on well with the partners in my department at work, even if we don't agree on everything.	
8	Incessant and noisy road works outside our house eventually pushed me to write a letter of complaint to my local council.	
9	It is generally believed that reducing the speed limit in cities will produce to fewer accidents on the roads.	
10	A proportion of students in my class have complained that they are being given too much work and not enough time to do it all.	

-------------------------------- **FOLD** --------------------------------

Part 2

A	My brother Tim is one of three <u>colleagues</u> in a law firm which specialises in company law.
B	Asked to estimate how much it now costs to bring up a child, we did our sums and the <u>amount</u> we arrived at was £200,000.
C	Eve wanted to become a pilot but her parents, who had other ideas for her, <u>drove</u> her towards a career in medicine.
D	He quickly discovered that training to become a professional musician <u>begged</u> a lot of dedication and hard work.
E	The director recently <u>achieved</u> filming his 29th feature film, probably the last in his long and illustrious career.
F	Having <u>known</u> the cause of the disease, scientists then set about finding a cure.
G	Research shows that people in their thirties spend a larger <u>number</u> of their income on entertainment than any other age group.
H	Increased investment in industry will <u>lead</u> a feeling of confidence in the economy.
I	After carrying out a thorough examination of the building, the investigating officer <u>settled</u> that the probable cause of the fire was faulty electrical wiring.
J	My cousin is coming over from the US next month to spend a couple of weeks with us, so we've decorated the spare bedroom in <u>hope</u> of his visit.

A

1 She's an excellent musician but she hasn't .... her full potential yet.
2 Everyone agreed that the police had .... their authority by randomly stopping and searching people in the street.
3 I really wish that I had .... the chance to travel while I was young.
4 By .... a better understanding of the cause of the disease, we may have a chance of finding a cure.
5 I'm not sure whether to study law or .... my true feelings and pursue a career in the theatre.
6 I'm prepared to .... any opportunity to help me get a good, well-paid job.
7 The expedition team .... serious problems when two of its members were injured.
8 The minister promised he would reduce crime and unemployment but we all .... his word.
9 I don't think we can .... these figures until we've done our own research.
10 Initial reports confirm that the military have .... control of the television station.

B

1 Fortunately, Tim .... his ambition of becoming a professional footballer.
2 James's remarkable performance in 'Romeo and Juliet' .... all our expectations.
3 When Susie asked me if I wanted to go to the concert, I naturally .... at the invitation.
4 We managed to break the user's password but .... access to his personal files was more difficult than we had anticipated.
5 I've never been much of a leader, preferring to .... the crowd and do whatever I'm told.
6 At first, we failed to .... the significance of what he was saying to us.
7 In the men's tennis final, Andy Murray .... stiff opposition from Novak Djokovic.
8 I knew that I would succeed where everyone else had failed – I never .... myself.
9 I can't tell you what to do but I think you should .... your instincts and do what you think is right.
10 If we had .... the opportunity when it was presented to us, we would have won.

1

The Dupont company thought they were on to a winner with Corfam, a synthetic leather substitute. It was cheap, easy to produce and looked exactly like the real thing. They decided it was especially well-suited to making shoes and that became the focus of their marketing campaign. Unfortunately, unlike real leather, Corfam wasn't flexible and didn't stretch, making it less than ideal for the product that was showcasing the material. Meanwhile, in response to the perceived threat from Corfam, real leather companies began reducing their prices. Corfam was never a commercial success and very few people today have even heard of it.

Message:
Make sure your product is fit for purpose. **(YES / NO)**

2

In 1976 Clairol introduced a new brand of shampoo called Look of Buttermilk. Test markets gave it a big thumbs-down. Everyone agreed there was nothing wrong with the product itself but Clairol found themselves continually answering the same two questions from their test consumers: 'What exactly is the 'look of buttermilk?' and 'Why should I want it?' Consumer brows were furrowed again a few years later when the company introduced Touch of Yogurt shampoo. Nobody liked the idea of washing their hair with yoghurt and there were rumours that some people had even mistaken it for food and eaten it.

Message:
The name of a product can sometimes cause confusion. **(YES / NO)**

3

Wall's make sausages and ice cream, and Rolls Royce make cars and aircraft engines. So if diversification works for them, why didn't it work for potato crisp producers Frito Lay when they introduced a new lemonade onto the market? It probably made sense at the time: when you eat our salty crisps, you get thirsty, so why not quench your thirst with our lemonade? Unfortunately, it never caught on, thanks to the simple reason that 'thirst-quenching' is not something people think of when they think of crisps.

Message:
A company that is well-known for one type of product shouldn't make other products. **(YES / NO)**

4

Some people are prepared to spend a fortune on their cats and dogs. Thanks to them, millions around the world are kept in employment grooming, boarding and providing food, healthcare and a myriad of other products and services for pampered pets. Unfortunately, the producers of Thirsty Dog! and Thirsty Cat!, bottled water for cats and dogs, failed to benefit from our love of animals. Inexplicably, although the drink came in mouth-watering flavours like tangy fish and crispy beef, it never caught on with pet owners or their feline and canine charges.

Message:
People are unwilling to spend money on unnecessary things. **(YES / NO)**

5

Ready meals are big business today. After all, why go to all the trouble of preparing a delicious, home-cooked curry or lasagne when you can buy one that's been made for you and all you need to do is pop it into the microwave for a few minutes? And if it works for food, why not for hot drinks? The creative team at Maxwell House may have been thinking that when they came up with the idea of Ready-to-drink coffee – a carton of prepared coffee with milk and sugar that you could put into the microwave. There was just one problem: it wasn't possible to microwave the coffee in its original container, which meant pouring the drink into a cup first. Customers found it just as easy to prepare their coffee the old-fashioned way.

Message:
Convenience food is not always so convenient.
(YES / NO)

6

In 1975 Sony introduced the first mass-market video recorder, using a format known as Betamax. The following year one of their main competitors, JVC, introduced their own recorder, utilising a different video format called VHS. Since the two formats were incompatible with each other, consumers had to choose between the two. Within a few months there was a fierce format war, with both companies trying to persuade the public that their version was the best. However, while JVC shared their technology with others, Sony refused to license Betamax technology. Consequently, with a far greater choice of models available, the public opted for VCRs, condemning Betamax to technological history.

Message:
Don't let other companies copy your technology.
(YES / NO)

Write sentences about …
- a criticism of something you didn't do in the past that you now regret.
- a past ability that you no longer have.
- something you are sure about in the present.
- something you are sure about in the past.
- something that is a possibility for the future.
- something that was a possibility in the past.
- something you need to do this week.
- something you don't need to do, but you do it anyway!

> needn't
> shouldn't/should
> could
> need to/have to
> must
> can
> might

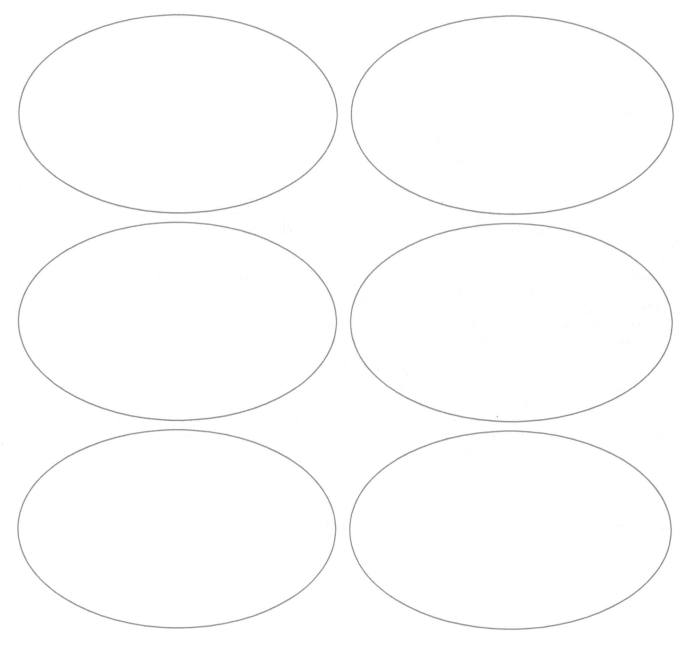

Part A
Complete the sentences with your own ideas.

1 I wish my best friend …

2 If only I had …

3 My parents would rather I …

4 I wish I'd …

5 It's high time politicians …

6 I'd rather people in my country …

Part B
Complete the sentences to fit your partner's story.

1 I wish my best friend …

2 If only I had …

3 My parents would rather I …

4 I wish I'd …

5 It's high time politicians …

6 I'd rather people in my country …

Team A

Your sentences

1 The information on my bank's website is very .... – it wasn't clear at all, and a lot of it seemed wrong. When I asked in the bank itself, the manager was very .... about it, and just said, 'Oh well!' like she didn't care.
2 I love the fact that my best friend is an incredible artist, but she's such an .... person. But sometimes her laid-back, modest attitude can .... appear disinterested, which has caused her problems with some galleries interested in exhibiting her work.
3 The students were .... of their new lecturer because his slides always had so many .... on them.
4 It's a .... that everything the chef cooks in this restaurant tastes good because this sauce is quite .... It doesn't taste of anything.

Your hits and misses

	A	B	C	D
1				
2				
3				
4				
5				
6				
7				
8				
9				

Your words for Team B

	A	B	C	D
1			misgivings	
2				misunderstanding
3		unassuming		
4				
5				
6	nondescript			disgruntled
7			misinterpreted	
8			misconception	
9		misguided		

✂ -

Team B

Your sentences

1 Laura didn't know what to think of the play. She said it wasn't bad, but it wasn't very good either. It was just .... Personally, I hated it, and was .... that I had to waste money on it.
2 There has been a big .... between my two colleagues at the laboratory. Jimmy .... some results, the head chemist found out, and Jimmy thought that Sara had told him. It's not the case, but he's convinced.
3 It's a .... that famous, best-selling authors always produce good work. I've just read something by one of the country's finest authors. It was .... from the start, with terrible ideas, and a story that didn't make sense.
4 Janet had some .... about joining the performance crew on the cruise ship. She's quite an .... person, so didn't like the idea of standing in front of an audience. But in the end, she loved it!

Your hits and misses

	A	B	C	D
1				
2				
3				
4				
5				
6				
7				
8				
9				

Your words for Team A

	A	B	C	D
1		inadvertently		
2				
3				
4	mistrustful		misleading	misspellings
5				nonchalant
6				
7		insipid		
8	misconception			unassuming
9				

Read the review quickly and tick what the writer liked or disliked about the film. Some of the things are not mentioned. Do you think the review is mainly positive or negative?

	Liked	Disliked
Plot		
Cast		
Special effects		
Jokes		
Cinema experience		
Costumes		

curiously   ironically   hopefully   oddly enough   understandably   unfortunately

★ ★ ☆ ☆ ☆

It'd been months since I'd been to the cinema because of work, so I was excited to get out on a Friday night and I was excited to watch Tom Grady's new film, *The Honour*. ¹........................ , I had seen the trailer the week before my sister had called to invite me, and I thought that it looked excellent. ²........................ , my one night out in a long time was spent watching something completely second-rate.

Due to its star-studded cast, *The Honour* ³........................ drew in the crowds, but we had booked in advance, so we had no problems getting good seats. ⁴........................ , a Tom Grady fan club had also decided to pick this specific Friday night to visit the cinema, so we had to endure various whooping moments and clapping moments throughout the showing.

The storyline wasn't so bad and it was entertaining and it was funny at least, if not a little predictable ⁵........................ , the trailer had given away most of the plot, so both my sister and I already felt as though we knew what was going to happen next.

....
....
....
....

Overall, we had a good night and we enjoyed being together, but I wouldn't necessarily recommend spending money on it or recommend watching *The Honour* on the big screen. The film itself was a bit dull and the acting was nothing to write home about. ⁶........................ , my next cinema visit will be a bit more successful and a bit more worthwhile.

Part A

1 The largest dinosaur was so ...., it almost always won when fighting other beasts.	**2** The new employee fit .... into the team and got on well with everyone.	**3** He was .... to prevent the merger even though he was the CEO of the company and was completely against it.	**4** When we conducted an investigation into the incident, we needed to take a number of facts into	**5** The zoo's new ape was strong and .... built.
6 The bomb squad were called in to .... the suspicious device.	**7** The pit was found to contain pieces of broken pottery along with some animal	**8** What .... me is that so much information is available online.	**9** The lecture was so boring that most of the audience left and only a handful of people	**10** There were thousands of these animals on the island until .... arrived in the early 18th century.
11 You must pay half the fee by 1 April and the .... at least two weeks before the course begins.	**12** Over the course of 200 years, the birds were .... almost to the point of extinction.	**13** Our trip to the nature park was really .... There were so many animals to see!	**14** The animals' .... ground is limited to the coast, where they feed on insects and small mammals.	**15** The chicken was cooked to .... Delicious!
16 Recent archaeological .... in the valley have shed more light on this ancient civilisation.	**17** I think I did extremely well in the exam .... I didn't do much revision.	**18** The city remained .... by European travellers until 1817.	**19** Craig has an .... to accept other people's ideas. He is so stubborn.	**20** Marie and Pierre Curie are best known for .... radium in 1898.
21 Going through some old boxes in the attic, we made an .... discovery.	**22** It was extremely .... of her to arrange a meeting without telling us beforehand.	**23** Once we had downloaded and .... the data, we were able to start work on the report.	**24** I'm afraid I'm .... to get you a table right now. We're completely booked up.	**25** Blood samples were sent to the laboratory for ....
26 'I can't believe you spoke to her like that!' he said, looking at me in	**27** Economic .... were consulted to see if they could understand how the economy was doing.	**28** The children were full of .... at the thought of visiting the dinosaur museum later that week.	**29** Despite the .... of the current political situation, we don't have much alternative, so will probably vote for the same government again.	**30** The adult dog didn't want to play with the puppy, who was too ....

Part B

analyse
able
perfect
hunt
consider
excite
remain
power
discover
astonish

Part A

You are a 19 year-old student. You love parties and going out with your friends. You like staying up late and when you aren't out in the evening, you are on your computer.	**You are a 64 year-old retiree.** You love spending time outside and are a fan of searching for treasure with your metal detector at the local beach. You enjoy your own company.	**You are a 30 year-old PhD student.** You are writing a thesis on video game design. In your free time, you like spending time with your closest friends at home having a nice meal.
You are a 25 year-old fashion graduate working for a magazine. You believe that the future of fashion is linked to technology and the importance of social media. In your free time, you like showing off your new clothes at expensive parties.	**You are a 40 year-old graphic designer.** You enjoy reading about the history of design and are inspired by famous designers from the past. You love nature and hate spending time at your computer when you aren't working.	**You are a 55 year-old history lecturer.** You are a technophobe and are quite introverted, except when discussing your subject.

Part B

almost a bit (by) far very much a lot much just a little a great deal

1   A natural history museum or a theme park for a day-out. (interesting)

....

2   A shopping trip to New York or a long walk in the English countryside. (exhilarating)

....

3   Watching TV or reading books. (educational)

....

4   History or computer game design. (useful)

....

5   Archaeologist or events manager (rewarding)

....

6   The internet or talking to friends. (informative)

....

> absolutely bitterly deeply disappointed emotional enormous exceptional fairly furious highly impossible
> perfect plausible practically predictable quite seriously somewhat surprised unremarkable worried

1 The spider in their living room last night was …

2 The meal they had last night was …

3 The film they saw at the weekend was …

4 They find getting up early in the morning …

5 They were … to discover that the museum they went to charged an entry fee.

6 They were … with their exam results.

7 They were … when they found that their email accounts had been hacked.

8 Their new English teacher is …

9 Their best friend was … when his pet goldfish died.

10 The storyline in the book they have just read was …

11 The latest album by their favourite group is …

12 They are … about the rising crime rate in their neighbourhood.

Mystery word

Part A

CAMPAIGN	LOYAL	MAIL
MARKETING	PRODUCT	RAPPORT
RETAIL	SALES	CUSTOMER(S)

Part B

1 The company is making a list of potential .... to try and increase sales this year.	2 The company changed names, so had to redirect all its .... to a different address.	3 .... friends are like family in many ways; they stick with you through thick and thin.	4 The new CEO was keen to come up with a new .... strategy for their luxury products since sales had dropped recently.
5 A well-thought-out advertising .... can make all the difference to the launch of a new product.	6 Sales people must establish a good .... with potential customers before attempting to make a sale.	7 The induction course included teaching a number of .... techniques to the new team.	8 The company tries to launch a new .... every couple of years to remain fresh.
9 .... sales in the USA contribute millions of dollars to the national economy – it's big business.	10 The use of television and radio can be a wonderful .... tool.	11 The local shop was lucky to have so many loyal	12 International .... always takes a few days to arrive.
13 The salesman was fortunate to have a number of repeat .... from previous customers.	14 It's annoying to receive junk .... from companies in my inbox.	15 The majority of the .... shops in town have moved from the high street to the newly built shopping centre.	16 The customers were .... and always returned to buy from her again.

The advertising company you work for has been asked to promote a new brand of potato crisps and you have come up with four mottos. You must now choose one of these. Which one would you choose? Alternatively, think of your own.

- *Add some crunch to your lunch.*
- *Taste the fun.*
- *Bet you can't stop at just one.*
- *Real potatoes, real flavour, real good.*

Your motto:

....

The advertising company you work for has been asked to promote a new airline and you have come up with four mottos. You must now choose one of these. Which one would you choose? Alternatively, think of your own.

- *Faster, cheaper, better.*
- *We'll give you the world without charging the earth.*
- *To us, you're more than just a piece of human luggage.*
- *Nobody gives you quality air time like us.*

Your motto:

....

The advertising company you work for has been asked to promote a new supermarket and you have come up with four mottos. You must now choose one of these. Which one would you choose? Alternatively, think of your own.

- *Eat to live, live to eat.*
- *Cheap food, cheap prices.*
- *Fill your trolley without emptying your purse.*
- *We put the fun back into shopping.*

Your motto:

....

The advertising company you work for has been asked to promote a new smartphone and you have come up with four mottos. You must now choose one of these. Which one would you choose? Alternatively, think of your own.

- *Get yourself connected.*
- *The whole world in the palm of your hand.*
- *It's much more than just another phone.*
- *The shape of things to come.*

Your motto:

....

The advertising company you work for has been asked to promote a new sports car and you have come up with four mottos. You must now choose one of these. Which one would you choose? Alternatively, think of your own.

- *It's not just a car – it's a whole new lifestyle.*
- *Love at first sight.*
- *Get in, start up, pull out and take off.*
- *Turning your fantasy into reality.*

Your motto:

....

The advertising company you work for has been asked to promote a new hotel chain and you have come up with four mottos. You must now choose one of these. Which one would you choose? Alternatively, think of your own.

- *Make yourself at home.*
- *Five-star luxury at two-star prices.*
- *Where every guest is a VIP.*
- *Whether it's for work or play, we're the place to stay!*

Your motto:

....

You have a meal in a restaurant and then leave. Halfway home, you realise you didn't pay for the meal. Do you return to the restaurant and pay?

A group of friends is coming over to your house to have one of your famous vegetable curries. You remember at the last minute that one of them is a vegetarian and you have used meat stock in the curry. Do you tell him/her?

You have an important test tomorrow. Worried about it, you decide to go to the classroom to talk to your teacher. She is not there but you see the test paper lying on your teacher's desk. Do you have a quick look?

You find a wallet on the bus. It has clearly been dropped by the man you saw getting off a few stops back. As there is no address in it, the only way you can return it is by getting off the bus and walking back a few stops. Do you?

While the waiter in the restaurant where you are having dinner is being very polite and helpful to you, he is being extremely rude to a couple at the next table. You suspect that this is because they are foreign tourists and aren't trying to speak the local language. Do you say something to the waiter?

You see a woman shoplifting in a supermarket. She looks like she has little money and has three small children with her. Do you report her to a shop assistant?

An unemployed friend has had a successful job interview and asks you for a reference. You know from past experience that your friend is not a good worker. Do you provide a reference for her?

While cycling down the street, you accidentally hit a parked car, leaving a long scratch down the side. Do you leave a note on the windscreen explaining what you have done and offering to pay for the damage?

Your friend didn't see a big film that was on at the cinema last month. It's not possible to buy or rent it yet, but another friend knows where you can download it for free. Do you download the film for your friend?

You are using your friend's computer without her permission and you accidentally erase some important files. Do you tell your friend what you have done?

You are using a cash machine to withdraw cash. You want to take out £100 but the machine gives you £150. The receipt says you have only withdrawn the £100 you wanted. Do you return the money to the bank?

A friend has bought a new suit and wants to know what you think of it. You think it looks terrible on him. Do you say so?

While walking down the street, you see a paper bag on the pavement. Looking inside, you find £500 in £20 notes. There is no indication who the money belongs to. Do you hand it in to the police?

The only parking space available outside the supermarket is for disabled drivers. You are only going into the shop for some milk, so won't be more than a few minutes. Do you park there?

Andy Watson

A The important thing is to not make comparisons with the way things are done in your own country. If something is different, it isn't necessarily worse.

B You've 'gone native', as the expression goes, but in the best way possible.

C It's perfectly normal to feel disoriented during your first few days in a foreign country but as long as you accept from the beginning that this is all part of the experience, you should get along just fine.

D Eventually, you'll start thinking and behaving just like your hosts.

E You should also remind yourself that you won't integrate overnight – that's something you need to work at and not give up if it all becomes challenging.

  1 A feeling of confusion is natural at first.

  2 It's common to have some negative feelings.

  3 You can quickly become part of your new community.

Alice Griffin

A They accept others and, in turn, they are accepted as one of them.

B When they arrive in their host country, many people have problems adapting.

C It can be three or four months before they tell themselves that they either have to accept the way things are or leave.

D Assuming they make the former choice – and it's much easier to do this when they start living and behaving like the locals – that is when things start changing for the better.

E The initial thrill of being somewhere different doesn't last long and they find themselves really missing their friends and family back home.

  1 The excitement of moving abroad is short-lived.

  2 Most people leave again after a short time.

  3 Integration is easier if you adapt to local ways of life.

Olivia Jenkins

A Providing they can maintain this momentum, they are certain to last the course and begin playing an active role in their community, even if they never fully become as much a part of it as they would like.

B What's more, they refuse to seek out the company of their compatriots or scour the streets looking for food from their own country.

C As soon as they arrive in a new country, many people make an active decision to make the most of their new situation.

D Instead, they throw themselves in at the deep end, going places, making new friends, joining clubs.

E They tell themselves from the start that they aren't going to sit around feeling homesick, avoiding strangers and complaining that 'they don't do things the same here'.

  1 Feelings of homesickness are common.

  2 Involvement in the community helps you to integrate.

  3 People who make an effort are able to integrate.

Peter Carter

A Then they start finding themselves getting irritated with little things, saying, 'We don't do things like this at home, so why do they?' and that's when homesickness sets in.

B Eventually, there comes that wonderful moment when they really feel that they are a part of things and they can say, 'I'm one of you now.'

C This doesn't happen straight away, of course, but perseverance and determination will ensure that it eventually does happen.

D However, they gradually begin to embrace their new surroundings, meet people, get involved in the local social scene and so on, and that's when they begin to feel a part of things.

E At first, people moving abroad experience a 'honeymoon' phase: everything is new and exciting.

  1 Making comparisons with home isn't a good idea.

  2 People become homesick when they can't integrate.

  3 Integration cannot always be achieved.

Questions

Which person ...

1 has a similar view to Peter Carter about the process people go through as they assimilate into a new life abroad?

2 shares Olivia Jenkins' view that a positive attitude from the start can help someone moving to another country?

3 has the same opinion as Andy Watson that becoming a part of a new community requires time and effort?

4 expresses a different view from the others regarding the extent to which people can integrate into their community?

Part A

A billionaire property tycoon.	An Olympic gold-medal winner.	An international supermodel.
The leader of a powerful country.	An Oscar-winning actor/actress.	A chart-topping classical musician.

Part B

Research questions
- *What are the secrets of the rich and famous?*
- *What are the best ways to become and stay successful?*

1 Ask for some simple personal details.
2 Ask for suggestions on how to become successful.
3 Ask about some of the possible downfalls of becoming famous.
4 Ask about some of their regrets.
5 Ask if they think women and men are treated differently in terms of salary and who they think is responsible for it.
6 Ask if they have any new projects they would like to announce in the near future.

Extra questions

....

....

....

....

....

....

....

Name of your City/Town ....

Introduction Include general introductory information about your city/town (e.g. population, where it is, industry, etc.)	
Possible benefits How would becoming *City of the Year* benefit the city? Use some (imaginary) numbers to support your ideas. Describe some trends (e.g. the number of jobs/amount of unemployment, population, number of children, etc.)	
How extra money could be spent Propose ideas as to how the extra investment into the city could be used to make improvements. Use language of speculation here.	
Recommendation to the board Make some recommendations to the board that chooses the *City of the Year*. What should they consider when making a decision? How can you convince them to choose your city?	

Team A

Read these sentences to Team B.

1 I failed my driving test yesterday.

2 I think that new restaurant on George Street is a bit expensive.

3 This new camera is absolutely fantastic!

4 I really fancy a coffee and a piece of carrot cake.

5 Are you OK? You look completely confused!

6 Why are there so few doctors and nurses in the UK these days?

7 I really don't know how we can afford to go on holiday this year. Any ideas?

8 Why does Sophia always defend the bosses at work when we are complaining about them?

Team B

Read these sentences to Team A.

1 What's your sister like?

2 Apparently, the new *Star Wars* movie cost $500 million to make.

3 Your talk was great, but I thought you spoke a bit too quickly.

4 Would you like another slice of cake?

5 I haven't seen Thomas since the accident.

6 How do you always come up with such excellent ideas?

7 Are you going to put the kids in nursery?

8 My brother keeps getting migraines.

Complete these sentences with the phrases in the box and match them with Team B's sentences.

> bear that in mind
> brain damage
> brainstorm
> brain scan
> childminder
> mind your language
> mind-boggling
> wouldn't mind

A Thanks, I .... It's really nice.

B They're sending him to have a .... next week.

C Very polite and proper, so .... when she's around.

D Oh, right. I'll .... next time.

E Amazing! That's a .... amount of money.

F I think they are a bit young yet. Getting a .... to come to the house would be a better option.

G I get together with the team at work and we .... ideas.

H He's still in a coma in hospital. The doctors fear he might have ....

Complete these sentences with the phrases in the box and match them with Team A's sentences.

> brain drain
> brain teaser
> brainwashed
> brainwave
> mind reader
> if you don't mind my asking
> mind you
> never mind

A No! I'm fine! Just trying to work out this .... in the newspaper!

B I agree. ...., it's worth it.

C Oh well, ... Better luck next time.

D I have no idea. I think they must have .... her!

E How much did it cost, ...?

F I've just had a .... Why not sell that old necklace of yours you never wear?

G Lack of investment has resulted in a ....

H Wow, you must be a ....! That's just what I was thinking!

Student A

- Something you were planning to learn when you got older, but never did.
- A move you were considering that never happened.
- A person you met on holiday once that you were hoping to keep in touch with (but didn't).
- An idea you had to make money that you were going to invest time in, but never did.
- An invention you assumed would be invented by now, but hasn't.
- A person you thought you'd never see again, but did (and you were pleased about it).
- Something you never imagined you would achieve, but have.
- A place you would have visited in the past, but you didn't.

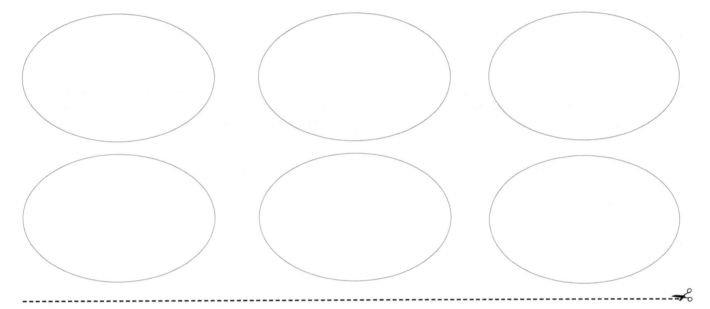

Student B

- Someone important you were going to keep in touch with, but never did.
- A personality trait from your younger years that you were hoping to change, but never did.
- A city you would have liked to live in in the past, but that doesn't appeal to you now.
- An object you never dreamt you would own, but now do.
- A career you considered going into once, but have decided is not for you.
- Something you were going to buy last year, but never did.
- A hobby you were going to take up, but never did.
- A person you predicted would become very successful (and maybe has or hasn't).

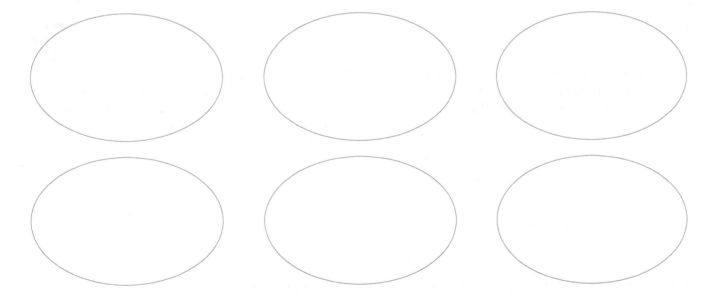

1 My dream last night was so unbelievably **preaken** that I'm actually quite worried that I've gone a bit mad! With all this stress at work, I think I'm losing it!

2 My father could sit for hours staring at the weekly **spartagle**. He insists on doing it every Sunday afternoon after lunch. He even keeps a little dictionary to hand to check his spelling!

3 I don't think that 50 years ago we could have imagined the rate at which **frayment** has developed and how much our world now revolves around new advancements.

4 Medical scientists are still hoping for a **trendile** in the search for a cure for the disease. The day that comes, the world will change for the better overnight.

5 As a young teen, I was always really **mattiable** about my voice, to the degree that, at times, I'd refuse to talk at all. Of course, this didn't last for long. By the time I was 15, you couldn't stop me talking in class!

6 I'm so indecisive. I find it impossible to make any sort of choice. Big or small, it doesn't matter if I'm **scallering** a course for university or just what ice cream I fancy on a hot day!

7 Tim's next-door neighbour has been accused of stealing from his work, but the whole street is completely convinced he is **ellitated**.

8 One of the worst parts of growing up as a musician was definitely when a parent or relative insisted on me performing to anyone who came to the house. It's like saying to a comedian, 'Make me laugh! Tell an **applie**!'.

Part 1

> However
> Wherever
> Whichever/Whatever
> Whenever
> Whoever

Some advice for planning a party

1 .... reason you have for throwing a party, remember that the main aim is to have fun.

2 .... you send an invitation to someone, remember to ask them to reply as soon as they can.

3 .... interesting the party is, remember that not everyone will be able to come.

4 .... comes, make sure you thank them.

5 .... you have the party, make sure that it's not too small for the number of guests you have invited.

Part 2

We would like advice on ....

> However
> Wherever
> Whichever/Whatever
> Whenever
> Whoever

1 ....

2 ....

3 ....

4 ....

5 ....

Ron

I like a challenge. In fact, the greater the challenge, the more I enjoy it. My motto is 'I don't do can't', which basically means that I'll do anything I'm asked to do. This can be exhausting, of course, and I've lost several nights' sleep working on things that are particularly difficult.

John

Many people go to pieces when they're working to a tight deadline, but not me. In fact, quite the opposite. That's when I'm at my best. My brain becomes more focused and I'm less easily distracted. The best essay I ever wrote I did three hours before it was due in.

Roberta

I'm not a solitary person, either in my personal or my professional life. I prefer being part of a team, especially when a job is particularly demanding or when I'm being put under a lot of pressure. I get on well with my colleagues, so this helps a lot when we're told to work together on something.

Amelia

I'm quite an imaginative person and I love inventing things. I recently designed a cover that protects my e-reader from damage, so now I can drop it on the ground or in a swimming pool and it's still OK. I'm also working on a device that waters your plants when you're away.

Jo

I think that people look up to me, respect me. It's nice to know that you're helping someone, even if you're just setting an example. One of the nicest things anyone has ever told me was that when they were given a difficult or challenging job to do, they wondered how I would do it. I must confess that made me feel really good about myself!

Teresa

My boss is always looking over my shoulder, breathing down my neck, asking me where my report is or if I've sorted out the accounts yet. This would put a lot of people off but, to be honest, I quite enjoy being pushed like that and I must admit it helps me to get the job done more effectively.

Jane

In a game or competition, I'm not happy unless I win. Second place just isn't good enough. After all, being second just makes you the first of the losers, doesn't it? I'll do absolutely anything to ensure I win; anything. Would I cheat? Probably not but perhaps if I was seriously pushed, I might.

Mark

I don't like it when someone gives me a difficult job to do and I'm left to struggle through it alone. However, put me with others and that's a different story. There's something about being in a group that helps you to focus more on the job at hand, exchange ideas, allocate tasks and so on. There's an English phrase that says, 'Many hands make light work,' and I think that's very true.

Alan

I don't think I'm any better or worse than my work colleagues but I seem to be alone on this one. It seems that I'm always being approached by one of them saying, 'You're always making good sales. How do you do it?' or 'What's the secret of your success?' I usually just tell them that it's not so much hard work as having confidence in yourself. I believe that's true. I really do.

Ollie

If you have a problem and want a solution, I'm your person! I'm especially good when it comes to improvising when you need something but haven't got it. The other day I went to a barbecue at my friend's and he didn't have any firelighters. I found the solution in his kitchen: a packet of Brazil nuts – they did the job perfectly!

Part A

Having offered	Needing
Not expecting	Not having seen
Being	Wanting
Walking	Being convinced/Convinced

Part B

Student A

1 a. I offered to look after my friend's flat while she was away and then decided that I could use her sunbed in her absence.

   b. .... to look after my friend's flat while she was away, I then decided that I could use her sunbed in her absence.

2 a. I needed to leave work early and asked my boss if I could finish my report at home.

   b. .... to leave work early, I asked my boss if I could finish my report at home.

3 a. I wasn't expecting any visitors last night, so was surprised when the doorbell rang.

   b. .... any visitors last night, I was surprised when the doorbell rang.

4 a. I hadn't seen my friend Keith for ages, so I was really pleased when he suddenly paid me a visit.

   b. .... my friend Keith for ages, I was really pleased when he suddenly paid me a visit.

5 a. Since I was a nervous flyer, I wasn't looking forward to the ten-hour flight to San Francisco.

   b. .... a nervous flyer, I wasn't looking forward to the ten-hour flight to San Francisco.

6 a. Because I wanted to text a few friends during my lesson, I decided to sit at the back of the class.

   b. .... to text a few friends during my lesson, I decided to sit at the back of the class.

7 a. As I was walking home the other day, I saw a large brown envelope lying in the road.

   b. .... home the other day, I saw a large brown envelope lying in the road.

8 a. Because I was convinced that my boss was up to no good, I hid a video camera in the office.

   b. .... that my boss was up to no good, I hid a video camera in the office.

Student B

1 a. Jenny and Carl weren't expecting so many wedding gifts and were overwhelmed by their friends' kindness.

   b. .... so many wedding gifts, Jenny and Carl were overwhelmed by their friends' kindness.

2 a. His mother wanted a break, so she booked a trip to New York for a long weekend.

   b. .... a break, his mother booked a trip to New York for a long weekend.

3 a. Marie offered to help with the party preparations earlier that week, so she arrived a couple of hours before everyone else.

   b. .... to help with the party preparations earlier that week, Marie arrived a couple of hours before everyone else.

4 a. Kurt was convinced by his brother to take up karate, so started a class for beginners at the local community centre.

   b. .... by his brother to take up karate, Kurt started a class for beginners at the local community centre.

5 a. Jude is a doctor, so she was calm in the emergency and helped when she could.

   b. .... a doctor, Jude was calm in the emergency and helped when she could.

6 a. Nate walked home slowly and called his best friend to tell her about his exciting day at work.

   b. .... home slowly, Nate called his best friend to tell her about his exciting day at work.

7 a. Chris hasn't seen his sister in over a year, so he's very excited about her visit next week.

   b. .... his sister in over a year, Chris is very excited about her visit next week.

8 a. I needed somewhere to stay while in Rome, so contacted an old friend from university who lives there.

   b. .... somewhere to stay while in Rome, I contacted an old friend from university who lives there.

Student A cards

START	**1** When his chair collapsed under him, he went bright red with	**20** You didn't do any revision. That's absolutely ....!' he said.	**6** Judy gave a deep sigh of .... 'This weather is just perfect.
21 Her brother was .... too because he hadn't seen his family in over a year.	**17** The .... welled up inside me until I started screaming and crying.	**13** 'I don't do it for your ....!' I said angrily. 'I do it so we can eat.'	**18** There seems to be some .... about the new dress code rules.

Student B cards

14 In fact, I don't think I've ever seen him look so	**11** 'It's so .... trying to make you see sense!'	**15** The final was .... , especially in the last few minutes.	**2** My maths teacher at school was a really .... man.
12 'Whether he fires me or keeps me on is a matter of complete .... to me,' he said.	**8** 'I find it really .... watching you try to cook. You haven't got a clue, have you?' said Julie.	**9** People are .... as to whether or not they can wear casual clothes like jeans.	**FINISH**

Student C cards

16 ... she shouted, storming out of the room and slamming the door in	**7** He looked at me in utter .... 'How on earth did you get an A in the exam?	**10** I would be .... to just sit here all day and soak up the sun.'	**5** The .... of the fans when their team won was huge.
4 His perpetual .... was reflected in his face, giving you the impression he had just been sucking on a lemon.	**19** Imogen was full of .... that her brother was home to visit.	**22** 'Oh, for goodness sake, don't be so ....!' my mother said. 'It's only a little spider!'	**3** Don felt completely .... about his boss's threats.

Pair A

1   It .... (say) that your mood .... (can/influence) by your diet, especially if you limit yourself to eating only healthy food.

2   Dogs .... (refer to) as Man's Best Friend for centuries because, as humans, we enjoy their loyalty and companionship and they are the most loving animals we can have.

3   These days, people get less enjoyment out of more common forms of entertainment and, for that reason, it .... (seek) through more extreme activities.

4   Millions of selfies .... (take) daily around the world and they .... (consider) to be a sign of modern-day narcissism, something new from this century. However, self-portraits .... (paint) for hundreds of years, and they aren't much different.

Pair B

1   In the world of employment, people .... (regularly/tell) what to wear and what not to wear. This isn't fair since employees .... (should/give) the opportunity to express themselves and their personalities through the way they dress.

2   Women .... (think) to put more emphasis on the importance of a partner's sense of humour than men.

3   In the past, we, as potential customers, ... (target) at random with products. On the other hand, with the advent of social media, marketing experts can now work out our personalities and interests by just checking our search history. This is a good thing because it means we .... (not show) items that don't interest us.

4   It .... (believe) that suddenly coming into a lot of money changes our lives for the worse.

Alternatively, …	Apart from …	As well as this, …	Besides this, …
Consequently, …	Despite this, …	Even so, …	For this reason, …
Furthermore, …	Given …,	In contrast, …	In view of …,
Moreover, …	On the contrary, …	On the other hand, …	What's more, …

Some teachers wear a suit and tie to work to confer authority.	Wearing socks with sandals looks really silly.	I usually dress very casually at the weekend.	Wearing smart, well-tailored clothes makes you feel good.
Wearing trainers with a suit is never a good idea.	Jolokia shoes are beautiful but unbelievably expensive.	I almost never wear a suit.	It's bad form to wear too much jewellery.
Wearing an ill-fitting or badly pressed suit does not make you look smart.	I think that some of the latest fashion designs are really over the top.	For quality clothes, you should go to Smart's on the High Street.	I believe that the secret of success is to always dress smartly, no matter what the occasion.
My brother has absolutely no taste when it comes to clothes.	I never have much money to spend on the latest fashions.	People who dress smartly for work are taken more seriously than those who dress casually.	The new sportswear shop on Rose Street is really good.
Buying designer clothes on the internet is cheaper than going to a department store.	Dressing well these days can be quite expensive.	They say that you shouldn't judge someone by the clothes they wear.	That shirt you're wearing really suits you.

1

When my classmates first established a litter patrol in my town, many people laughed at us. Our local newspaper, which seems to take delight in making people look stupid, even ran an article in which we were referred to as 'the Dirty Dozen'. I guess we were a bit discouraged at first but we decided to ignore the jokes and just got on with it. Gradually, as we began making a difference, ridicule turned to respect. That, I guess, is the secret to life: don't give up and lose heart just because others poke fun at you.

2

With crime becoming a big problem in my town, I decided it might be a good idea to set up a neighbourhood watch scheme on my street. The idea was that the residents would all keep an eye on one another's properties and report anyone behaving suspiciously to the police. I put the idea forward at our annual residents' meeting but my initial enthusiasm was replaced by a sense of disappointment at their lack of interest.

3

The environment is in big trouble, and has been for many years. What worries me is that so few of us seem to have any concern about things like global warming, pollution and all the other environmental problems that are damaging our planet. I believe that people are aware of these problems but need to be encouraged to actually do something about them. It's all too easy to do nothing in the belief that others will take care of it for you.

4

When it came to homelessness in my city, I was a bit apathetic. I felt sorry for homeless people, of course, but I didn't feel there was anything I could do to help. However, visiting London one evening, I came across a group of volunteers who spend their nights roaming the city streets giving food, help and support to those unfortunate enough to live rough. The inspiration they gave me to do something was remarkable. So, when I returned home, I set about starting up a similar organisation.

5

The other day I saw a young man drop an empty crisp packet on the street. I hate litter, so I politely asked him to pick it up and put it in the bin. The rebuke I received was alarming but not altogether unexpected. 'Mind your own business!' he said and then, somewhat illogically, 'Show me some respect!' I explained that I couldn't do the former because his littering was everybody's business and I could only do the latter once he had done something to deserve it – like using a litter bin, for example. This merely earned me more abuse and the feeling that some people just don't care about their environment.

6

When I suggested to my local council that the town set up a public bicycle-sharing scheme similar to those in places like Paris and London, I came up against a lot of opposition. The main argument was the cost and the belief that it would be money wasted. Using data obtained from public research into the viability of these schemes, I was able to prove to the council that not only would it cost less than they thought but, in the long run, it would actually make them money. And, of course, it would help to cut down on motor traffic in the town, making it a more desirable place to live in, work in and visit. That seemed to work and so far the scheme has been a great success.

7

When congestion charges for privately owned vehicles were first introduced to my city, many people complained that the system was rather confusing. It didn't matter to me at first, since I took the bus into the city. However, when I was promoted, I was given a company car, which meant I would have to drive. I quickly found out that the system was in fact pretty straightforward. Drivers of private vehicles had to pay £10 to drive into the city centre, unless they were carrying two or more passengers or if their vehicle was an electric-hybrid one, and charges weren't applied at the weekend. Very simple, really.

1   The speaker thinks that you shouldn't be .... when people fail to take you seriously. (letters 1 and 10)

2   The speaker expresses his/her .... at the apathy of others. (letters 1 and 8)

3   The speaker thinks that when it comes to the state of the environment, people's lack of .... needs to be addressed. (letter 4)

4   The speaker found a great deal of .... in the people he/she met. (letter 7)

5   The speaker says the man dropping litter wanted .... that he hadn't earned. (letter 7)

6   By persuading the council of the benefits of his/her plan, the speaker managed to overcome his/her .... (letter 6)

7   The speaker found the congestion charge scheme less .... than he had heard. (letters 2 and 8)

Mystery word

If you want to succeed in something, what you need above all is …

Student A

Clues

1 down: ....

4 down: ....

5 down: ....

8 across: ....

9 across: ....

Student B

Clues:

2 down: ....

3 down: ....

6 down: ....

5 across: ....

7 across: ....

Part A

Hardly	At no time	No sooner	Under no circumstances
Not only	Rarely	Scarcely	Seldom

-- ✂

Part B

How often did you get involved in extracurricular activities when you were at school? What were they?	Should we encourage children to have an interest in science? Why? How can we do this?
Did you ever go on a school camp when you were younger? What kind of camp? Did you learn a lot?	What do you remember about the science experiments you did in school with your teachers? How often did you do them?
Did you study science at university or school? What advice would you give to young people who are thinking of going into science now?	In your opinion, what is the most important invention that has ever been created? What do you know about the history of this invention?
Why do phone companies bring out new models so often? How often do you buy new products that come onto the market?	Why are fewer people studying sciences at university these days? In your experience, is this the case?
Which technological devices are the most useful? Would you ever give them up in order to live more simply?	What are the most useless inventions you have seen on the market and why?

Pearson Education Limited
KAO TWO, KAO Park, Hockham Way, Harlow,
Essex, CM17 9SR, England
and Associated Companies throughout the world

www.pearsonELT.com/gold

Teaching notes by Clementine Annabell

Photocopiable activities by Louise Manicolo and Rawdon Wyatt

New edition first published 2019
Third impression 2019

ISBN: 978-1-292-21775-8

Set in Frutiger LT Pro Light
Printed and bound by CPI Group (UK) Ltd, Croydon CR0 4YY

Illustrated by Oxford Designers & Illustrators and Integra Software Services Pvt. Ltd.